Contents

Are evolution and creation irreconcilably opposed? Is "intelligent design" theory an unhappy compromise? Is there another way of approaching the present-day divide between religious and so-called secular views of the origins of life?

Jacob Klapwijk offers a philosophical analysis of the relation of evolutionary biology to religion, and addresses the question of whether the evolution of life is exclusively a matter of chance or is better understood as including the notion of purpose. Writing from a Christian (Augustinian) point of view, he criticizes creationism and intelligent design theory as well as opposing reductive naturalism. He offers an alternative to both and an attempt to bridge the gap between them, via the idea of "emergent evolution." In this theory the process of evolution has an emergent or innovative character resulting in a living world of ingenious, multifaceted complexity.

JACOB KLAPWIJK is Professor Emeritus of the Department of Philosophy, Free University, Amsterdam.

PURPOSE IN THE LIVING WORLD?

Creation and emergent evolution

09

JACOB KLAPWIJK

TRANSLATED AND EDITED BY HARRY COOK

CAMBRIDGE
UNIVERSITY PRESS

CAMBRIDGE UNIVERSITY PRESS
Cambridge, New York, Melbourne, Madrid, Cape Town, Singapore, São Paulo, Delhi

Cambridge University Press
The Edinburgh Building, Cambridge CB2 8RU, UK

Published in the United States of America by Cambridge University Press, New York

www.cambridge.org
Information on this title: www.cambridge.org/9780521729437

First published 2008

Printed in the United Kingdom at the University Press, Cambridge

A catalogue record for this publication is available from the British Library

Library of Congress Cataloguing in Publication data
Klapwijk, Jacob.
Purpose in the living world? : creation and emergent evolution / Jacob Klapwijk.
p.   cm.
Includes bibliographical references and index.
ISBN 978-0-521-49340-6 (hardback) – ISBN 978-0-521-72943-7 (pbk.)
1. Evolution (Biology)–Religious aspects–Christianity.   2. Evolution (Biology)
3. Creation. 4. Teleology. 5. Creationism. I. Title.
BL263.K53 2008
231.7'652–dc22
2008028871

ISBN 978-0-521-49340-6 hardback
ISBN 978-0-521-72943-7 paperback

100656964X

Figures

viii

Preface

In writing this book and preparing it for publication many have been of great help to me, some with punctilious corrections of the text, others with penetrating commentary on its content, and others again with very useful support of a practical nature. I want to express my deep appreciation to Kate Brett, Roy Clouser, Henk Geertsema, Gerben Groenewoud, Bas Jongeling, Ronald Meester, Wim van der Steen, Dick Stafleu, Tony Tol, Henk Van Andel, Nick Wolterstorff, and Uko Zylstra. This appreciation I also want to extend to Cambridge University Press for its compliant co-operation.

One name I have not yet acknowledged: namely, Harry Cook. He is Professor Emeritus of The King's University College in Edmonton Alberta, Canada. What Harry has meant for bringing this book to completion cannot easily be overstated. Some years ago, after he initially gave careful commentary on the first Dutch concept, he was prepared to translate the whole manuscript into English. Due to the large time difference between the Netherlands and Alberta, Canada, there was an intensive exchange of e-mailing which spanned day and night. Translating was for Harry the occasion to do much more: he expended a great deal of effort on this project. He is, after all, an expert on the theory and history of biology and as such he kept a close eye on the comprehensibility of the argumentation, especially for the benefit of all non-philosophical readers. He offered much bibliographical material from many sources. Indeed, Harry made so many valuable suggestions to improve the content that I simply had to acknowledge in the course of time that as well as a knowledgeable translator, I also had the use of an eminent editor for the book. Who knows, perhaps this book has profited more from his material contributions than simply from his work as translator. I consider it an honour that through this book his name will remain associated with mine.

Introduction

How delightfully simple it would be if the word "evolution" did not refer to anything but facts: the factual descent of biological species and their mutual relationships. Then we could leave the evolution debate to the professional insights of biologists, geneticists, biophysicists, and paleontologists with nary another thought.

Things are different. The problem of evolution does not only concern the phylogenetic succession of species. It also touches the world where the species originated, the becoming of the planet Earth, and the origin of stars and galaxies. It even has to do with the Big Bang and the early inception of time and space. For life did not originate in complete isolation. It gathered itself out of cosmic energy and organic molecules. It nestled itself in an expansive time–space reality. Vexing questions arise here. How could life make a place for itself in a world of energy and radiation? How was it able to survive in the midst of a shattering surplus of matter?

Evolution, beyond the cosmic past, also has to do with the continuation of the story: the self-maintenance of the species on earth and their expansion in the biosphere. Life manifested itself in bacteria and algae, moulds and sponges, plants and animals, in short, in an overwhelming array of new life forms. Yes, it organized itself in a taxonomic diversity of increasingly complex kingdoms. Nettlesome questions arise again. Whence this newness, this abundant wealth of life forms? What explains the fundamental difference between the kingdoms?

The evolution problem finally brings us to the phenomenon of human beings. Who is *Homo sapiens*? Having come forth from the irresistible drive of life, we humans appeared on the world stage at the eleventh hour. As creatures with self-consciousness we have begun to think about ourselves and the evolutionary past of our existence. The genesis of *Homo sapiens* is not only related to hominids of millions of years ago but also has to do with the birth of technology, science, art, morals, and religion. Perhaps we have here the most vexing question. Are humans exceptional creatures on earth? Or can we still see them as representatives of the animal kingdom?

All these questions make clear to us that, while the theory of evolution is based on facts, facts as hard as nails, it is clearly not limited to that. A full-fledged theory of evolution not only requires knowledge of the facts but also mastery of what these facts imply. For how do we string together the evolutionary facts into a believable story? Natural scientists, geologists, biophysicists, and neurologists bring information forward. Social scientists and his-torians place these insights into a larger framework. But even then, science does not have a monopoly on the truth. To the contrary, we as people are convinced of all kinds of things outside of science. And there is always a degree of uncertainty and provisionality that clings to scientific propositions.

The respectability of science is beyond doubt. But we do have to ask ourselves whether science is the exclusive source of knowledge out of which insight into the mysteries of life wells up. Do we not have to draw from extra-scientific sources also? Do we not have to listen to what the traditions of the nations, the wisdom literature of the past, and the origin narratives of the religions tell us? In this book I particularly want to pay attention to the creation account of the Bible. In the final analysis it is this story that has functioned as a standard orientation point for all of Western culture for nearly two thousand years. Do creation and evolution exclude each other or is this a misunderstanding that short-sighted Christians and equally short-sighted seculars attempt to convince us of?

Once again, the life sciences bring forward impressive evolu-tionary facts but these facts need to be put together. They need to be incorporated into a convincing, coherent story without ideo-logical prejudice. Step by step, we go on a search for this unknown story. Thus the present study is no biological treatise, no presen-tation of hard research results, as published in *Science* or *Nature*. Nor is it a biological textbook in which all evolutionary facts have been thrown together, as one can find in Peter H. Raven's voluminous work, *Biology*. This book, esteemed reader, is different. It offers reflection, philosophical reflection on the possible meaning of all these things. It reflects on what the evolutionary facts could mean for us, taking note of what scientific specialists have brought to light, and taking note of what extra-scientific sources of wisdom bring forth.

Is philosophy sufficiently equipped for such a search for meaning? My answer can be short. Let us honor philosophy as the mother of all sciences, as has been done since the days of Confucius, Laozi, Buddha, Parmenides, and Plato. As such, she shows a twofold sensitivity. On the one hand she has a feeling for all that goes on in all those theoretical disciplines to which she gave birth, even if the offspring subsequently has gone its own way. On the other hand, she draws from the pre-theoretical intuitions and practices that one encounters in daily life experience, a circuit of knowledge from which she stepped forward in an ancient past. By way of this twofold cognitive interest, philosophy may indeed be in an appropriate position to present the exciting story of humankind and of the evolution of species in a scientifically justifiable manner. I am going to make an attempt.

CHAPTER I

Does life on earth have a purpose?

On Saturday, October 22, in the year 4004 BC at six o'clock in the evening God created heaven and earth, and in the days that followed, he created plants, animals, and human beings. This was the opinion of Archbishop Ussher, memorable seventeenth-century Irish church historian.[1] The bishop based his calculations on biblical genealogies. Ussher was not the first or only theological calculator. Over time, more than 140 biblical scholars have attempted to reconstruct, on the basis of holy writ, the date on which God called the world into being.[2] I have always found it a charming touch of these chronologians that they situated the origin of the world in the autumn. From the start, fruit must have been available to the first human pair, including, significantly, Eve's "apple." Thus, their piety shaped their pondering.[3]

I A QUEST FOR MEANING

Is belief in the biblical creation story in agreement with science or, to be more specific, with the modern theory of evolution? When

[1] James Ussher, Anglican Archbishop of Armagh in Ireland (1581–1656), published his calculations in *The Annals of the World Deduced from the Origin of Time* (London: E. Tyler, 1658). See M. Gorst, *Aeons: The Search for the Beginning of Time* (London: Fourth Estate, 2001), ch. 2; D. Young, *Christianity and the Age of the Earth* (Grand Rapids, MI: Zondervan, 1982).

[2] Genealogies in the Bible are related to history. They do not serve chronological calculations but witness to matters of faith. They have often been adapted to become stylized symbols (Matt. 1:17). Thus Joseph can be called "son of David" and a faithful Jew "a child of Abraham" (Matt. 1:20, 3:9). Compare the genealogies of Jesus in Matt. 1:1–17 and Luke 3:23–38, written from the point of view of Joseph and Mary respectively. In Luke 3:23 Joseph has the role of adoptive father; see P. Feine, *et al.*, *Introduction to the New Testament* (Nashville, TN: Abingdon Press, 1965), p. 36. In this book all references to the Bible are from the New International Version, unless otherwise indicated.

[3] That the forbidden fruit was an apple is not mentioned anywhere in Scripture. The misunderstanding arose because the Latin word "malum" means apple as well as evil.

Darwin first published *On the Origin of Species* in 1859, it caused a storm of controversy in religious circles, especially in England, where the faithful widely held to Ussher's chronology.[4] Is the idea of a chance-based origin of species through a process of change that spans hundreds of millions of years – ever since Darwin this has been the question – not in conflict with the creation account in Genesis? Is it compatible with the story in which the Lord God, "in the beginning," created heaven and earth and all earthly creatures in a time frame of six days?

Creationism, the very symbol of conservative Christianity in the United States, and other countries too, would say yes. Evolution is in conflict with creation, with the belief in God as the almighty creator of heaven and earth. The theory of evolution assumes a gradual development and progressive modification of earlier life forms, while the Bible teaches the constancy of species, created by God in a few days "according to their kinds."[5] To creationists the earth is really very young, even though the fossils seem old and weathered. In their Flood Model Theory they suggest that this weathering is the understandable result of a global catastrophe: the Genesis flood at the time of Noah.[6] This young age is in agreement with the Orthodox Jewish calendar which begins with the creation of the world in the year we know as 3760 BC.

I will not go into all these dating intricacies, often symptoms of a literalistic and intellectualistic interpretation of Scriptures. The topic that shall engage us in this book is a question of an entirely different order. It is the question: how should we think about the theory of evolution in the light of the never-ending quest of humankind for meaning? Is there purpose or meaning in life on earth, or does the theory of evolution exclude any awareness of directionality?

I want to elaborate on this question. Many people, whether they are Christians, Jews, or Muslims, believe that God has created the

---

[4] Ussher's chronology continued to receive support well past the time of Darwin, e.g. in the marginal notes of the popular Scofield edition of the King James Version, first published in 1910.
[5] God created all living beings "according to their kinds" (Gen. 1: 21, 24–25).
[6] Such a view is proposed in J. C. Whitcomb and H. M. Morris, *The Genesis Flood: The Biblical Record and Its Scientific Implications* (Philadelphia: Presbyterian and Reformed Publishing Co., 1962).

world and humankind. But – so reason quite a few of them – since fossils of sable-tooth tigers, dinosaurs, and other strange creatures have been found on earth, an evolutionary process of some kind must also have taken place, at least to a certain extent. At least to a certain extent? I doubt whether creation and evolution can be combined by limiting the range of evolution. What many people don't realize is that in the Darwinian theory evolution is an aimless process of development that actually comprises all forms of life. There are no discontinuities in the tree of life. Living nature selects continuously and in all circumstances from completely random variants, devoid of any underlying plan. Is evolution, indeed, a universal process without a plan? Is life, with its abundant diversity of forms, by definition a chance product of blind natural processes? Or is there an alternative? Can evolution also give evidence of a purpose, perhaps even of a creational design? Can evolutionary developments be the world-wide expression of blind experiments and simultaneously a clear manifestation of divine intentions?

The question of purpose is crucial, especially when it concerns human origins. For if plan or intent lies at the basis of human life on earth, then this would parallel what the Bible states about humans as the crown of creation and as God's partners in history. Then we may discover in the baffling world of minerals and microbes, of plants and animals, a pathway of meaning: a development that may be considered meaningful because it is not devoid of ends and purposes and appears to be a precursor to the human search for meaning. But if life on earth is the product of pure chance, then human existence would be also. Then Darwin's theories of blind selection and chance evolution would, in the final analysis, throw overboard all our human expectations of meaning, the religious ones being the first to go.

Do not think that the quest for meaning is an exclusively religious, not to mention an exclusively Christian, interest. To the contrary, it represents a general human interest. It is a quest that even affects the place of theoretical science. To put it more strongly, the idea that life on earth would have developed without any direction, and that human existence represents the result of a lucky draw, saddles us with a thorny theoretical question. If human beings are no more than chance products of nature, then this must also be true for the human mind, and everything that this mind has produced, evolutionary theories and creationist counter-theories included. In this view a theory is no more than a secretion product of the brain, an aid to the survival of *Homo sapiens*, like a jaw, or a claw, or an impressive chest-beating in other creatures. The one is no better than the other, just so long as it helps in the battle for survival. In short, a theory of evolution that trumpets forth the view of an evolution that is totally due to chance has, in the final analysis, little or nothing to do with truth, and everything with imposing behavior and survival.[7]

Our big question is this: should a believer take advantage of this relativistic result of evolutionary theory and develop arguments for the opposite, that is, a creationist concept of origins that is based on the traditional notion of constancy of species? Or shall we – believing that we are pilgrims on this earth, with all of creation on the way to the kingdom of God as its blessed destination – develop an alternative view of evolution? Is it possible to reformulate Darwin's theory of phylogenetic development of species in such a manner that it has academic respectability and nevertheless leaves room for the notion that the development of life on earth gives evidence of direction? I want to be more specific about this dilemma. Do we have to assume as self-evident that the living world is a cosmic accident? Or are there indications that, in the evolution of life forms, in spite of the blind indifference of nature, a pathway or perspective of meaning manifests itself?

2 PLANNED APPROACH

Here follows my plan of approach and the content of the following chapters. In chapter 2 I focus on creationist views of origins, and Dembski's theory of intelligent design, comparing these views with what I, inspired by Augustine's vision of time, defend as the biblical idea of creation. In chapter 3 I discuss Darwin's theory of descent,

---

[7] See A. Plantinga, *Warrant and Proper Function* (New York: Oxford University Press, 1993), p. 218: "what evolution guarantees (at most) is that we behave in certain ways – in such ways as to promote survival . . . It does not guarantee mostly true or verisimilitudinous beliefs."

and the modern synthetic theory of evolution that is grafted upon it. In chapter 4 we discover the hidden premises and category mistakes behind the evolution debate that spell the difference between a scientific theory of evolution and the ideology of evolutionary naturalism. We examine the biological concept of species and the consolidating effect of natural selection in chapter 5. In chapter 6 I introduce the theory of emergence as it was formulated by the British philosophers Conwy Lloyd Morgan and Samuel Alexander at the beginning of the last century.

The second half of this book takes a systematic turn. In chapter 7 I reformulate the theory of emergence as based on the distinction between entities and modal functions and as oriented on the key concept of idionomy; the theory is applied to the different organizational levels in living nature. In chapter 8, in a discussion with John Searle and Peter Checkland, I make clear the relevance of this theory for an understanding of the different levels of being in human culture; I introduce a general theory of emergent evolution. Chapter 9 clarifies the idea of distinct levels as a conceptual framework for the variety of theoretical disciplines; it ends in a discussion of the philosophy of mind. Chapter 10 is about the relation of faith and science, about Augustinianism and Thomism, and in particular about the hermeneutic significance of the biblical notion of creation for understanding evolution. In chapter 11 the holistic and ecological implications of the theory of emergent evolution are brought to the fore. In chapter 12 I unfold my own philosophical starting-points in a critique of the essentialist species concept of the Christian philosopher Herman Dooyeweerd. In chapter 13 we consider remaining questions to which the theory of emergent evolution calls attention. I conclude, in chapter 14, with a comparison between the meaning perspectives disclosed in the theory of emergent evolution and the closed world picture of evolutionary naturalism.

CHAPTER 2

Creationism, Intelligent Design, and Augustine's idea of time

Creationism presents itself, and has done so for over a century, as a biblically oriented critique of Darwinian evolution theory. It wants to expose its naturalistic and atheistic premises. Rightly so, for in the evolutionary camp we find all kinds of thinkers who give evidence of dogmatic prejudices. How creationists present themselves is another story, on which we shall focus in this chapter (section 1). As we continue, we shall turn our attention to the Intelligent Design movement (section 2), and to the scholastic tradition out of which this movement has arisen (section 3). Then we shall consider the significance of the creation account in Genesis and of creation narratives in general (section 4). Finally in this chapter, we shall reflect on the Church Father Augustine and his pioneering interpretation of time as a creature of God (section 5).

I CREATION AND CREATIONISM

Creationism I take to mean the view that the creation story in Genesis is not only a believing witness regarding God as the source of all being and the origin of all that lives, but also a scientifically reliable representation of the manner in which He brought the world and the diverse forms of life into being at the beginning of time. That the text in Genesis has also been shaped by the ancient, oriental world picture that prevailed at the time the narrative took shape, creationists will only admit with much hesitation and reserve.

Creationism is accustomed to use the Bible as an encyclopedia, a reference work that supplies to believers, or at least to the exegetes among them, accurate information about all areas of life, even about basic questions that modern sciences pose. Thus it has developed a biblicist view of the relation between faith and science. Biblicism denotes the search for a synthesis, in the sense of a mutual adaptation and harmonization, between the biblical message and scientific knowledge. One the one hand the Bible, in this case the biblical creation account, is seen as a dependable source of information and frame of reference for science. On the other hand all kinds of scientific insights are "discovered" or (to be more precise) inserted into the Bible, after which Scripture is interpreted accordingly. Through this process of eisegesis and exegesis creationism gives rise to a mixture of biblical and scientific opinions in regard to the becoming of the world, the origin of life, and the peculiar nature of human beings. And often it is not clear which of these opinions are warranted by the authority of Scripture and which by the authority of science.[1] A widely respected authority on creationism and "creation science" is the American historian of science, Ronald L. Numbers.[2]

Also in the Muslim world creationist views present themselves. This creationism is not based on the text of the Bible but on the creation message of the Koran. The center of the Islamic creationism movement is located in Turkey. One of the proponents of this creationism is Harun Yahya, pseudonym of Adnan Oktar. His Bilim Araştırma Vakfı (Science Research Foundation) organizes conferences with leading American creationists. Yahya's latest study, and imposing tome, carries the characteristic creationist title *Atlas of Creation* (2006); one can download it from the Internet. In this book, Yahya takes a forceful stand against Darwinian evolution theory and, in particular, against what he regards as its atheistic and materialistic foundations.[3]

In the creationist movement of Christian origin, three phases can be distinguished which, at the same time, continue to exist as three rather independent schools of thought. Originally the movement read the Genesis story as literally as possible, as if it were a set of

[1] Typical of this biblicist eisegesis and exegesis are books such as H. M. Morris, *The Biblical Basis for Modern Science* (Grand Rapids, MI: Baker Book House, 1987) and *Scientific Creationism* (El Cajon, CA: Master Books, 1985); A. A. Roth, *Origins: Linking Science and Scripture* (Hagerstown, MD: Review and Herald Publishing Association, 1998).

[2] R. L. Numbers, *The Creationists: The Evolution of Scientific Creationism* (Berkeley: University of California Press, 1992).

[3] Harun Yahya, "Atlas of creation," http://www.harunyahya.net/V2/Lang/en. Yahya shows himself to be an adherent of so-called Old Earth creationism.

minutes or a newspaper account. In the spirit of Bishop Ussher and in accordance with traditional views in science, creationism defended the thesis that the world with all its inhabitants came into being six to ten thousand years ago, created by God in the span of six days. This view is still very much alive, in particular on the American and African continents. It is often named Young Earth creationism.

Creationists of the second phase accepted the challenge posed by modern science. Here the biblicism is less strict. The Bible is still the authoritative source of knowledge. But noting the geological and paleontological insights into the great age of the earth and of fossilized forms of life, it is suggested that the six days of creation should be interpreted as cosmological and geological periods of hundreds of millions of years. In these periods God would have successively called into being the cosmos, the earth, the heavenly bodies, the plant and animal kingdoms with the entire diversity of biological species, and finally would also have created the human soul and incorporated it into the highest existing form of life. This position is known as Old Earth creationism.

Since the 1990s a new movement has come to the fore, in the United States and in other places, under the significant name Intelligent Design, or ID in short. It is seen by many as a third phase of the creationism tradition. This is only partially correct. The new theory reformulates the creationistic objections against evolutionary naturalism but it does not seek its authority in a biblicist synthesis of scriptural givens and scientific data. The movement prefers to avoid an appeal to the Bible, a choice between an old or a recent earth, and other controversial topics from the creationist camp. The adherents of ID want to form a broad front that communally will provide new insight into the origin of life and of species. The ID movement prides itself on having a "big tent."

Intelligent Design announces itself as an independent scientific theory; it profiles itself as an alternative scientific program. It holds current theories about evolution unsatisfactory, as products of an incomplete explanatory model or a "failed scientific research program."[4]

[4] W. A. Dembski, "Introduction: Mere Creation," in Dembski (ed.), *Mere Creation: Science, Faith, and Intelligent Design* (Downers Grove, IL: InterVarsity Press, 1998), pp. 13–32; p. 22.

For this purpose proponents point to phenomena in organic nature that are so specific or so complex that they cannot be the result of natural causes and evolutionary developments. Thus they must be regarded as the result of a design that has been purposefully brought into cosmic evolution and development on earth. It is this ambitious program that William Dembski, Michael Behe, and others have named "Intelligent Design."[5] The question of whether design theory itself, given its rejection of biblicist attempts to harmonize Bible and science, seeks a synthesis between the two remains to be seen.

To complete this survey I mention that in Germany a special branch of contemporary creationism has formed around the work of Werner Gitt, Siegfried Scherer, and the study community "Wort und Wissen." Creationism in Germany does not so much focus on a synthesis of faith and scholarship as on an analysis of the spiritual motives that impel evolutionary theories. It offers a penetrating critique of naturalistic reductionism.[6] In biological systematics, Scherer and co-workers are engaged in a taxonomical project to reclassify the "basic types of life"; not at the level of species but at the higher levels of genera, families, and orders. These types are presented as irreducible units, i.e. as possible representatives of the units of life as God created them in the beginning. *Within* these basic types there would be room for an evolutionary development of species.[7]

2 LIFE BASED ON AN INTELLIGENT DESIGN?

Earlier I raised the question: do we have to assume as self-evident that life on earth has developed completely by chance, or are there

[5] See Dembski (ed.), *Mere Creation*, also for the views of other representatives of ID. See further M. J. Behe, *Darwin's Black Box: The Biochemical Challenge to Chemical Evolution* (New York: The Free Press, 1996). For a general critique of ID see E. B. Davis, "Debating Darwin: The 'Intelligent Design' Movement," *The Christian Century*, July 15–22, 1998, 678–81.

[6] Gitt especially, as an information scientist, has an eye for the distinctive levels of created reality. He states correctly that the semantics of the information system that functions in the DNA of every living organism is not translatable into the language of physics. W. Gitt, *In 6 Tagen vom Chaos zum Menschen: Logos oder Chaos* (Neuhausen/Stuttgart: Hänssler-Verlag, 1998).

[7] S. Scherer, "Basic Types of Life," in W. A. Dembski (ed.), *Mere Creation*, pp. 195–211. A comparable taxonomic approach can be found in Michael J. Behe's newest book *The Edge of Evolution: The Search for the Limits of Darwinism* (New York: The Free Press, 2007).

indications that purpose also manifests itself? It is especially the Intelligent Design movement that takes a clear position on this topic. It states that the origin and development of life are based on a design and thus indicate a purpose. With this thesis it has attracted much attention, also in scientific circles. In this section I will examine its scientific position. In the section that follows I will investigate how it attempts to construct a bridge between science and faith.

Contrary to creationists, ID adherents do not appeal directly to the text of the Bible. They also recognize that the earth is older than 6,000 years, reject flood-geology, and support the view that evolution is not lacking in nature. But for the rest, they want little or nothing to do with Darwinism. They are especially against the view that the complexity of the living world is a strictly fortuitous result of blind powers of nature, explainable on the basis of the Darwinian double principle of genetic variation and natural selection. Over against this they defend the view that "certain features of the universe and of living things are best explained by an intelligent cause, not an undirected process such as natural selection."[8]

For Christians who have an eye for the unimaginable miracles of nature and wrestle with the evolution problem this is an intriguing position. Isn't the person who believes that God, in his inscrutable wisdom, created the world not also prepared to believe that this wondrous world came into existence on the basis of an intelligent design?

Be careful with hasty declarations of agreement and for an identification of creation belief with intelligent design. The design theory emphasizes that it does not want to be understood as a testimony of faith. It wants to be judged as a scientific theory. It announces itself as a new scientific theory about the origin of life, based on a notion of intelligent design in nature. To be sure, an Intelligent Design does point to an Intelligent Designer. And an Intelligent Designer of nature does make many think of God. On this point, however, ID would have itself know as agnostic: "Unlike

[8] The citation originates in the Center for Science and Culture, the Discovery Institute, Seattle: "Top questions," http://www.discovery.org/csc/topQuestions.php.

creationism, the scientific theory of intelligent design is agnostic regarding the source of design and has no commitment to defending Genesis, the Bible or any other sacred text." Adherents do speak of design but the designer is kept anonymous. The proponents of ID state, if science is not to deteriorate into uncontrollable metaphysics, the designer should remain unnamed. The center of the movement, the Discovery Institute in Seattle, presents itself therefore as a "secular think tank."[9]

Speaking of complexity, Intelligent Design wants to account for the complex character of living organisms, a complexity that biochemists and molecular biologists have uncovered over the last few decades. They have encountered organisms with millions or billions of body cells, body cells with thousands or tens of thousands of genes, and numerous intricate interactions between all these cells with their DNA molecules, proteins structures, etc. ID poses the following penetrating question: can evolution theory give a complete and satisfactory explanation of the riddle of life? Did all organisms originate by chance according to the model of natural selection? Or must we reject this totality claim and conclude that the beginning of life, the origin of the genetic code, the advent of the cell, the becoming of multicellular organisms, etc., surpass every natural explanation and result from a non-natural cause, a clever design that has been inserted, as by an invisible hand, into the regular order of nature?

William Dembski's book *The Design Inference* gives a clear example of this train of thought. Dembski is the theoretician of Intelligent Design. From this book, do not expect insights into the concrete research of the evolutionary sciences. Dembski raises a methodological question. It is the question whether, and under which circumstances, in the explanation of processes in nature, we could come to the conclusion that we are not dealing with natural factors but with a purposeful design. I can only indicate some of the major points from this formal, mathematical analysis.

Dembski's thesis is that a natural event or phenomenon, regardless of the underlying causal mechanisms, can be explained in

---

[9] For the citations see, once again, the explanations of the Discovery Institute.

one of three ways that complement each other and that are, at the same time, mutually exclusive (I add some examples):

(1) As a regular and thus very probable or even necessary course of events. One could think here of the expansion of iron upon heating, or of the rising of the sun every morning.
(2) As a fortuitous and thus somewhat unlikely happening. An example here would be that it is snowing at the moment or that, in a place not known to me, I run into an old classmate.
(3) As designed according to a unique and independently originated pattern and thus as a specified and simultaneously highly improbable phenomenon. In this category one could include the origin of life on earth.[10]

In *The Design Inference* and publications that follow, Dembski concentrates on phenomena of the third type. Design phenomena are exceptional, if not singular, in nature and, for this reason, of particular significance. From a statistical point of view, Dembski, a statistician and philosopher, calculates for us that the beginning of life was a process of such extraordinary and specific complexity that it cannot be categorized as a regular occurrence or as a chance incident. According to the standards of probability calculations the origin of life was so improbable that one has to conclude that a unique phenomenon came into being here, a phenomenon that is only explainable on the basis of a conscious design.

How can one detect phenomena with an evidence of design? Dembski develops an "explanatory filter," a negative selection procedure based on the three options mentioned above of regularity, chance, and design. In an explanatory process one assumes in the first place that a phenomenon or process at hand is of a regular character. If this regularity is untenable then it is likely that the phenomenon occurred coincidentally. If this option, too, cannot be maintained one is justified to draw the conclusion that design is involved. In other words, one can only conclude that a phenomenon displays the feature of design if the other two options can be filtered away by logical elimination. Using the jargon of modern

---

[10] W. A. Dembski, *The Design Inference: Eliminating Chance through Small Probabilities* (Cambridge: Cambridge University Press, 1998), p. 11.

symbolic logic, Dembski states: "To attribute an event to design is to say that it cannot reasonably be referred to either regularity or chance. Defining design as the set-theoretic complement of the disjunction regularity-or-chance guarantees that the three modes of explanation are mutually exclusive and exhaustive."[11]

Thus, Dembski bases the inference of an intelligent design not on religious intuitions or special texts in the Bible but on logical reasoning. It is reason that brings forward, with the aid of an explanatory filter, arguments for the existence of phenomena that are of such small probability that they cannot be ascribed to regularity or chance. They must therefore have been originated from a specific design. Dembski admits that only the notion of an intelligent design, not of an intelligent designer, can be deduced by formal mathematics from the negation of regularity and chance. But he is prepared to connect this notion, if not on formal then certainly on practical grounds, to the notion of an intelligent designer.[12] As he sees it, it cannot go further than that. The words "design" and "designer" do not necessarily imply a divine author.

Many will ask themselves why Demski nevertheless colors his account with the suggestive term, "intelligent design." For this phrase is a metaphysically loaded concept. In all of Western philosophy, from Plato to William Paley, design arguments have been brought forward to prove the existence of a divine master builder of the world. Dembski rejects such proofs of the existence of God as metaphysical speculations. Correctly so! Science is not able to discover the creator of heaven and earth. If we know God, we only know Him through faith. But then, why reintroduce the concepts of design and designer in a scientific argument? In regard to singular events, such as the origin of life or of the DNA molecule, couldn't Dembski have been satisfied with the stimulating conclusion that the theory of evolution is not a complete theory, or that the evolution process brought forth phenomena that cannot be fully explained by regularity or chance? Couldn't he have earmarked these irreducibly new phenomena as "complex specified information" or

---

[11] *Ibid.*, p. 36.
[12] *Ibid.*, p. 9: "design as inferred from the design inference does not logically entail an intelligent agent."

something similar, and avoided the use of terms that suggest something that cannot be ascertained scientifically?

Questions also arise about the mutual exclusiveness of the three explanatory options. The exclusivity is, in the first place, questionable from a biblical point of view. The Bible sees God's hand in unique events, such as the origin of life on earth, but as much in events that we ascribe to chance or regularity.[13] Speaking of chance, the Bible shows, for example, God's governance in the life of Joseph, who, although a slave, came in contact with the Pharaoh and through this chance encounter was put in charge by Pharaoh of the whole land of Egypt.[14] And speaking of regularity, there are numerous psalms that praise God as the origin of the regular order of nature.[15] Isn't this also the religious experience of ordinary people? They see the presence of God not only in the things that they do not understand, such as the resurrection of Jesus or the coming of God's kingdom, but also in things that are easily understood, such as the gift of daily bread or a good night's rest.

Also from a logical point of view the question can be raised whether the three explanatory possibilities exclude each other. Especially questionable is the exceptional position of the third explanatory option. Dembski does not make clear why a regular process (e.g. the expansion of iron when it is heated) or a fortuitous event (e.g. the liberation of an oppressed people) does not rely as much on an intelligent plan as a one-time event such as the origin of life. Doesn't every laboratory experiment, because it is repeatable, give evidence of regularity and, at the same time, because it is planned, evidence of design? And if regularity can be paired with human planning, then why not with a divine plan?

[13] Representatives of ID do not deny that God also works through natural factors. For this purpose they make use of the scholastic distinction between primary cause and secondary causes. God manifests himself directly or as "first cause" in cases where natural explanations fall short and where we must speak of a special creation or supernatural intervention. Natural factors are indicated as indirect or "secondary causes."

[14] Joseph experienced the events of his life as governed by divine guidance (Gen. 45:5). Even processes that are based on chance are described in Scripture as being under God's control (Prov. 16:33).

[15] God's presence in the regular orderings and in the explosive violence of nature is spoken of in Psalm 8, 19, 29, 65, 93, 104, 147, and 148. They show that in the religious consciousness of Israel a regular or contingent natural occurrence on the one hand, and God's acting on the other hand, were not experienced as mutually exclusive.

There are, finally, also philosophical objections that can be brought forward against Dembski's representation of affairs. On this point I have to elaborate. Dembski's explanatory filter suggests that events, regardless of the causal factors that play a role, lend themselves to an explanation on the basis of regularity, chance, or design. In Dembski's mathematical model these are mutually exclusive, but are they also in the real world? In reality, an event can be an illustration of regularity and, at the same time, a random hit. One day I wanted to go to see a sunset over the ocean; for many this is an epitome of regularity. But through circumstances I almost missed this phenomenon. At the moment I arrived at the beach I saw the sun disappear below the horizon; for me this was an epitome of chance.

As soon as a formal explanatory model, such as Dembski's, is applied to the real world, it has substantive implications. It then unfolds as a specimen of what is called in philosophy a one-level ontology. It makes the world a one-dimensional reality, in which all phenomena fall neatly into three explanatory categories. The results are far reaching! If phenomena appear that in this one-level ontology do not lend themselves to a typical explanation in terms of regularity or chance, then they have to be labeled, per definition, as improbable and exceptional. And for these exceptional phenomena it follows that an exceptional, non-natural cause has to be contrived, in terms of a design and a related designer.

It must be clear that there is something amiss with this kind of explanation. A one-level ontology is, by definition, contradictory. It assumes a natural reality but it simultaneously presupposes knowledge regarding it. And the latter, the cognitive level, cannot be reduced to the natural level. In this world, cognitive processes represent a reality all of their own. They are not determined by natural laws but by universal laws of a different sort, logical principles, such as those of identity and contradiction. Well, cognitive reality demands a redefinition of the standards of regularity, chance, and exception. Imagine that shells have washed ashore somewhere and together they form a meaningful word. In a natural context this is a highly improbable, even an exceptional happening. But on a cognitive level or in a cognitive setting – perhaps children played on the beach – this unexplainable phenomenon could be classified as a regular and easily explainable phenomenon.

Let me make this argument more specific. It cannot be excluded that also within nature itself, differences in levels assert themselves. Assume – we'll examine this point more closely later – that in living nature independent laws assert themselves that are different from the laws of physical nature: biological principles of cellular organization, self-conservation, and reproduction, which cannot be found in physical reality. Also in this biological setting we are forced to re-examine the classification according to the three proposed explanatory options.

Here, too, I take an example: the protein molecule, hemoglobin. This respiratory enzyme in higher animal species (mostly vertebrates) is so ingenious and complex that design theorists like to bring it forward as originating from a design. But is this correct? Experts in biophysics have calculated that the probability of a spontaneous origin of hemoglobin in molecular nature is one in 10^{190} (i.e. a one with 190 zeroes).[16] That is to say, in a physical explanatory context, the probability of the origin of hemoglobin is practically nil. But in a biological explanatory context, measured by the principle of self-conservation, the calculations have a different end result. Improvements that increase the probabilities of survival, no matter how small, are incorporated in living beings over a span of hundreds of millions of years. The living world consolidates them in favor of posterity. In this new framework the chances are reversed. An enzyme that, on the basis of physical laws would not be attainable and in Dembski's one-dimensional account would have to be explained in terms of a design, can, on the basis of biological laws, have developed itself normally and in steps. It can be explained in terms of regularity or chance.

Compare the chance of the evolutionary origin of hemoglobin with a dice-player with five stones trying to throw five sixes at once. The prospects of these attempts soon prove to be hopeless, for the theoretical chance of succeeding in one throw is one in 6^5, i.e. the player will, on average, have to throw 7,776 times to reach the goal.

[16] R. Dawkins, *The Blind Watchmaker: Why the Evidence of Evolution Reveals a Universe without Design* (New York: W.W. Norton, 1986), pp. 45–49. Dawkins uses this "cumulative selection" as an argument *for* Darwinian naturalism. In what follows it will become clear that the peculiar nature of biological principles and explanations forms an argument that, in fact, turns against such naturalism.

The dice-thrower comes to the conclusion, after innumerable futile attempts, that he (or she) may never reach his goal unless he applies a trick: an "intelligent design." For instance, he could make the dice heavier on one side. But there is also an alternative solution that suggests itself to him. He could imagine that a new situation has arisen with modified rules for the game. The new rules allow the dice-player to proceed step by step. That is to say, once the desired result is obtained (a six), it remains in effect; the dice-thrower continues to play with the remaining dice. It will be clear that within this new context and with these new rules he will reach his goal without tricks within a minimum of time.

I come to the conclusion that Dembski's explanatory filter in its uniformity is not applicable to reality in its multiformity. One could even generalize this result. It would then imply that explanations based on probability calculations, developed outside the formal uniformity of logic and mathematics for the benefit of events in the real world, are always dependent on different contexts and on the rules that hold for them. I admit that this analysis does not solve all puzzles that surround the living world and the origin of its complex structures. To the contrary, new puzzles arise. For suppose that in the organic world, in the passage of hundreds of millions of years, time and again new biological groups and kingdoms with their own rules, rituals, and practices came to the fore; how must we explain the origin of these new orderings? The only thing I want to emphasize at the moment is that the complexity of the living world is not of such a nature that a statistician must necessarily conclude that a purpose or goal is in play in terms of an intelligent design.

3 A BRIDGE BETWEEN SCIENCE AND FAITH?

Above I discussed the legitimacy of the reasoning that gives rise to the design inference. Is scientific reason, which has built up credit in the entire world by empirical investigation and methodical discipline, entitled to simply apply Dembski's formal and uniform trio of necessity, chance, and design to nature in all its multiformity? And may it, on this basis, demand room for natural phenomena with an "intelligent," in the sense of non-natural or supra-empirical, cause?

With the recognition of phenomena of this type, isn't the definition of empirical science artificially stretched? Isn't science made subservient – as many evolutionary biologists suspect – to religious purposes? We stand before the question: how do science and faith relate within the framework of the design theory?

Dembski accommodates us in this new problematic. In the collection of essays *Mere Creation* (1998), he outlines a rather ambitious research program for Intelligent Design with the following four components (I quote it verbatim):

(1) A scientific and philosophical critique of naturalism, where the scientific critique identifies the empirical inadequacies of naturalistic evolutionary theories and the philosophical critique demonstrates how naturalism subverts every area of inquiry that it touches;

(2) A positive scientific research program, known as Intelligent Design, for investigating the effects of intelligent causes;

(3) A cultural movement for systematically rethinking every field of inquiry that has been infected by naturalism, reconceptualizing it in terms of design; and

(4) A sustained theological investigation that connects the intelligence inferred by Intelligent Design with the God of Scripture and therewith formulates a coherent theology of nature.[17]

This program still lacks concrete elaborations. But no matter how brief, it does show that the aforementioned agnosticism does not detract, as far as Dembski is concerned, from the Christian intentions that play a role in proposing Intelligent Design. The agnosticism appears to be of a methodological nature. It wants to emphasize that the theory of design does not depend on religious intuitions or biblical notions but leans on the objectivity and independence of reason. The theory argues on strictly scientific grounds, Dembski suggests.

Scientific reason and scriptural faith are, in the first instance, presented as two independent sources of knowledge. Yet this dualism does not have the last word; Dembski does not choose a dichotomy between reason and religion. But the creationism we

---

[17] Dembski (ed.), *Mere Creation*, p. 29.

mentioned earlier, i.e. the biblicist intertwinement of biblical and scientific knowledge, is also not an option for him. Instead, Dembski pleads for an alternative model of Christian synthesis. In the final analysis, as shown above, he wants to relate reason and faith to each other with the help of a "theology of nature." In this, the notion of a higher intelligence, inferred from the concept of design, must create a bridge between the world of empirical science and the so vastly different world of the Christian faith.

Here Dembski follows a respectable but controversial strand in the Christian tradition. Earlier I referred to the English theologian William Paley, who, already in pre-Darwinian times, strove for a synthesis between reason and faith on the basis of the notion of design. Paley, too, made a case for a "natural theology"; he derived arguments for the existence of a divine architect from designs in nature.[18] However, the striving toward a synthesis between faith and reson on the basis of a design in nature has much deeper roots in the Christian tradition. It has arisen from medieval scholastic philosophy; at that time it concentrated itself in what is usually indicated as the theory of the divine Logos. Dembski connects with this on major points. To bring the problematic sides of the design argument into sharper focus, I venture to make some comments both about this scholastic synthesis and the Logos doctrine.

Scholastic synthesis   In the philosophy of Scholasticism, which gained prominence in the Middle Ages in the thought of Thomas Aquinas and which still has its defenders in Christian circles, reason and faith are two separate but nevertheless mutually attuned sources of knowledge. Reason sets its sights on the natural or empirical world; it is an ability to know that is inherent in human nature, available to all people. Faith, on the other hand, is aimed at the supernatural reality of God and the secrets of salvation mediated by God's church; it is a cognitive ability that has to be granted to human beings, a form of knowing that is exclusively Christian. Although separate in principle, natural and supernatural knowledge are complementary: reason supports faith and faith perfects rational insight.

---

[18] W. Paley, *Natural Theology or Evidences of the Existence and Attributes of the Deity, Collected from the Appearances of Nature* (London: Wilks and Taylor, 1802).

The intended synthesis comes to the fore in knowledge of God. Full knowledge of God can only be obtained on the basis of biblical revelation and church dogma. Only the Bible, the church, and Christian theology can explain to us who God, the father of Christ Jesus, is in the deepest sense. But natural reason can provide valuable support: Aristotle would already have proven the existence of God. The final aim of philosophical reason is to present itself – as Dembski's program also indicates – as a "theology of nature." This natural or philosophical theology is seen as preparing the way for supernatural or Christian theology. For, insofar as philosophy discovers vestiges of a divine design in the natural world, it makes the existence of God rationally acceptable and can thus help non-believers to find the way to church, faith, and Christian theology.

The Logos doctrine   ID theory is affiliated, in particular, with the Logos doctrine. Medieval thinkers saw in ancient philosophy, and especially in the classical doctrine of the divine Logos, a *praeparatio evangelica*, a connecting point and preparation for the Christian message. The Stoics and Plato were leading lights in this doctrine. The medieval masters emulated the Stoics in that they saw the Logos (divine reason) as the ground of natural reality. They emulated Plato in that he taught that all natural things originated as a shadow of ideas, i.e. of supratemporal arch models that lie at the basis of the temporal world. In short, nature is a reflection of divine wisdom. But the truth, which the ancient Stoics and Platonists saw as through a veil, thanks to reason, was only preparatory. Now it is disclosed for those who believe, according to the medieval scholars. The Logos of the Stoics is, in fact, the God of the Bible, the creator of the world, the source of all wisdom and understanding. And the ideas that Plato had in mind are, in fact, *ideae in mente Dei*, ideas in the mind of the God of the Bible: the intelligent blueprints or designs according to which this Logos created the world, human beings included.

The medieval Logos doctrine can thus be seen as a form of Stoic–Christian Platonism, a synthesizing theory of design in embryo. Just as human ideas lie at the basis of cultural products, say of every cup and saucer, so divine ideas lie at the basis of all things in nature, say of every tree and tree frog. They are intelligent designs sprung from the mind of the divine creator. This also sheds light on the hidden Christian character of empirical science. Thinking about things, as scientists do, seems to be a secular undertaking but it is really thinking God's thoughts after him. Later adherents of Logos thought therefore could summarize their view in the phrase "things are thinks."[19]

In my view, it is this tradition of Scholasticism and the Logos doctrine on which Dembski falls back. He, too, assumes the distinction between natural reality, as the more or less autonomous domain of science and philosophy, and that other reality that transcends nature: the domain of Christian theology. He, too, strives for a synthesis of both, being of the opinion that scientific research can only fully unfold itself when a bridge is built between the two domains: "the bridge between science and theology."[20] And Dembski, too, intends to build this bridge on phenomena with a design character. He is convinced that in nature, especially on the molecular level, exceptional phenomena present themselves and that serious science cannot deny that these exceptional phenomena have arisen from designs of a higher intelligence. Yes, serious science can be seen as the fact that one (human) intelligence attempts to think after the other (divine) intelligence: "Intelligent design is one intelligence determining what another intelligence has done."[21]

I do not forget that there are also differences between the scholastic Logos theory and the modern design theory. Logos theory sought a synthesis and accommodation with theories from antiquity about the origin of things. The design theory seeks a connection and accommodation with the evolutionary insights of modern science. Thus, in the design movement we are dealing not so much with a Scholastic but a neo-Scholastic paradigm of synthesis.

Substantive differences go together with this. The most striking difference is that the Logos theory was inclusive: it saw all things in

[19] J. Klapwijk, 'Honderd jaar filosofie aan de Vrije Universiteit', in M. van Os and W. J. Wieringa (eds.), *Wetenschap en Rekenschap 1880–1980: Een eeuw wetenschapsbeoefening en wetenschapsbeschouwing aan de Vrije Universiteit* (Kampen: J. H. Kok, 1980), pp. 528–93; pp. 542–44. (The phrase was coined by George Berkeley in a different context.)
[20] See the subtitle of Dembski's book, *Intelligent Design: The Bridge between Science and Theology* (Downer's Grove, IL.: InterVarsity Press, 1999).
[21] Dembski (ed.), *Mere Creation*, p. 19.

the world as rooted in the creating ideas of the Logos. Dembski's conception is exclusive: he does not deny God's creating power, but he will only speak of design in cases where natural explanations of origin fall short. This difference corresponds with the shift in primacy in the synthesis of faith and scholarship in modern times. In the medieval synthesis, faith was paramount and science had to adjust. In the modern synthesis – insofar as modernity still strives for a synthesis with the Christian faith – science has the primacy; here faith has to adjust. Thus, the complementarity of reason and faith did not lead to a competition between explanations based on empirical observations and explanations based on intelligent design in medieval Logos theory, but does in modern design theory. Modern explanations of origin based on design can only be introduced in a supplementary way. They are for Dembski, by definition, exceptional and incidental.

The incidentalism of Intelligent Design has far-reaching effects. Given Dembski's explanatory filter, design theory is in the uncomfortable position that, in order to detect design, it must make use of lacunae in science. For it is only in those cases where no scientific explanation is available in terms of regularity or chance that phenomena can be based on design. This incidental referral to a design thus necessarily leads to a God-of-the-gaps argument, an appeal to a divine intervention or a metaphysical cause in places where empirical science has holes. The attempt to synthesize faith and reason has become dependent on the progress of modern science.

I know that many design theorists, but not all, reject the notion of God as the filler of gaps. They suggest that such gaps would not occur at all if scholarship would only make room for the new, scientific paradigm of design. Dembski even announces a paradigm shift or "a new kind of science."[22] I think that the elaboration of such a new type of science will be less novel than he has in

---

[22] W. A. Dembski, *The Design Revolution: Answering the Toughest Questions about Intelligent Design* (Downers Grove, IL: InterVarsity Press, 2004), last section. Some suggest that the recognition of gaps in nature is desirable; it may indicate a new type of science, sometimes called "theistic science." See J. P. Moreland, "Complementarity, Agency Theory, and the God-of-the-Gaps," *Perspectives on Science and Christian Faith* 49 (1997), 2–14.

mind. It will probably only be a modernized version of traditional metaphysics.

Within ID, many are aware of this metaphysical temptation. Thus, in many cases the explicit striving after a synthesis of science and faith, as brought forward in Dembski's research program, is pushed back. The term "intelligent design" plays an ambiguous role here. To avoid metaphysics – there are also political reasons at stake[23] – the adherents of ID will discuss intelligent design but would rather not mention the intelligent designer, let alone a divine agent. For with the latter, so the argument goes, one would cross the boundaries of empirical science. But only with the latter? I am of the opinion that as soon as scientists start to explain natural phenomena on the basis of a non-natural design, one has already crossed the bounds of legitimate science.

To be sure, one can defend the thesis that living phenomena display such a specific complexity that it cannot be directly derived from the laws of inanimate nature. With the defense of this thesis – I shall return to it later in connection with Michael Behe (see ch.7, section 6) – Intelligent Design would have more than its hands full. However, the thesis that phenomena are based on design reaches further. It includes, if not the explicit proof, then certainly the implicit suggestion that a divine author is involved and that true science can provide insight into this: "scientists discover the creator."[24] I see this implicit synthesis as a hidden metaphysics and this hidden metaphysics as the Achilles heel of the ID theory.

Nowadays, the search for a synthesis of faith and science with the aid of metaphysical arguments is very disputable, both from the standpoint of faith and from the standpoint of science. From the standpoint of faith, questions such as this arise: is professing God as "the almighty creator of heaven and earth" not preeminently an

---

[23] In the United States there are also political reasons why ID people want to discuss the design but do not want to discuss the devine designer. "Disestablishment" rules prohibit public schools from teaching religion. So the movement attempts to get a foot in the door by offering ID as an alternative theory without referring to God.

[24] The deeper intentions of ID are effectively pictured in the subtitle of J. M. Templeton (ed.), *Evidence of Purpose: Scientists Discover the Creator* (New York: Continuum Publishing, 1994).

article of faith? Is the God of the Bible, the father of Jesus Christ, the same as the intelligent cause to which the design theoreticians conclude? Does reason, in search of design in the world, offer an alternative access to God in favor of an intellectual elite? And what do the words of Hebrews 11, a hymn not to reason but to faith, mean: "By faith we understand that the universe was formed at God's command, so that what is seen was not made out of what was visible" (Hebr. 11:3)?

From the standpoint of science, entirely different questions arise. Is human intellect capable of transcending empirical reality and of looking for non-natural or supernatural causes? Is it in a position to prove the existence of a supra-human designer and to think his creative thoughts after him? Can science be extrapolated to metaphysics? Space prevents me from going into the devastating critique by David Hume and Immanuel Kant of the credibility of metaphysics. But their argument, that metaphysical propositions cannot be subject to any kind of empirical control, as is demanded in science, is still as solid as the Rock of Gibraltar.

One can consider the above considerations theoretical, but they do lead to an incisive practical conclusion. This conclusion is that it is not evolutionary science but Intelligent Design that endangers faith in God as the creator of all life on earth. I must express myself even more precisely and emphatically. Research programs such as Dembski's seem to support the truth of the Christian faith, but I fear that they unwittingly aid atheism. For if the lack of an evolutionary explanation for a complex phenomenon of life can be considered as a proof for the existence of a divine designer, then the reverse, the finding of such an explanation, can be considered as an argument for the fact that this God does not exist, or that His existence is, at least, irrelevant. Then the irresistible forward march of the evolutionary sciences cannot be regarded other than as a triumph of atheism and as a defeat for faith in creation. I fear that many, consciously or unconsciously, have drawn this conclusion long ago.

Finally, a comment to avoid misunderstandings. I have questioned the search for a synthesis in the sense of a bridge between faith and science based upon the pillars of metaphysical design arguments. With this, I do not suggest that faith and scholarship are separate terrains, or that religion is irrelevant for reason. Although science represents a type of knowledge all its own, it is not autonomous in the sense of being self-sufficient. It is involved in a comprehensive, historical, and societal process of understanding. Science is a project of people who form their theories out of historical and philosophical traditions (Wilhelm Dilthey), on the basis of paradigmatic models of science (Thomas Kuhn), and as a practice connected with daily life (Hilary Putnam). Besides, the results of this investigation are encompassed in a yet wider context of understanding, a hermeneutic matrix determined by religious convictions that can be Judeo-Christian but also from humanistic or naturalistic nature (Hans-Georg Gadamer). Thus we shall have to think again about the coherence of faith and science, traces of God in nature, models of synthesis, and a Christianity-inspired scholarship in a non-Scholastic context. Creation stories can help us on our way.

4 CREATION STORIES AND THEIR PRACTICAL INTENT

There are good reasons to relate faith and science in a way that differs radically from the synthesis model that is characteristic of the Scholastic and neo-Scholastic tradition.[25] In a later chapter I hope to examine this alternative in a more fundamental sense (see ch. 10, section 2). Here I focus on the concrete question of how, in relation to evolutionary science, we should read the creation narrative in Genesis 1–2:4a. I would suggest: not as a historical research report or as a scientific account, but as a testimony of faith, cast into the form of a hymn of praise to the Creator of the universe, with all the expressive abilities this genre provides. Genesis 1 is a narrative and poetic composition, a ballad about the origin of the world, recognizable by the constantly recurring refrain: "And there was evening, and there was morning – the first (second, etc.) day." It is an imaginative referral to the one God who is for the Bible writers the unfathomable source of all being. And the symbolic representations

---

[25] In the history of Christian thought one can, beside the biblicist and scholastic model, discover many other models of Christian synthesis. See J. Klapwijk, S. Griffioen, and G. Groenewoud (eds.), *Bringing into Captivity every Thought: Capita Selecta in the History of Christian Evaluations of Non-Christian Philosophy* (Lanham, MD: University Press of America, 1991).

that are shown to us in this chapter (e.g. waters above and below the firmament) are – how else could it be – determined by the ancient, oriental world picture of the authors.

Previously, I have hinted that I have not always been happy with the appeal that some Christians make to the literal meaning of bible texts. There are reasons for this. For the "*sensus literalis*" (Martin Luther), i.e. the literal or real meaning of a text, is often not unambiguous or obvious. It cannot be determined simply with the aid of grammatical rules and a dictionary. The meaning of a text often depends on the character of the context in which such a text functions. For it makes an enormous difference whether this context is an eyewitness account, a narrative, or a poem. A text in the Bible must also be seen as a function of the context. First we have to know what this text originally meant in the world of the Bible authors before we can say what its meaning may be nowadays, in the world of our experiences. The exegesis of a text in Genesis 1, too, should be determined by the hermeneutical understanding of the context: the character of this chapter as a creation narrative. In other words, the exegesis will have to let itself be led by the possibilities of expression that are peculiar to the genre of creation narratives. What is a creation narrative?

Creation stories abound in religious literature. Noteworthy are their excess of symbolism and their shortage of factual information. The stories recount how, in the religious consciousness of a people from primeval times on, practical relationships among creator, human beings, and the world are regulated. They make mention of the greatness of the creator, the mandates for human life, and the divine ordinances that support the cosmos. They also tell of the human condition, of challenges and temptations, of evil and its consequences, and of shame and guilt. They point, finally, to an avenue of salvation, reconciliation, and happiness, and they emphasize the necessity of celebrating the monumental primal beginnings on days of remembrance with fitting rituals. In short, creation stories confront us with a worldview, a pattern of values, and a practice for life that are wholly determined by an existentially lived communion with the divine.

Let us keep these things in mind as we consider the biblical creation story. This story involves us emphatically in the practical relationships of life among God, humans, and the world. It does not present us with a factual account, and certainly not with a primitive theory about the origin of the cosmos or of humankind. The days of creation do not order created things in a historical succession, but in a sequence of ascending practical importance. For this reason in Genesis 1 the earth appears first, then plants, then the diversity of animals, and finally humans as the crown of creation. For this reason, too, the creation of the sun follows the creation of the earth and the plants, as if it were an interim provision of God. For it is only after dry land has appeared, and life has budded forth, that the sun becomes of eminent importance as a source of light and warmth.

This practical intent is particularly noticeable in the paradise story that follows. Genesis 2 and 3 confront us with Adam, the earth man, and Eve, the bearer of life. We are told of their divine origin, their naming of all things, their fall into sin and guilt, and their subsequent life under God's judgment, but also of God's promise of a new future. The paradise story is a touching account of the human condition. Any person sensitive to drama and symbolism should be able to recognize himself or herself in the story. In Adam a mirror is held before our eyes. In Adam we are created, we have sinned, we have need for salvation, and in him God has cleared a new way for us.[26]

The creation account and the paradise story deal with historical facts, says the orthodox believer. That is as true as it is not true. Creation and the fall into sin are not historical facts in the modern scientific sense of the word, events datable in an era far removed from ours. We don't get off that easily! We are dealing with real facts in the form of primeval events that are handed down from generation to generation; stories that are from far, yet near. From far because they speak of events in the distant past. And near because they are within our reach. In the primeval story I stumble over my own roots. I run into my most distant ancestors and I run up against myself. God's work in creating is history, yes, but not in the form an objectifiable history in the usual sense of long ago. It is

<hr>

[26] In the New Testament this new way is depicted more precisely as the way of Christ. Compare Gen. 3 with Rom. 5. In the Romans passage Paul gives a new, practical meaning to the paradise story. His message is: in Christ God makes a new start with humanity.

an involving primeval history, recognizable in faith.[27] The biblical creation stories have a corporative and inclusive significance; they give direction, also for our times. And what about history in its usual sense, all those datable events from long or not-so-long ago, right up to this very day? These events form the creaturely continuation, the continuing episodes that the drama of Genesis brings to the fore.

All in all, Genesis 1, with its six days of creation and one of rest, is one great song of praise to God as the Lord of heaven and earth, a song that is of great practical bearing. When the sovereign God creates and then rests, it is fitting for human beings to mirror him and to observe a work week and times of rest, and thus to remain human instead of becoming workaholics. To put it another way, the meaning of creation manifests itself in the Sabbath, the day of shalom and recreative rest. A similar point is made in Genesis 2 and 3, for these chapters also do not contain strictly historical, objectifiable facts. The paradise story, also, is a primeval story. It sketches paradise and the fall into sin as original forms of existence, related to the first human pair. It sketches, at the same time, the basic situation of every person as being entangled in shame and guilt, or in anguish and uncertainty, and yet not without hope and promises in this world.[28]

In short, the biblical interest is completely different from the interest of science. The book of Genesis does not offer a (primitive) theory of origins of a world that has gone for ever. On the contrary, it presents to us a reality that is not past but touches us all. Compare

---

[27] Christ's death and resurrection, too, are not historical events in the usual sense. They also form a primeval event that includes us. In Christ again, a mirror is held up to our faces. In Rom. 5 the resurrected Lord Christ is presented as the new Adam. He symbolizes the new humanity, the human being that answers to God's intentions. In him lie our new roots.

[28] For an illustration of the exemplary and inclusive nature of the creation story see Ex. 20:11. Here we are exhorted to six days of labor and a day of rest in imitation of God's days of creation. For the exemplary and inclusive nature of the paradise story in Gen. 2 and 3 see Rom. 5:12–21. Here we read that in Adam all people have sinned. Adam's fall into sin is in other words a corporate event, just as Christ's salvation is a corporate event; we become part of it by faith. The doctrine of "an original sin, inherited from our first parents" is a dogmatic misinterpretation of people who do not know what to do with history as an involving process and thus separate such sin from personal responsibility, depicting it as a heritable ailment. Such people have problems not only with the appropriation of Adam's sin but also with the appropriation of Christ's righteousness.

this with those noble, postwar German people who after half a century of shame and repression felt a need to make amends (*Wiedergutmachung*) and who thus went to ask for pardon from the victims of Nazi terror inflicted by a previous generation. Or compare it with the former Pope John Paul II, who in the year 2000 at the Wailing Wall in Jerusalem made a similar gesture when he asked Jews to forgive all the evil that Christians had perpetrated against them through the ages. It is strange but true: there is a past that catches up with the present and hammers on our conscience. So, too, does the creation account.

5 AUGUSTINE: TIME IS A CREATURE OF GOD

Creation stories abound, but the biblical account of creation distinguishes itself in four ways:

(1) It is monotheistic. It summons all creatures to service of the one God who does not wrestle with matter, with idolatrous rivals, mythical monsters, or pre-established time, but who is sovereign and calls everything from naught into being: *creatio ex nihilo.*[29]
(2) It is anti-spiritualistic. Matter, fertility, and reproduction are not of lesser mettle than spirit or thought. All that comes into being is described as "good," human beings with the breath of life in their nostrils even as "very good."
(3) It is anti-mythological. Amon-Re and Shamash, worshiped by Egyptians and Sumerians as sun gods, are stripped of their divinity and put on display as heavenly lights, i.e. ordinary creatures.
(4) It is focussed on the stewardly task of humans. They become the representatives of God. They are given responsibility for the governance and care of the earth and its inhabitants. Culture is raised to the level of *cultus.*

If God is the origin of the entire cosmic and earthly reality, then what does this mean for our understanding of time? In this regard a

---

[29] See 2 Maccabees 7:28: "observe heaven and earth, consider all that is in them, and acknowledge that God made them out of what did not exist, and that mankind comes into being the same way" (Jerusalem Bible).

literal reading of the Bible often stands in the way of perceiving the proper meaning of Scripture. Thus, it is written that on the fourth day God created the heavenly lights "to separate the day from the night"; that is to say, God created day and night on the fourth day. If one takes these words literally one is faced with a glaring paradox, for how can days come into existence on a certain (i.e. the fourth) day? The days as *framework* of God's creating acts are of an entirely different order than the days as *result* of God's creative acts, i.e. as periods of twenty-four hours. For us, time-bound creatures, it is impossible to imagine that God created the world, including time, without doing so in a framework of time. This time frame is, therefore, a representation *for us*. Nowhere does the Bible suggest that God, in his creative acts, was himself bound to work days of twenty-four hours or, in a less literal interpretation, to periods of hundreds of millions of years.[30]

To be more specific, the drama of creation cannot be located in time at all. The Eternal One is not bound to time and the temporal. No one has stated this more strongly than the Church Father Augustine in the eleventh book of his *Confessions*, in the famous discourse about time. This discourse – in fact a prayer to God – is of great import for what follows. Here Augustine makes a sharp distinction between God's creative activity, which is from eternity, and time, which is a result of God's creativity. He comes to the remarkable conclusion that not only all things that originated in time, but *time itself* is a creature of the God who is eternal and precedes all periods of time. With profound insight, he writes:

How could those countless ages have elapsed when you, the Creator, in whom all ages have their origin, had not created them? What time could there have been that was not created by you? . . . You are the Maker of all time . . . for time could not elapse before you made it . . . But if there was no time before heaven and earth were created, how can anyone ask what you were doing "then"? If there was no time, there was no "then" . . .

Furthermore, although you are before time, it is not in time that you precede it. If this were so, you would not be before all time. It is in eternity, which is supreme over time because it is a never-ending present,

---

[30] Gen. 1:14. The paradox is already built into the first day of creation. We read that God created light on the first day and called it day; Gen. 1:3. In a comparable way we can ask here: how can God create a day on the first day?

that you are at once before all past time and after all future time . . . It is
therefore true to say that when you had not made anything, there was
no time, because time itself was of your making . . . What then is time?
I know well enough what it is, provided nobody asks me; but if I am asked
what it is and try to explain, I am baffled.[31]

Augustine develops here an impressive vision of time. In this vision,
time in all its puzzling complexity is itself a creature of God. And in
the course of that time, the world – which was created together with
time – comes to its dynamic disclosure. Everything that God
created "in the beginning" comes to light in the process of time. If
I understand Augustine correctly, time is for him the temporal disclosure and realization of everything that was enclosed from the onset
in the secret of God's creative activity. In short, time is the showroom
of creation. In time God exhibits his plans with the world. In the spirit
of the Church Father one could say: even the things that come to light
in the universe and on earth, after billions of years, were from the very
beginning marked as creatures with which God has an intention. The
human being, too, is a creature with a purpose, even if we know
nowadays that in evolutionary history this creature has appeared on
the world stage as a complete latecomer.

Here the question arises: has Augustine's concept of time also
importance for our topic? Is the process of evolution with all its
contingent developments strictly random, or could it accord with
the realization of a purpose? When one looks with Augustine's eyes,
one is convinced of the latter. The intentions of the creator precede
the developments in time; to put it more strongly, they manifest
themselves in time. Time is the gradual disclosure of the creation.
Augustine's vision, grandly painted in his book *The City of God*,
implies the notion of a divine edict or design that effectuates itself
irresistibly in the processes of nature and in the occurrences of world
history. But don't forget, for Augustine this notion of design is no
theoretical conclusion, no supra-natural intervention, no inference

---

[31] The quotations in this paragraph are from book XI, sections 13, 14, of Augustine,
Confessions, trans. by R. S. Pine-Coffin (Harmondsworth: Penguin Books, 1961). In contrast to the mainstream of Western philosophy since Parmenides and Plato, time in
Augustine's view is an integral component of reality. In modern physics Einstein confirmes
this insight by presenting time as a fourth dimension of the space and time continuum.

from the calculated measure of improbability of particular things in nature, *à la* Dembski. It is a religious vision that encompasses all events of the world, a result of his faith in God as "the Maker of all time."[32] The troublesome question that will force itself upon us in the chapters to come is this: is the concept of time of the great patriarch a purely religious intuition, or can support or recognition also be found for it in scientific discourse?

Augustine's view of time lifts us, in one fell swoop, also above the calculations of the early creationists, the worthy Bishop Ussher included. The six days of creation are neither a historical measure of time nor a chronological table in which we can place God, founder of the ages. We may not measure God's days by ours. Instead, we are invited to mirror our days to his. In that respect we cannot take the days of creation literally enough. For, if we assume that the Bible invites us indeed to experience the practical Christian life from day to day as a *cultus*, a spiritual act of worship to God, then the creation story presents itself as a liturgy that returns every week. Thus it becomes a text that does not reveal God's agenda as creator but that indicates how *we as creatures* are to arrange our days and weeks in order to commemorate God's great deeds. As it is written in the Torah: "Six days you shall labor and do all your work, but the seventh day is a Sabbath to the Lord your God . . . For in six days the Lord made the heavens and the earth . . . but He rested on the seventh day."[33] The American Christian philosopher Roy Clouser correctly suggests: if it is true that God brought to existence not only space, matter, and the laws that govern the universe but also time, then every creation account is necessarily anthropomorphic.

---

[32] For the Augustinian vision on time as a disclosure of creation, see J. H. Diemer, *Natuur en wonder* (Amsterdam: Buijten & Schipperheijn, 1963) and, in a more critical approach, C. E. Gunton, *The Triune Creator: A Historical and Systematic Study* (Grand Rapids, MI: Eerdmans, 1998), pp. 79–96.

[33] Ex. 20:9–11. For a description of the Christian life as a "spiritual act of worship" see Rom. 12:1. In the New Testament, too, creation story and Sabbath command are seen, practically, as a proclamation of faith. They are a call to labor, rest, and celebrate; yes, to enter the land of rest: the heavenly Canaan (Hebr. 4:9). The description of the creation story as a "liturgy that returns every week" was suggested to me by Dick Stafleu. He remarks: "Note the Jewish tradition to marry on Tuesdays, because it is twice said of the third day of creation that it was good" (personal communication).

Then it is written in terms that can only be drawn from human experiences and practices.[34]

We do not have to experience everyday life as an endless circle. The liturgical text of Genesis 1 invites us to experience our work week as a celebration of light, life, labor, humanity, etc., given by God the creator, and culminating in the Sabbath, a day of recreation. In other words, I read the first pages of the Bible as a trumpet voluntary celebrating the majesty of God as creator of heaven and earth, source of all life, maker of humankind, origin of dethroned heavenly bodies, and the author of time and history. And for human beings this voluntary becomes an *Aufforderung zum Tanz*, an invitation to dance, a summons to lend our voices and join the music of the spheres, a call to tune the restless rhythm of our work week to the beat of God's works. Six days of labor with their ups and downs, and then: *basta, fiesta!*

I want to conclude with a comment to clarify my position. In the chapters that follow I hope to clear away the immensely popular but disastrous misunderstanding that there is a conflict between religious faith in creation and the scientific theory of evolution. But let one thing be clear. Even if I am of the opinion that the conflict is based on a serious misunderstanding, I am not an adherent of what is often called "theistic evolution" in the evolutionary debate. Does God create through evolution? If that were true, then my struggling with Augustine has been in vain. Worse, then the festival of recreation is over.

---

[34] Roy Clouser, "Is Theism Compatible with Evolution?," in Robert T. Pennock (ed.), *Intelligent Design Creationism and Its Critics: Philosophical, Theological, and Scientific Perspectives* (Cambridge, MA: MIT Press, 2001), pp. 513–36.

CHAPTER 3

Darwin, neo-Darwinism, and the naturalistic continuity claim

In the preceding chapter we explored the world of religion. We requested attention to the narrative of creation and to the practical function that this story has in the life of believers and in the liturgy of the church. We also paused to examine the intellectualistic interpretation that the creation message has received in creationist circles.

In this chapter we turn our sights to the world of science, particularly of evolutionary science. Can the belief that God created the world, including living organisms, be harmonized with the scientific idea that life on earth developed through natural selection, and as such represents an evolutionary continuum? First I recapitulate a number of key points in Darwin's theory (section 1). Then I refer to neo-Darwinism or the modern synthesis of evolutionary theory and genetics; at the same time I introduce a sharp distinction between the theory of evolution and the ideological claims of so-called evolutionism (section 2). This distinction will lead us into a discussion of the naturalistic implications of evolutionism (section 3). We conclude this chapter with a critical analysis of the continuity postulate and the reducibility postulate that are both presupposed in the evolutionistic ideology (section 4).

I DARWIN'S THEORY OF EVOLUTION: THE CVST ALGORITHM

The theory of the origin of biological species by selective natural breeding and hereditary transmission is a monumental one. One could see it as one of the greatest scientific breakthroughs of the nineteenth century. It was carefully formulated by Darwin on the basis of years of investigations during his voyage on the *Beagle*.

The young Charles Robert Darwin (1809–1882) set sail in 1831 holding traditional views about the constancy of species. He soon began to doubt when on his journey along the various continents he was struck by greater or smaller dissimilarities between related plant and animal species that came from segregated areas. Paleontological finds in South America, among others of sloths and armadillos, strengthened his doubts, because he encountered among earlier specimens characteristics that differed, even in size alone, from what is observable today. Finally, the subtle differences that he noticed between finches, mockingbirds, and tortoise populations from the various Galápagos islands set him thinking.[1]

All these differences among species gave him the luminous idea that in living nature gradual changes must have occurred over time. Apparently there are species that are related in origin, but which gradually differentiated from each other as they adapted to divergent environments. In his autobiography Darwin recalls the three lines of evidence that led him to his theory.

From September 1854 onwards I devoted all my time to arranging my huge pile of notes, to observing and experimenting, in relation to the transmutation of species. During the voyage of the *Beagle* I had been deeply impressed [firstly] by discovering in the Pampean formation great fossil animals . . . secondly by the manner in which closely allied animals replace one another in proceeding southwards over the Continent; and thirdly by the South American character of most of the productions of the Galápagos archipelago, and more especially by the manner in which they differ slightly on each island of the group.[2]

How had these vegetative and animal-like productions become different? What was the mysterious force in the process of evolution – evolution understood as "descent with modification"? Initially

---

[1] Darwin, in his description of the tortoises of the Galápagos Islands, writes: "I have not as yet noticed by far the most remarkable feature in the natural history of this archipelago; it is, that the different islands to a considerable extent are inhabited by a different set of beings. My attention was first called to this fact by the Vice-Governor, Mr. Lawson, declaring that the tortoises differed from the different islands, and that he could with certainty tell from which island any one was brought." *Journal of Researches into the Natural History and Geology of the Countries Visited During the Voyage of H. M. S. Beagle round the World* [1845] (New York: Ward, Lock and Co., n.d.), p. 375. The work is known as *The Voyage of the Beagle.*

[2] C. R. Darwin, *The Autobiography of Charles Darwin: 1809–1882* [1887], N. Barlow (ed.) (New York: W. W. Norton, 1958), p. 118.

Darwin had no idea. He found an explanation in 1838, two years after his return to England, when he read the famous *Essay on Population* by Thomas Robert Malthus. In this book the moody Malthus, demographer and economist studying processes of population growth, created a sensation with the thesis that human existence hinges, in the final analysis, on success in a relentless struggle to survive. This was an eye-opener for Darwin. The origin of biological species, he saw at once, was a powerful demonstration of Malthus' thesis, applied to the entire plant and animal kingdoms.[3]

Darwin's theory of descent, presented in *The Origin of Species* and later applied to human beings in *The Descent of Man*, is still of basic significance for the life sciences.[4] I would summarize his views in the following four theses:

(1) In view of the exponential increase of offspring due to reproduction – e.g. from 2, to 4, to 8, to 16, etc., but often the rate of increase is much greater – in plant and animal organisms, when not disturbed, population pressure quickly leads to overproduction and, in the words of Malthus, to an inevitable *struggle for life.*

(2) In view of the small variations in heritable characteristics that randomly occur in the reproductive process, the struggle for existence leads to a selective advantage for those organisms possessing characteristics that are more adapted to external circumstances than those of other organisms; in short, the struggle for existence leads to *natural selection.*

---

[3] Thomas R. Malthus, *An Essay on the Principle of Population as it Affects the Future Improvement of Society* (London: J. Johnson, 1798). Malthus states that increasing prosperity results in a population explosion, and this, in turn, to an excessive increase in labor supply and a serious decrease in incomes. This would lead to a struggle for survival and massive death rates which result in a decrease in population pressure and a gradual recovery of prosperity. With this the cycle would start to repeat itself. Malthus concludes that this cycle would result in a level of prosperity that oscillates around a minimal subsistence. In recent times this trend is no longer inevitable, thanks to technological progress, at least in the privileged West. Whether technological renewal, also in the rest of the world, can end the stark struggle for life is still open to debate.

[4] C. R. Darwin, *On the Origin of Species by Means of Natural Selection* (London: John Murray, 1859), and *The Descent of Man, and Selection in Relation to Sex* (London: John Murray, 1871), are still in print today in a variety of editions.

(3) In view of the adaptive advantage that some of these traits confer on the organisms that possess them, the spontaneous and undirected selection by nature – which Darwin often contrasted with the artificial and purposeful selection by plant and animal breeders – leads, in terms he borrowed from Herbert Spencer, to a *survival of the fittest.*

(4) In view of the heritability of the aforementioned traits, the reproductive success of the fittest organisms ('fit' in late medieval usage already meant adapted) leads, if the populations are isolated, to an increased diversity within species, and, ultimately, to new plant and animal species: the *origin of species.*

These four theses give a short summary of what is included in the process of evolution according to Darwin's presentation of affairs. To this I would like to add the following. When one reads popular representations of Darwin's theory, then the principles of variation and selection mentioned under points 2 and 3 are usually regarded as central. Evolutionary biologists present them as "Darwin's double principle" and as the most important "mechanisms of evolutionary change." The theses show that in Darwin's thought not two but at least four principles can be distinguished, here indicated as competition, variation, selection, and genetic transmission.

It is helpful to see these four principles in mutual context, as a chain of principles. For without competition there would be no evolutionary advantage in the variation of characteristics. Without variation, there could be no selection for more adapted characteristics. And without selection, no transmission of characteristics with the greatest reproductive success could take place. For this reason, I have named the four aforementioned principles the CVST algorithm.

The CVST principles operate in a biological context. They are universal laws, yet they are not laws of a physical nature. The CVST algorithm is exclusively applicable to living nature, i.e. to typically biological phenomena. Competition, variation, selection, and transmission have no points of contact with material nature, nor in cosmic space, nor in geological processes, nor in abiotic reality. Thus they do not explain the origin of life; rather they presuppose the presence of life. Darwin, too, applied these rules in relation to evolutionary changes in the living world; he did not venture an opinion about the question of how life originated.

Naturally one could also speak, in a certain context, of cosmic evolution; one could also formulate laws to explain processes of modification in material nature. But that is another story. In Darwin's account, such laws do not come up for discussion. And Darwin certainly does not suggest a continuum between cosmic and biological evolution. For this reason I do not find it advisable to describe the principles of mutation, selection, etc. as "mechanisms of evolutionary change." With a terminology of this type one builds, perhaps unintended, a mechanistic framework that will not be able to do justice to the uniqueness of life and to the unique character of biological or non-mechanistic principles.

2 EVOLUTION THEORY AND EVOLUTIONISM

Modifications to Darwin's theory were inevitable. They successively came to light in the last century and came especially from the side of population ecology and genetics. Thus, ecologists concluded that the process of selection in nature was less dependent on sexual selection and intraspecific competition than Darwin thought; it was found to be much more dependent on environmental factors, such as mimicry, genetic drift, and interspecific group advantages. And the discipline of genetics, completely unknown to Darwin, has been able to determine, among other things, the manner in which natural selection gains a foothold in reproduction. Milestones in this development were the hereditary laws of Gregor Mendel, published in 1864, almost totally unknown in Darwin's time; the gene and mutation theories of Hugo de Vries of 1889–1901; the population genetics theses of G. H. Hardy and W. Weinberg (1908); and the double-stranded DNA model of J. D. Watson and F. H. C. Crick (1953). From the 1970s, genetics received powerful support from molecular biology, which gave access to the complex world of the biological cell. Molecular biology demanded attention to the disparate forms of mutations that can occur in DNA, such as point mutation, deletion, insertion, duplication, transposition, endosymbiosis, and hybridization. This suffices to make clear that cell turbulences have been discovered in the interior of the cell, of which neither Darwin nor Mendel had the faintest inkling.

The contributions of paleontology, population ecology, comparative anatomy, immunology, and molecular biology have not only considerably modified but also fundamentally confirmed the Darwinian theory of evolution through natural selection. During the middle of the last century the theory reached a measure of completion through its alliance with genetics and molecular biology. Since that time, the phrase "evolution theory" represents an impressive combination of theories about the descent of species that begins with Darwin's view of genetic variation and natural selection, and takes into account all its modern modifications up to the gene frequencies in the DNA. This cluster of theories is referred to as neo-Darwinism or, more specifically, as the synthesis theory or the modern synthesis (of evolutionary theory and genetics).[5] Major figures in the development toward this synthesis include Thomas Hunt Morgan, J. B. S. Haldane, Theodosius Dobzhansky, Ernst Mayr, George Gaylord Simpson, and G. Ledyard Stebbins.

Thus "evolution theory" refers to the modern synthesis. But "evolution theory" can also denote something entirely different. Then it is not a cluster of theoretical disciplines that seek a step by step confirmation of evolutionary hypotheses. Then it is a *worldview*: an a priori view of the world as an evolutionary reality having the material world as its self-evident and all-explaining origin. Then it would have us believe that the magnificent diversity of life forms on earth, right up to its most complex systems, is necessarily a product of pure chance, of blind powers and random regulatory mechanisms, and thus without any design, purpose, or meaning. This worldview, too, adorns itself with the name of evolution *theory*, but it is in fact a dogma: a belief implying that evolution theory, once and for all, has solved the mystery of life. Later on I shall give many examples of such a worldview conviction. Philosophers would detect an *ideology* here, i.e. a view that can no longer be called theory or science, because it has become a rationalized belief system, although it proceeds under the banner of science.

---

[5] Neo-Darwinism is a rather ill-defined concept. The term was used around 1900 for a strict form of Darwin's theory developed by August Weismann. He posited that natural selection is the only means of evolutionary change and that the heritability of acquired characteristics is not possible. He was wrong on the first count and correct on the second, while his argument in favor of this viewpoint (the separation of germ- and soma-plasm) is also questionable. The incorporation of Hugo de Vries' mutation theory has also been named neo-Darwinism.

In the analyses that follow I accept evolution theory as a respectable cluster of hypothetico-scientific theories. I distantiate myself from it whenever it turns out to be a belief system, a transfer medium for ideologies of a naturalistic provenance. A major problem in evolution debates is that theory and ideology are often inextricably intertwined. Many authors interlace their scientific arguments with ideological expectations or season their ideological expectations with scientific arguments. Readers who have such expectations are often inclined to swallow the argument hook, line, and sinker. For those who do not share these expectations critical distinctions are needed.

In this book I introduce a strict distinction between evolution theory and evolutionism.[6] Evolutionism is for me suspect. The suffix "ism" points to an absolutization of a particular insight. Thus the term "psychologism" is an overestimation or absolutization of the explanatory power of psychology, as we find in Freud. And the term "economism" is an overestimation or absolutization of the explanatory power of economics, as we find in Marx. In our case we deal with an absolutization of evolutionary science. In short, when I speak of *evolution theory* I refer to that cluster of theoretical disciplines that so many geneticists and evolutionary biologists around the world work at with methodic diligence and dedication. On the contrary, when I mention *evolutionism* I refer to that view of evolution that pretends to be the definitive solution to the riddle of life. Evolutionism is a naturalistic ideology that has impregnated evolution theory in the past century, and that is packaged as scientific truth. For that reason "evolutionism" is for me equivalent to "evolutionary naturalism."

The distinction between evolution theory and evolutionism can help us to determine a thinker's position in the evolution debate. At the same time there is reason to apply this distinction carefully, and to not apply labels without careful thought. There are three particulars that we need to keep in mind. First, evolutionism is in the life sciences more a tone-setting trend than a sharply demarcated position. Secondly, it is with some authors a dominant theme, with

[6] The same distinction is made by J. Lever, *Creation and Evolution* (Grand Rapids, MI: International Publications, 1958), ch. 6.

others just a subconscious presupposition. In the third place, we have to admit that ideological stories, too, can contain important elements of scientific truth.

3 THE AMBIGUITY OF NATURALISM

In the above I designated evolutionism to be a "naturalistic ideology." What does this indicate? Previously, I stated what I understand "ideology" to mean: a belief system disguised as science. But what is "naturalism"? Often writers distinguish between ontological and methodological naturalism; I will deal with this distinction in a later chapter.[7] I confine myself here to naturalism as an ontology, an overall view of reality.

Ontological naturalism often gives rise to confusing discussions. This is because the word "naturalism" is, in itself, already ambiguous. It has a traditional and a modern meaning, and the two are often mixed up. In early modern times the word acquired its traditional meaning. "Naturalism" was seen as the counterpart of the ontology espoused by medieval scholastics, namely, supernaturalism, the doctrine that there is a natural and a supernatural (or divine) reality (see ch. 2, section 3). Thinkers who did not acknowledge this double reality, and wrote off the supernatural, became subsequently known as naturalists.[8] Today many people consider this scholastic dualism to be a thing of the past; besides, many Christians consider it to be in conflict with an integral Christian view of life. Still, the dualistic pattern of thinking continues to color the traditional meaning of the word. Thus, this naturalism indicates a scheme of thought that excludes the supernatural, and that declares any

---

[7] Ontological naturalism is a view of reality based on the idea that nature is the all-encompassing principle of all that exists. Methodological naturalism is a view of science based on the idea that the method of the natural sciences, in particular the physical method, is foundational to all theoretical disciplines. Both views often go hand in hand but this is not necessarily the case (see ch. 9, section 5).

[8] I cite Gisbertus Voetius, the theological opponent of Descartes: "alios philosophos naturae omnia adscribentes aut supra naturalem cognitionem vix assurgentes plerumque Naturalistes vocant" (other philosophers, who attribute everything to nature, or who hardly rise above natural knowledge, are usually called Naturalists). G. Voetius, "De atheismo," in *Selectarum disputationum theologicarum*, 5 vols. (Utrecht: Waesberge, 1648–1669), vol. 1 (1648), p. 123.

speaking about God to be taboo. This naturalism is synonymous with philosophical atheism.[9]

In the last few centuries a modern meaning has come into vogue. The word "naturalism" is no longer defined from out of a scholastic dualism as a rejection of the supernatural. The modern view is based on a monistic idea of the world, a unitary optic in which nature is presented as the all-encompassing basis of reality. Naturalism represents the conviction that all that is is, in its very essence, material nature, determined by universal laws and physico-chemical causes, and in the final analysis explicable according to the paradigm of the natural sciences.[10] This naturalism is not associated with philosophical atheism but with philosophical materialism. At present, depending on how God and nature are defined, one may therefore even encounter theistic variants of this type of naturalism.[11]

Which definition of naturalism shall we retain? Earlier I reacted against scholastic dualism, the assumed duality of a natural and supernatural reality. The supernatural is, upon closer analysis, a non-biblical concept, formulated in the Middle Ages, probably of Neoplatonic origin. For this reason the scholastic definition of naturalism as counterpart of supernaturalism is not very attractive. Furthermore, I do not wish to consider all naturalists as atheists. Therefore, I prefer the modern definition of naturalism. I do so, however, without agreeing with its content. I consider it incorrect to take the physical concept of nature as the ultimate principle of reality. Naturalism in its modern expression is a misconception of the nature of physical reality, based on an overestimation of the explanatory abilities of modern physics.

Let us return to our point of departure. We concluded that present-day evolutionism rests on basic views of naturalism. Thus

---

[9] C. S. Lewis, *Miracles: A Preliminary Study* (New York: Macmillan, 1947), p. 16: "Our first choice, therefore, must be between Naturalism and Supernaturalism."

[10] A. C. Danto: "Naturalism, in recent usage, is a species of philosophical monism according to which whatever exists or happens is *natural* in the sense of being susceptible to explanation through methods which, although paradigmatically exemplified in the natural sciences, are *continuous from domain to domain of objects and events*" (my emphasis). From "Naturalism," in *The Encyclopedia of Philosophy*, vol. v (New York/London: Macmillan and The Free Press, 1972), p. 448.

[11] See W. B. Drees, *Religion, Science and Naturalism* (Cambridge: Cambridge University Press, 1996).

that is to say, it rests on basic views of naturalism in its modern expression. What do these basic views include? I can now mention four elements:

(1) The starting-point of evolutionary naturalism is the self-evident identification of nature in general with the one-sided and abstract concept of nature that is used in modern physics.

(2) Contrary to Darwin, who had no explanation for the origin of life, this naturalism claims that the physical concept of nature can serve as the ultimate explanatory basis, also for all phenomena of life.[12]

(3) On to this theoretical basis it has built an explanatory scheme of organic nature in the style of neo-Darwinian selectionism.

(4) From this scheme it draws the twofold conclusion that all life forms have originated in a strictly fortuitous manner from material nature in a gradual and uninterrupted line of development, and that these life phenomena are complex and completely reducible variants of physical phenomena.[13]

4 CONTINUITY AND REDUCIBILITY?

Thus evolutionary naturalism is based on two postulates: (a) there is a fundamental continuity between inanimate and animate nature; (b) all non-physical or higher level phenomena are in the final analysis reducible to physical phenomena. In what follows I shall refer to these two correlated principles as the naturalistic continuity postulate and the naturalistic reducibility postulate.

A postulate is an axiomatic claim, a presupposition that is considered to be so evident that it can be brought forward as a basic statement without further proof. Evolutionism claims without proof that all of earth's phenomena of life, by virtue of miniscule variations and mutations in the genetic material of the species, have

---

[12] The closing sentence of the sixth edition of *On the Origin of Species* states: "There is grandeur in this view of life, with its several powers, having been breathed by the Creator into a few forms or into one." Naturalists often interpret this sentence as an accommodation to the feelings of his deeply religious wife, Emma.

[13] A continuous line of development to the present does not exclude that numerous phylogenetic lines of development were interrupted: according to modern estimates 90 to 98 percent of all known fossil species is now extinct.

developed by chance in a continuous line caused by purely material processes. It claims, furthermore, that the typical characteristics of living organisms, human beings included, can be completely translated in terms of the properties of the molecular building blocks that constitute these organisms. Of course, all evolutionists will immediately agree that much water has to go under the bridge before this ultimate goal is reached.

I do not wish to be misunderstood here. Some positive remarks can be made about these two postulates. Evolution presupposes change and innovation but it also presupposes continuity. In the phylogenetic development of every biological species, if it is to be truly evolutionary, a certain form or a certain measure of continuity must be present. This is comparable to the continuity that is present in the ontogenetic development of a living individual, no matter how drastic the changes are in its development: e.g. from caterpillar to pupa, or from pupa to butterfly. And to the extent that a development is continuous it is, in principle, also explainable. That is to say, the latter state of affairs is reducible to the former.

The difficulties are hidden in the exclusivity of both claims. They are formulated in such an exclusive way that every irreducible novelty or fundamental discontinuity in the development of species is dismissed out of hand. However, when we consider the precipitous distance between mind and matter or between human freedom and the necessity of nature, why could an element of saltational change or evolutionary disruption not have accompanied evolutionary continuity? Why is the idea of evolutionary discontinuity such a totalitarian taboo?

This dismissive attitude is, in my view, inspired by a faith: the faith that science can, in principle, furnish a full explanation of everything. When new phenomena present themselves, sooner or later, science should be able to account fully for the new in terms of the old, the unknown in terms of the known. Higher life forms, too, should be reducible to the characteristics of lower systems. The exclusivity of both postulates is supported by reductionistic expectations, and this reductionism is ultimately prompted by *scientism*, i.e. the belief that science is not an abstract and thus one-sided approach of reality but the final standard of all knowledge and the deepest source of all truth. Thus the British evolutionary biologist Richard Dawkins states without hesitation: "Science is the only way we know to understand the real world."[14] Dawkins does not realize how much we know about the world without any scientific legitimation.

Which science will have pride of place on the evolutionistic playground? Nominated to be the final arbiter of knowledge is natural science, with physics assuming the first place. Physics has earned its laurels in inanimate nature; at the moment it also takes a prominent place in the domain of animate nature in terms of biophysics and molecular biology. For this reason naturalistic scientism is often designated as "physicalism." Its continuity principle flows from the a priori faith that living beings are just extremely complex molecular aggregates and that even the human mind is fully determined by those molecular regularities to which physical science holds the key. Ultimately it is to physical theories that we must look to solve the riddle of life. That's the very reason why Dawkins, in his controversial book on evolution, *The Selfish Gene*, portrays the living organism as a robot, a "survival machine" constructed by its genes to maximize their chances of replication.[15]

One of the most forceful defenders of a stringent physicalist worldview in the United States is the philosopher Paul Churchland. Churchland denotes physicalism as "eliminative materialism." He states that the neurosciences of the future can only give a real evolutionary explanation of everything that goes on in the brain when they eliminate the immaterial ideas that we form daily, of beliefs, feelings, desires, etc. He observes in this context: "The important point about the standard evolutionary story is that the human species and all of its features are the wholly physical outcome of a purely physical process."[16] Also his life-partner, the neurologist Patricia Churchland, embraces this eliminative materialism. She goes even one step further in this approach. In her book, *Neurophilosophy*, she renews the old ideals of logical positivism: the ideals of a "scientific worldview" and of a "unified science." She pleads for that one science in which the fundamental differences

[14] R. Dawkins, "Thoughts for the millennium: Richard Dawkins," in *Microsoft Encarta Encyclopedia 2000* (1993).
[15] R. Dawkins, *The Selfish Gene: Why the Evidence of Evolution Reveals a Universe Without Design* (Oxford: Oxford University Press, 1976, 2006).
[16] P. M. Churchland, *Matter and Consciousness* (Cambridge, MA: MIT Press, 1984), p. 21.

between mind and the neural and molecular network of the brain have been totally eliminated. Mind and brain form an evolutionary continuum.[17]

One of the most remarkable weaknesses of physicalism, as it is promoted by the Churchlands and kindred spirits, is that it does not succeed in any way in describing the theoretical arguments in favor of this position in the language of physics. Thus through the years numerous evolutionary thinkers have raised their voices against this radically reductive physicalism, often as a voice in the wilderness. Ernst Mayr, the venerable American zoologist who died in 2005, taxonomist and one of the authors of the modern synthesis, writes:

This reductionism has led to what David Hull calls "the arrogance of the physicists." They say, yes, you biologists deal with complex things, but the ultimate explanation will be supplied by the level at which we study . . . I strongly disagree. They might find out all about particle physics, but it won't shed a single bit of light on, for instance how the nervous system works or how ontogeny works. Complex systems have to be studied at high levels of complexity . . . Physical scientists must understand that biologists are not disclaiming physical phenomena. We are not setting up vitalism. We are not trying to produce a metaphysics. We simply claim that in complex, historically formed systems things occur that do not occur in inanimate systems. That is all that is being claimed.[18]

In spite of such warnings on the part of authoritative biologists, the influence of physicalism is not negligible. In many cases the naturalistic continuity claim and its counterpart, the naturalistic reduction claim, hold the evolution debate in an iron grip. Their advocates dictate what in academic discussions can be accepted as a scientific argument and what must be dismissed as unscientific verbiage. Regrettably there are precious few proponents of the continuity and reducibility principles who realize that their own position is open to debate, and that they themselves can be considered as "believers."

---

[17] P. S. Churchland, *Neurophilosophy: Toward a Unified Science of the Mind-Brain* (Cambridge, MA: MIT Press, 1986); R. Llinás and P. S. Churchland (eds.), *The Mind-Brain Continuum* (Cambridge, MA: MIT Press, 1996).
[18] Ernst W. Mayr, quoted by Roger Lewin in "Biology is Not Postage Stamp Collecting," *Science* 216 (1982), 718–20.

One of these exceptions was the famous English anatomist and anthropologist Sir Arthur Keith, in his time a certified authority on evolution (he thought modern human beings had evolved from Neanderthals). Keith admitted that his scientific opinions about evolution were based on a belief. To him is ascribed the often-cited pronouncement: "Evolution is unproved and unprovable. We believe it only because the only alternative is special creation and that is unthinkable." I do not exclude the possibility that this citation is a product of creationist imagination; I have not been able to trace its original source.

The naturalistic continuity principle puts a heavy stamp on what the concept of evolution may contain. Its proponents apply it to the three phases in the development of life on earth. As a start, they assume that the most elementary life forms have developed out of inanimate matter by strictly mechanical impulses and by chance. Jacques Monod states: "Pure chance, absolutely free but blind, [lies] at the very root of the stupendous edifice of evolution."[19] Next, they suggest that not only unicellular organisms, but also plants and animals, have developed from these elementary life forms in a purely undirected and entirely fortuitous process, with human beings as an unintentional end result. George Gaylord Simpson writes: "Man is the result of a purposeless and natural process that did not have him in mind. He was not planned."[20] Finally, many evolutionists also claim that this process of contingent events does not only explain the origin of human beings but also the miracle of human culture, morals, and civilization. Richard Dawkins suggests: "our own existence once presented the greatest of all mysteries, but . . . it is a mystery no longer because it is solved. Darwin and Wallace solved it."[21]

The question arises as to what such apodictic pronouncements by leading figures of evolutionism have to do with the empirical facts of evolutionary science, which should be our point of departure. It will become clearer as we continue that these statements are not

---

[19] J. Monod, *Chance and Necessity*, trans. A. Wainhouse (New York: Vintage Books, 1972), pp. 112–13.

[20] G. G. Simpson, *The Meaning of Evolution*, revised edition (New Haven: Yale University Press, 1967), p. 345.

[21] Dawkins, *The Blind Watchmaker*, p. ix.

evidence of science but of science-belief. And science-belief – this
we have to grant the creationists – is difficult to reconcile with
creation-belief, i.e. the belief that God has purposefully created all
life on earth, that He elevated human beings to be the crown of his
creation, and that He propels this creation in a meaningful way in
the direction of his Kingdom. Thus, in contrast to the hesitant,
agnostic Darwin, a seasoned evolutionist (like Dawkins) is often an
atheist, someone who does not hesitate to declare even faith in God
to be the result of the evolutionary process. With this much axiomatic
certainty, a sense of wonder evaporates, the scientific precision is
undermined, the debate on worldviews is impaired, and, yes, our
quest for purpose and meaning should immediately be abandoned.[22]

Let me conclude this chapter with a final question. In the debates
about evolution one often sees the naturalistic science-belief go
head-to-head with the biblical creation-belief. Faith against faith.
An impasse seems unavoidable. Wouldn't it be better to make a
clean sweep of it, to carry on the discussion with purely theoretical
arguments, and to keep all messy faith presuppositions, whatever
their origin may be, out of academic discourse?

Don't do that, say present-day theories of science. Science needs
vision and inspiration. Faith-based views can supply these. They can
be of heuristic significance for science, i.e. they can make science
inventive, imaginative, and resourceful. By virtue of their own take
on things and their specific patterns of expectations they can put
science on the track toward new insights. I have appropriated this
approach with reference to the biblical view of creation. This view,
not in a creationist but in an Augustinian sense, can indeed have
heuristic significance. I hope to show this in detail later. At the
same time I acknowledge without hesitation that the naturalistic

---

[22] With his axiomatic certainty Dawkins is far removed from the nuanced views of Darwin.
Darwin had difficulty accepting the biblical creation story but he also had an eye for the
limitations of the human intellect. In his autobiography of 1876 he recounts how, after the
voyage of the *Beagle*, he abandoned his faith because he could not reconcile Paley's proof
of the existence of God (based on the presence of design in nature) with the law of natural
selection. Nevertheless, he questions, for example in a letter written to a correspondent in
Utrecht in 1873, the thesis that "this grand and wondrous universe, with our conscious
selves, arose through chance" and he concludes "that the whole subject is beyond the scope
of man's intellect."

continuity faith, which I don't share, also has heuristic value. I will also return to this point (see ch. 10, section 2).

The heuristic of faith does call for a watchful eye! The vision inspired by faith should give rise to fresh ideas, engender discussions, and not exclude opponents. In this regard, naturalistic evolutionism is a disappointment for me. I would suggest that the postulates of continuity and reducibility may be advanced as inspiring articles of faith, as long as no one imposes them as scientific arguments. For faith disguised as science – this is how I would define "ideology" – no longer functions in the context of discovery, i.e. as a challenging research perspective; instead, it functions in the context of justification, as the final authority. By claiming a scientific monopoly for their postulates, the proponents of evolutionary naturalism make them non-negotiable and wipe all competing opinions from the table.

CHAPTER 4

Miller's pre-biotic broth and the premises of evolutionism

To gain clarity in the discussion on origins, we distinguished in the previous chapter between evolution theory and evolutionism. There is, on the one hand, *evolution theory* as a strictly scientific analysis of the evolution process, a cluster of theories about the descent of biological species. On the other hand, there is *evolutionism* as the elevation of these theories to an ideological complex, a worldview of naturalistic character. Also this ideological edifice is often designated as "evolution theory" but it rests on pre-theoretical foundations. It offers naturalistic explanations, in the first place for the origin of life on earth (section 1), then for the development of all lower and higher life forms (section 2), and finally for the unfolding of *Homo sapiens* in the direction of human culture, morals, and science (section 3). In this chapter let us, using the work of Stanley Lloyd Miller as a starting-point, examine these naturalistic explanations on their scientific merits. They appear to be affected by problematic premises.

I ORIGIN OF LIFE: A CATEGORY MISTAKE

Did inanimate nature originate life on earth entirely by its own means? That chemical chaos, typical of the young earth, gave rise to life – in the form of unicellular micro-organisms – and that in a completely random and unordered manner, has never been proven scientifically. Some scientists even reject this option completely. On August 6, 1996, NASA announced with great fanfare that a meteorite from Mars, found in Antarctica, contained the fossil remains of bacteria.[1] The information is as suggestive as it is controversial. It does connect, however, with opinions held by Fred Hoyle and Francis Crick, the one an astronomer and exobiologist,[2] the other a biochemist and discoverer of the structure of DNA. Both suggested that life on earth must necessarily be of extraterrestrial origin. Why is it assumed to be of extraterrestrial origin?

This view stems from the extremely short time in which life on earth has configured itself according to present-day calculations. This fact has puzzled scientists for years. Suppose the earth is approximately 4.5 billion years old, and suppose that the first signs of life appeared approximately 3.8 billion years ago.[3] Then, if one also takes into account the time necessary for the glowing globe to cool, there were probably less than 200 million years available for the development of the first forms of life. On a geological timescale, this is an improbably short time period! Present-day molecular biology only adds to the puzzle. The more molecular biologists understand the bewilderingly complex microstructure of the living cell, the more incomprehensible becomes the question how in such a short time, under such adverse circumstances, such delicate life forms could arise from inert material.

Contrary to Richard Dawkins' assertions (see ch. 3, section 4), Darwin did not solve the mystery of the origin of life and did not claim that he did. His *magnum opus* did not discuss the origin of life but the origin of species, as the title indicates. Not insensitive to the naturalistic continuity postulate, he guarded himself against making overwrought statements. Thus he wrote: "The mystery of the beginning of all things is insoluble by us."[4] Indeed, the so-called

---

[1] The controversial information from NASA is reported in D. S. McKay *et al.*, "Search for Past Life on Mars: Possible Relic Biogenic Activity in Martian Meteorite ALH84001," *Science* 273 (1996), 924–30.

[2] Fred Hoyle is the astrophysicist who sarcastically coined the phrase "Big Bang theory." His views about the extraterrestrial origin of life on earth, sometimes referred to as the panspermia theory, no matter how unbelievable, gained some respectability through the NASA announcement.

[3] The first signs of bacterial life forms are commonly thought to be 3.45 billion years old.

[4] Darwin concluded, in his autobiography, "The mystery of the beginning of all things is insoluble by us; and I for one must be content to remain an agnostic." *The Autobiography of Charles Darwin*, p. 94. In the well-known concluding paragraph of *On the Origin of Species*, at least in the sixth edition, he states that life is "breathed by the Creator into a few forms or into one."

"mechanisms" of competition, variation, selection, and transmission cannot explain the origin of life. There is a simple reason: the CVST principles are not mechanical operations of matter leading to life, but, instead, are functional procedures of life itself. They are not inanimate mechanisms; they are biological or, more accurately, biotic ordering principles, principles that presuppose and constitute the presence of life.[5] Right from the start, processes such as mutation and selection are woven into a ruthless struggle *for life*, a struggle which is unknown to mechanical nature.[6]

It is biochemistry, not evolutionary biology, that has made important contributions to a better understanding of the origin of life. I think here of the famous Urey–Miller experiment at the University of Chicago in 1953. Stanley Lloyd Miller, working in Harold Urey's laboratory, took a mixture of chemicals (hydrogen, ammonia, methane, and water vapor) to begin his experiment. According to the so-called Oparin–Haldane hypothesis this mixture was characteristic of the reducing atmosphere of Jupiter and thus, perhaps, of that of the young earth. In this combination of gases he created an electrical discharge, simulating lightning, and, behold, a number of amino acids were formed.[7] Supporters enthusiastically praised these experiments as if the secret of life had been solved, once and for all. Actually, the experiment brought forth neither bacteria nor the building blocks that make up a bacterium (proteins, nucleic acids, polysaccharides, or lipids), but it did produce ingredients of these compounds: some of the twenty amino acids

[5] As such, biotic ordering principles and phenomena have nothing to do, of course, with biology as a science. Speaking of bio-*logical* principles, phenomena, and the like is an unavoidable adaptation to current scientistic ways of speaking.

[6] Evolutionists bring even "survival of the fittest" forward as a "mechanical" principle; I suggest that this is a misuse of the word "mechanical." Mechanical causation is purposeless and aimless. Life is not aimless; it strives for survival, has a functional urge for self-maintenance that manifests itself differently on different levels of complexity. Plants distinguish themselves by survival practices, animals by survival instincts, and human beings by survival strategies. The evolutionary reduction of survival values to natural causes has an ideological basis.

[7] S. L. Miller, "A Production of Amino Acids under Possible Primitive Conditions," *Science* 117 (1953), 528–29. This work and the hypotheses of A. Oparin and J. B. S. Haldane are discussed in P. J. Bowler, *Evolution: The History of an Idea* (Berkeley: University of California Press, 1983), pp. 318–21.

necessary for forming proteins in a living cell (*a*- and *β*-alanine, glycine). Subsequently, other researchers have also determined experimentally that organic compounds can be formed spontaneously out of gas mixtures.[8] The question of whether the atmosphere on the young earth contained the cocktail of these gases is still unanswered; the Oparin–Haldane hypothesis is now rather dated. Unanswered, too, is the question of how, from the conditions assumed to prevail on the young earth, such experiments can be a bridge to the living cell. Miller's major contribution is that he was one of the first to show that a simulating experiment can produce substances characteristic of the biochemical conditions necessary for life.

Since Miller's work, research has focused on the transitional stages on the way to living organisms. How did the cell acquire the ability to make a purposeful selection from alternative chemical reactions? This trait can only begin to function when long molecular chains exist. With this in view many laboratories have made concerted efforts to create complex bio-molecules by the aggregation of amino acids or of nucleotides. Sydney W. Fox at the University of Miami showed that when a mixture of amino acids and polyphosphates are heated and cooled, polymers can be formed in the form of proteinoids – protein-like compounds with the functional characteristics of a primitive enzyme.[9] For his part, Manfred Eigen, working at the Max Planck Institute in Göttingen, showed that a solution of nucleotides, enzymes, and salts may occasionally form short nucleic acids in the form of RNA molecules and that these may even multiply to some extent.[10] However, we have to note that in both cases these macro-molecules still lack an essential quality of life: the mutual coordination that is so typical of the self-regulating and self-reproducing ability of the living cell.

---

[8] Formation of these compounds has been called "molecular evolution." The organic molecules that can be formed in this way are carbon compounds and are not living cells or organelles of such cells, of course.

[9] See S.W. Fox and K. Dose, *Molecular Evolution and the Origin of Life* (New York: Marcel Dekker, 1977).

[10] This work, carried out in the eighties, is described in M. Eigen, *Steps Toward Life: A Perspective on Evolution* (Oxford: Oxford University Press, 1992).

How did life come about in that ancient chemical broth when in the oceans organic compounds started to accumulate? During the last century two theories gained popularity: the aggregate hypothesis of Oparin and Fox, and the gene hypothesis of Hermann Joseph Muller and Eigen. According to Fox, life began with the formation of proteins. In the laboratory, proteinoids show they are capable of aggregating into small protein-like micro-globules that can multiply spontaneously by clumping followed by division. These "life-like" properties and "cell-like" behaviors would have been the first faltering step in the genesis of life. According to Eigen, however, living organisms had their first beginnings in nucleic acids. From the mix of nucleotides, enzymes, and salts, nucleic acids appear to be able to form an RNA strand of sorts. This RNA strand would be able to replicate as if in a matrix by virtue of its ability to recognize corresponding nucleotide components and to incorporate them into a new strand.[11]

The protein-first theory as well as the RNA-first theory are controversial and, in view of their point of departure, they also contradict each other. For in the concrete reality of a living cell, proteins and nucleic acids work in mutual interdependence. Furthermore, Fox's aggregation hypothesis could be criticized because protein-like macro-molecules would lack the ability of adaptation, growth, and self-replication as soon as the environmental substances to be aggregated are depleted. In that regard, the gene hypothesis has more going for it, because it allows for mutation, and thus for selective advantages, adaptation, and growth. But here the objection has been raised that the idea of a pre-biotic replicator is unrealistic: the energy-rich mixture of enzymes and nucleotides would not be available in the sparse resources originally circulating on the earth. And quite apart from the question of what came first, genes or proteins – or possibly cell membranes as a third option – biologists

---

[11] In the 1980s Thomas Cech and Sidney Attman already called attention to the special significance of RNA. They posited that RNA is more than a passive courier of genetic information and that it can sometimes function like an active enzyme, just as a protein can. H. F. Noller, in 1992, stated that the coupling of amino acids can be catalyzed by RNA only. Thus, DNA molecules and proteins would be derived in an evolutionary sense from RNA. See H. J. J. Nijkamp, *Genetica: Opwindend perspectief voor de samenleving* (Amsterdam: VU Boekhandel, 1992), p. 4.

still wrestle with the question of how the necessary bio-molecules could have been packaged into the cell, and how metabolism and reproduction could have developed in these cells.

A stumbling block in both hypotheses is the question of whether key biological concepts such as adaptation and selective advantage are applicable in the case of initially freely floating macro-molecules. In cellular systems adaptation is a direct result of natural selection and reproduction. But what can "adaptation" mean in a situation where molecules float aimlessly outside a living cell? And what is "selective advantage" when macro-molecules replicate themselves but are, in the first instance, lifeless, and thus have no innate drive to reproduction and selective advantage? Indeed, how can molecules that are not alive manifest selection if selection is differential survival and survival is a characteristic of life? Isn't this a case of attaching biological categories to a non-biological reality? Or, to put it differently, do not both hypotheses assume what they are trying to explain?[12]

Whatever is the case, the controversy is extremely instructive. Biochemists have succeeded in finding a link between living cells and chemical substances. They have shown that it is plausible that life has originated *from* chemical processes. They remain stuck in the question of how life could have arisen *by* chemical processes. Proteins and nucleic acids have shown themselves to be *necessary conditions*; they have not shown themselves to be *sufficient conditions* for the origin of life. Apparently, the physical and the biotic are connected in an intrinsic structural coherence, yet there is, at the same time, an incisive structural difference. In other words, life presents itself to us as a phenomenon in its own right. Which is not to say that it just fell out of heaven as the Kaabah in Mecca. Even if it would be correct to say that life came into existence in a process all its own, science has made it plausible that this could only occur because proteins or, more likely, RNA molecules had been formed in advance, creating the necessary basic conditions.

[12] In S. L. Miller and L. E. Orgel, *The Origins of Life on the Earth* (Englewood Cliffs, NJ: Prentice Hall, 1974), the authors write on p. 223: "We are convinced that natural selection, acting on a system of polymers (some of which are able to replicate), was responsible for the emergence of organized biological structures." The circularity of this argument seems to have escaped the authors.

Consider the wreck of a ship on the ocean floor.[13] Usually such a wreck rusts away over the years in its salty grave, but every so often the hulk is overgrown with corals and sponges. Something new develops: a coral reef. Wreck and reef each have their own history, the one nautical, the other biotic. The one cannot be reduced to the other. Yet, besides differences there is also coherence. For the presence of the wreck was an indispensable condition for the formation of the reef. So, too, the presence of materials is an indispensable condition for the origin of life. Research in biochemistry and cell biology has shown all of this. It throws light on the ingenious basic conditions under which life came to be. It also makes clear, however, that one should not use key concepts from the life sciences to force entrance into a reality that has not yet been opened up for life. The attempt to use key concepts that are not appropriate to open up a new empirical domain is referred to by philosophers as a *category mistake*.[14]

2 SURVIVAL OF THE FITTEST: A TAUTOLOGY

Did the lower organisms, in particular bacteria and archaea, give rise to the higher life forms entirely by their own means? According to the premises of neo-Darwinian evolutionism, scientific evidence shows that life developed spontaneously into increasingly complex biosystems, from protozoa to primates, and that randomly and all by itself. This happened thanks to the algorithm of competition, variation, selection, and transmission, with the universal principle of natural selection taking the lead.

---

[13] The metaphors I occasionally bring to this discussion have rhetorical rather than argumentative value. They are aids to break the closed thinking of one-dimensional evolutionism with a bit of imagination.

[14] A "category mistake" is a semantic or ontological error by which a characteristic is incorrectly ascribed to a type of phenomena to which it is not applicable. Gilbert Ryle introduced this term in *The Concept of Mind*. Category mistakes were common in literature shortly after Darwin's discoveries. Wilhelm Preyer spoke of "competition in the chemical changes in nature"; Leopold Pfaundler of "struggle for existence among the molecules"; Carl du Prel about the efficacy of the solar system as a consequence of "the origin of the efficacy through natural selection." Darwin's son, George Howard Darwin, even applied Du Prel's *Der Kampf ums Dasein am Himmel* (The Struggle for Life in the Sky) (Berlin, 1874) to his theory about the tides. See H. A. M. Snelders, *Darwins "strijd om het bestaan" en de evolutie in de niet-levende natuur* (Amsterdam: Vrije Universiteit, 1984).

Here, too, questions arise. How universal is the mechanism of natural selection? Evolution implies that by selection on heritable characteristics organisms have been produced that are more fit than others, better adapted to their environment and with greater reproductive success. But be careful, for terms like "selection," "fitness," "better adaptation," and "greater success" are treacherous. They suggest a norm derived from the experience of humans, while humans belong to the objects to be explained! Even when biologists are able to formulate their concepts in strictly functional terms – i.e. in terms of the processes that enable the organism to adapt, live, and behave in its environment in accordance with its nature – suspicions of circular reasoning seem almost unavoidable.

Take the concept of survival of the fittest, in which the CVST processes are supposed to culminate. In population genetics it is customary to define "fitness" in functional terms as the reproductive success to be expected. "Survival," too, is defined functionally, as a continued existence that is assured by reproductive success. Where does that leave us? Does the concept say that organisms with the greatest expectation of reproductive success have the greatest reproductive success? Does it say: the survivors survive? That is not a general principle, not a universal law. As Karl Popper has already noted, it remarkably resembles an empty formula, a tautological phrase, a truism.[15]

Is "survival of the fittest" indeed a tautological formula without empirical content, something akin to two times two equals four? In his book *The Sceptical Biologist* Bas Jongeling, a theoretical biologist in Zimbabwe, has proposed the thesis that one can salvage the principle, provided it is understood to be an ideal model that is given concrete content by practical research. He formulates the difference between a tautology and a model as follows. A tautology is an equation that is always balanced, an empty formula that is thus not empirically testable. A model, however, requires concretization.

---

[15] K. R. Popper, *Objective Knowledge: An Evolutionary Approach* (Oxford: Clarendon Press, 1975), p. 241: "the trouble about evolutionary *theory* is its tautological, or almost tautological character . . . For we have, I am afraid, no other criterion of fitness than actual survival."

A model can be given content by attaching empirical claims to it, in practical situations, that are testable indeed.

Take the thesis that antelopes with long legs are survivors, as they have greater fitness than antelopes with short legs. This is more than an empty slogan; it is an empirical claim that is indeed falsifiable in practical situations, e.g. by the presence of large numbers of short-legged antelopes. Even if the long-legged fitness design were of vital importance for all antelopes, even then this importance would still not be universal; it would not be decisive, say, in the case of mice. The rule is that the fittest individuals in nature survive, but this principle has such different end-results in various species that it's impossible to capture it under one phenotypic concept of fitness.[16] In short, what Jongeling teaches us is that principles such as natural selection and survival are not universal laws in the sense of uniform laws, such as we find in physical nature. Biological principals are not an extension of physical laws, comparable to the law of gravity. Thus they offer no support for the continuity hypothesis of evo-lutionary naturalism. They are ordering principles of their own, and they only obtain a concrete meaning in their application to the diversity of biological species.

Perhaps even more encompassing are the views of Wim van der Steen, of the Free University in Amsterdam. In *Evolution as Natural History* he ruthlessly typifies concepts such as natural selection, design fitness, and the like as empty shells that need to be filled. This filling is by definition context dependent, also in an ecological sense.[17] In this regard Van der Steen is extremely critical. In evo-lutionary processes the diversity of empirico-historical factors is so overwhelmingly great that the formulation of an overarching theory such as we find in physics, applicable to all living organisms, must

---

[16] T. B. Jongeling, *The Sceptical Biologist: An Inquiry into the Structure of Evolutionary Theory* (Amsterdam: Vrije Universiteit, 1991), sect. 20.1.

[17] With the use of mathematical equations, population genetics can assign standard fitness values to genetic factors that variant organisms possess. The explanatory power of these models is limited because for the explanation of evolution one needs to take into account not only population genetics but also ecology, which relates the genetic properties of organisms to selective environmental factors such as predation, moisture, and temperature. It seems infeasible to categorize genetic and ecological factors under an overarching explanatory model with standard values. Thus argues W. J. van der Steen, *Evolution as Natural History: A Philosophical Analysis* (Westport, CT: Praeger, 2000), ch. 3.

be considered to be impossible. Darwinian theory is handy as an auxiliary framework, but it is guilty of overwrought generalizations when, in explaining the development of earthly life, it invokes Darwinian principles as if they were universal laws of nature. With some exaggeration he states: in biology laws have, at most, a "container status."[18]

Hence van der Steen's proposal for moderation which is, at the same time, a proposal for concretization. Let us reformulate modern evolution theory as a natural history. Let us reinterpret it as a continuing progression of empirico-historical descriptions of concrete phenomena; descriptions that refer to laws and governing principles in only a limited way, for these are "bodies of theory at low levels of generality, which often contain non-universal claims."[19]

In chapters to come we shall have to examine more deeply the nature of biological laws and their relationship to physical laws. Methodological considerations such as those raised by Jongeling and van der Steen already indicate that, in bacterial as well as plant and animal systems of life, the originally physical reality has reorganized itself in accordance with new ordering principles that appear to be less comprehensive than physical laws. However much it is entangled with physical processes, life manifests itself as a domain that observes rules of its own.[20]

Do we have to consider biological rules such as of cellular organization, homeostasis, and reproduction to be universal or particular? My answer is: in biological rules universality and particularity are interwoven. To the extent that they are determinative for the being and well-being of living organisms as such, we can designate them as universal: the rules of cellular organization, reproduction, etc. are applicable to all of living nature. But to the extent that they are distinct to the special modes of life and survival

---

[18] Van der Steen refers to these laws as "placeholder concepts," *ibid.*, p. 3 and ch. 2.

[19] *Ibid.*, p. 3.

[20] Animate nature is a domain obeying its own laws but it has mechanical nature as its substratum. Thus the frequent molecular mutations in the genetic material of living organisms occur mechanically and by chance. At the same time it is striking that in the struggle for existence these mutations offer no advantage, as a rule. The mutant usually dies, but not always! In the evolutionary process chance mutations can, in some cases, be put to use for the self-maintenance of the biological group. But we can only draw this conclusion on a level of complexity that is above mechanical reality.

strategies of specific groups or species in their habitat, they are particular: in the phylogenetic process they have got a particular elaboration. In short, biological rules are simultaneously universal and particularized. For that reason I designate them as "principles," or even as "germinative principles," i.e. universal laws with a particular application.[21]

Thus biological principles are initial laws that in the living world germinate in different directions. They are universal but also specified into differential guiding codes or rules of life *in loco*. I take as an example the universal principle of reproduction. There is no life form without reproduction, yet we are confronted in different living contexts with a heterogeneous diversity of reproductive systems. There is, for instance, sexual but also asexual reproduction. This particularization of universal laws makes it nearly impossible to get to the bottom of a living thing; it makes a living phenomenon extremely complex. In the status of biological principles we find also, in my view, the proper reason why scientists of life find it so difficult to make universal statements or exact predictions as is customary in physics. They can only lift tips of the veil that is spread over the mysterious history of life on earth.

That numerous evolutionary biologists – not just dyed-in-the-wool naturalists – bring principles such as variation and selection into the discussion as "mechanisms" has increased the misunderstanding concerning the status of biological laws considerably. Speaking here of "mechanisms" is a category mistake in the opposite direction. In the preceding section we saw that biological concepts are sometimes attached to mechanical nature to explain the origin of life. Here we see the opposite, the attempt to attach mechanistic concepts to organic nature to explain the development of life. This is an approach without prospects. Animate nature, with its diversity of living organisms, has indeed realized itself in physical or mechanical nature as the basic condition of its existence. Yet in what follows it will become clear that the peculiarity of biological

---

[21] I derive the term "germinative principle" from Edward Caird, *The Evolution of Theology in the Greek Philosophers*, Gifford lectures, vol. II (Glasgow: J. Maclehose, 1904), lecture 20. I do not share Caird's neo-Hegelian interpretation. I also take distance from the speculative connotations with the Stoic doctrine of the λόγος σπερματικός as a germinative principle of reason which manifests itself in the universe.

phenomena cannot be adequately explained in mechanistic terms any more than the peculiarity of mechanical phenomena can be adequately explained in biological terms.

The explanatory mode of biology as a paradigm of the life sciences is different from the methods that are applied in (bio)chemistry and (bio)physics. The biological approach can be designated as a functionalistic one. It is tuned to the typically biotic way of being of unicellular and multicellular systems, directed at functional purposes: the transmission of genes, the adaptation of organisms, and the survival of the species. This functional directedness is absent in the physical world. The functionalistic explanations of biology are based on and differ from the mechanistic explanations of all physical and chemical disciplines.[22] The mechanistic way of thinking is instrumental, focussed on the *how*: the behavioral pattern of natural systems. The biological way of thinking is functionalistic, focussed on the *for which*: the purpose of natural systems and processes. Given the fact that living organisms can be seen as a realization of life in mechanical nature, in the world of living organisms both types of explanation complement each other. Thus science is more than natural science. It has to be understood as a pluralist methodological approach, as *Wissenschaft*. Especially the sciences of life manifest this variety of methods.[23]

As soon as we pretend that living phenomena and evolutionary processes are *fully* explicable in a mechanistic way, we give evidence of a naturalistic bias. For though inanimate nature is the basis for biological processes such as cellular organization, adaptation, and survival, the naturalist cannot make the case that these processes are in themselves mechanical procedures and that the principles

---

[22] The ethological explanations of zoology are even further removed from the mechanistic model of explanations. The behaviors of animals are more complex than the reactions of bacteria and plants, co-determined by an inner center of experience; sensitive impulses mediate the animal's reactions to the world in which it lives. The interpretative model of explanations in the human sciences is even more complicated. Interpretative explanations supersede the methods of zoology in that human behavior is intentional, not only sensitively determined but also interpretable as mental and normative actions.

[23] There is a great variety of scientific methods and this implies an inclusive and pluralist concept of science (German: *Wissenschaft*), i.e. of theoretical disciplines. The ideal that neo-positivism developed a century ago, of a unified science, is a fundamental category mistake.

involved are just logical consequences of uniform laws of nature. On the contrary, as soon as the naturalist attempts to deduce life principles from the laws of physical nature or represents them as uniform laws for animate nature, a philosopher will raise the critical question in which respect those laws would differ from *tautological*, i.e. meaningless, statements.

3 EVOLUTION OF SCIENCE: A PERFORMATIVE CONTRADICTION

In the preceding sections I have tried to make the case that both the naturalistic explanation of the origin of life (section 1) and the naturalistic explanations for the development of lower and higher life forms (section 2) are entangled in logical fallacies. In conclusion, what is the state of affairs in regard to human beings? The appearance of *Homo sapiens* on the world stage and its unequalled accomplishments since then in culture, morals, and science strikes many as a unique phenomenon that must be based on a well-considered plan or perhaps even on a divine design. Others will deny this. They see, on naturalistic grounds, the origin of the human species and the unfolding of its remarkable cultural competencies as nothing more than a "glorious accident," to use the phrase of Stephen Jay Gould.[24]

"[T]he biosphere looks like the product of a unique event . . . The universe was not pregnant with life nor the biosphere with man. Our number came up in the Monte Carlo game." That is the wisdom of the molecular biologist, Jacques Monod.[25] Is humankind indeed a wild gamble of Mother Nature? Has her addiction to gambling produced not only the human body with its erect gait, oppositional thumb, and over-sized brain, but also, as a stroke of unprecedented luck, the human mind? Are the domains of science, culture, and morals to be considered "epiphenomena," unintended by-products of natural processes that proceed at random? Here we touch on the naturalistic credo of Monod and his colleagues. They

[24] S. J. Gould, *The Flamingo's Smile: Reflections on Natural History* (New York: W. W. Norton, 1985), p. 431.
[25] Monod, *Chance and Necessity*, pp. 145–46.

defiantly assert that all of human culture and civilization can be derived from the competitive and selective operations of nature. And if we are to go by the socio-biological perspective of Michael Ruse, the same would be the case for human morals: "Morality is just an aid to survival and reproduction and has no being beyond or without this."[26]

Does this hold true? Darwin himself certainly had the greatest of problems with this naturalistic and selectionist view of things as soon as he had to apply it to humans. When he discusses the human species in the *Origin*, it is chiefly from the perspective of natural selection. But later, in the anthropological context of *The Descent of Man*, in crucial cases he pushes the principle of selection aside. Here, in the discussion of the human species, he often inclines toward the alternative evolutionary theory of Lamarck: the principle of the inheritance of *acquired* characteristics. Of all things, he invokes a theory overtaken by his own work! Of course, Darwin's embarrassment was rather pronounced. He felt the explanatory deficiency of his selectionism as soon as he considered what the humanity of humans really encompasses. He found it contradictory that the bloody slaughter he witnessed in nature should be used as a believable explanatory basis for what we have in mind when we appeal to human virtues and morals.[27]

We can demonstrate the contradictions that beset a naturalistic explanation of humanity as they relate to the phenomenon of morality but also – as John Haught recently did – in regard to the phenomena of science, cognition, and truth.[28] Darwin also

---

[26] M. Ruse, "Evolutionary Theory and Christian Ethics: Are They in Harmony?," *Zygon* 29 (1994), 5–24, 20.

[27] In later editions of the *Origin* Darwin added Lamarckian notions to his selectionist view. For an informative summary of Lamarck's influence on Darwin and on modern biology, see H. Cook and H. D. Bestman, "A Persistent View: Lamarckian Thought in Early Evolutionary Theories and in Modern Biology," *Perspectives on Science and Christian Faith* 52 (2000), 86–96. Molecular genetics, upon close examination, does not exclude the possibility that – with or without human involvement – acquired characteristics are paired with genetic changes. Not only recombinant DNA technology (Cook and Bestman, "A Persistent View," p. 93) but also the nuclear disaster in Chernobyl are penetrating examples.

[28] J. Haught, *Is Nature Enough? Meaning and Truth in the Age of Science* (Cambridge: Cambridge University Press, 2006), and "Theology and Evolution: How Much Can Biology Explain?," http://www.metanexus.net/magazine/ArticleDetail/tabid/68/id/9598/Default.aspx.

attempted to account for these contradictions. He asked himself: what does the human mind do? Does it bring us closer to the truth, in and outside science, or does it only increase reproductive fitness? That the problem alarmed him is shown by what he wrote in a letter to W. Graham: "With me the horrid doubt always arises whether the convictions of man's mind, which has been developed from the mind of the lower animals, are of any value or at all trustworthy. Would any one trust in the convictions of a monkey's mind, if there are any convictions in such a mind?"[29]

Applied to the practice of science, evolutionary naturalism is hobbled by the following logical inconsistency. It announces its views as a scientific theory. Science is based on methodical presentation of proof. Every step of the proof has to stand the test of critique. This critique requires that the data are relevant, the theses formally consistent, the arguments logically valid, the theories empirically confirmable, the conclusions open to falsification, etc. In other words, arguments of scientific proof presuppose universal standards such as lack of ambiguity, relevance, coherence, consistency, validity, formal correctness, and truth of content. To put it another way, scientific theories must be testable by an international forum of scholars on the basis of criteria that humankind holds in communal trust and that can thus be considered to be part of our humanity.

Now, evolutionary naturalism wants to be scientific but it cannot derive universal standards from nature. Take, for instance, George Gaylord Simpson, whom I put center stage before. He is considered by some to be "the Darwin of the twentieth century" but he lacks the intuitive feeling for the self-refutational inconsistencies of a rigorous naturalism that we find in Darwin. Simpson posits the naturalistic thesis that "man" with all of his intellectual baggage "is the result of a purposeless and natural process that did not have him in mind. He was not planned" (see ch. 3, section 4). The question arises: is science not also part of the human intellectual baggage, aimlessly brought forth by material particles? It's one or the other. A scientific theory – Simpson's own opinions included – is either in

[29] "Letter to W. Graham, July 3rd, 1881," in F. Darwin (ed.), *The Life and Letters of Charles Darwin* (New York: Basic Books, 1959), p. 285.

the final analysis a purely random product of nature, a secretory product of the cerebral lobes of a bipedal primate, adaptively developed in the struggle for life. In that case it serves, who knows, to brag or to bully, but in any case it makes no claim to truth. Or, alternatively, a scientific theory is the conclusion of an argument with an implicit claim of validity. In that case a super-arbitrary standard is presupposed, and the theory is not prompted by blind powers of nature, but formulated in freedom by responsible people over against a universal norm of truth that is part of the imperative to be human. Whatever the situation may be, Simpson's naturalistic thesis contradicts itself, for in the one case it proves to be false, and in the other case it proves not to be naturalistic.

The famous British geneticist J. B. S. Haldane brought up this dilemma with disarming honesty. Despite a strong affinity with materialism, which he even defended later in life with renewed energy, he wrote:

I am not myself a materialist, because, if materialism is true, it seems to me that we cannot know that it is true. If my opinions are the result of chemical processes going on in my brain, they are determined by the laws of chemistry, not those of logic.[30]

There we have the Achilles heel of naturalism, also known as materialism. It tries to explain away what is typically human and humane for so-called scientific reasons. However, in doing so it implicitly refers to a standard. It appeals to the norm of truth as an indispensable, typically human, touchstone for scientific arguments. For, in science, when someone does not argue logically, he or she is unmasked as a blockhead. Yes, indirectly naturalism also appeals to other norms as indispensable, human touchstones for science, especially cultural and ethical norms. For if someone in science does not also give evidence of carefulness and trustworthiness, that person is unmasked as a charlatan. In short, scientific arguments, including those of a thoroughgoing naturalist, depend on logical, cultural, and ethical standards, standards that manifest the

---

[30] J. B. S. Haldane, *The Inequality of Man* (1932; Harmondsworth: Penguin Books, 1937), p. 157. Haldane later retracted this position: "I repent an error," *Literary Guide*, April 1954, 7. Haldane's positions are discussed in K. R. Popper and J. C. Eccles, *The Self and its Brain: An Argument for Interactionism* (Heidelberg: Springer Verlag, 1985), pp. 75–81.

humanity of humankind. Thus evolutionary scientists cannot pass off mental processes – for isn't that what scientific arguments are? – as purely material processes without endangering their own credibility or, to put it more strongly, without destroying the possibilities of communication and argumentation.[31]

Of course, I do not want want to deny that in the human brain mental processes correlate with material (in the sense of neuro-physiological) processes. I shall return to this point in more detail. No one can assert, however, that mental processes are identical or totally reducible to material processes without getting bogged down in a logical contradiction. Philosophers call this contradiction a *performative self-contradiction.*[32] That is, if someone asserts that scholarship, culture, and morals can be totally reduced to nature, then this statement as a lingual performance is in contradiction to the content of this statement. It is a contradiction because, as a lingual activity, this assertion strives to be a contribution to our knowledge and as such it lays claim to the truth; it implicitly refers to a criterion of truth. But explicitly and in its content it wants to appeal only to the brute facts of material nature; from the brute facts, however, it is impossible to derive a standard or criterion of truth.

Enough has been said about category mistakes, tautologies, and performative contradictions! I want to conclude this chapter with a more general comment about the position of biological theory. In the past century the sciences have made us witness of a remarkable and paradoxical scene. On the basis of general relativity theory and quantum physics, modern physicists came to the insight that nature, at its most basic level, is different from a Newtonian, mechanically driven reality. This insight was not taken to heart by many biologists, however, for they committed themselves instead to a consistent mechanization of their world picture. More and more emphatically, they presented organisms and living cells as complex

[31] See A. Plantinga, *Warrant and Proper Function* (Oxford: Oxford University Press, 1993), last chapter.
[32] See K.-O. Apel, "The Problem of Philosophical Foundations in the Light of a Transcendental Pragmatics of Language," in K. Baynes *et al.* (eds.), *After Philosophy: End or Transformation?* (Cambridge, MA, and London: MIT Press, 1987), pp. 250–90; *Towards a Transformation of Philosophy* (Milwaukee, WI: Marquette University Press, 1998; German edn., 1973).

mechanical systems. With the spectacular advancements that molecular biology has made – think of the discovery of the structure of DNA, and of the disclosure of the human genome around the turn of the century – they suggest that science has not only uncovered the material basis of all life forms but has also solved the mystery of life.

This suggestion makes no sense whatsoever! For if it becomes clear anywhere that the world is more than matter, it is in living nature. Even if it is true that life phenomena can be described as material things or mechanical processes, this does not imply that they can be exhaustively described as material things or mechanical processes. On the contrary, there are numerous indications, as we shall see, that life cannot be equated with the material nature out of which it originated long ago, and in which it has realized itself since that time. Thus I say, with the well-known bacteriologist Carl Woese, we await "a new biology for a new century."[33]

---

[33] C. R. Woese, "A New Biology for a New Century," *Microbiology and Molecular Biology Reviews* (June 2004), 173–86.

CHAPTER 5

A cold shudder along Darwin's back

The great challenges of modern evolution theory do not lie in the bumptious claims of radical evolutionary naturalists but in the painstaking proofs that empirical investigators have brought to the table. It is these proofs that have made the traditional theory of the constancy of species extremely unlikely. First there are the fossil finds, slowly surrendered by the soil. Despite numerous fissures and disturbancies of the earth's crust these fossils testify, from layer to layer, to the reality of evolutionary change. Then there are the morphological differences between closely related, yet isolated populations, first observed by Darwin in the finches and giant tortoises in the Galápagos archipelago. Furthermore, there are the structural similarities between homologous body parts, such as the bones of the wings of birds and the front legs of mammals, even when these body parts now have different functions. Finally, there are the remarkable parallels between the phases of development through which an embryo goes, and the phylogenetic development that species have undergone, even if Ernst H. Haeckel's "biogenetic law" has, in general, been abandoned.[1] All these phenomena suggest evolutionary change and a common origin of all life forms.

But there is even more! Nowadays the idea of phylogenetic relationship and common ancestry receives a strong support from the laboratory observations of biochemists and molecular biologists.

---

[1] Haeckel's law, which has been succinctly summarized as "Ontogeny recapitulates phylogeny," states that the ontogenetic development of an individual is a shortened repetition of the phylogenetic (evolutionary) development of the individual's species. Thomas Huxley, who had a way with words, summarized the theory: "In the womb, we climb the ladder of our family tree." Although the law is no longer held to be true, there are nevertheless some interesting parallels. Thus an early stage of a human embryo makes one think of a fish and then, later, of an amphibian.

Biochemists have found that when inorganic compounds are exposed to sparks in a chamber, the resulting amino acids are a racemic mixture. Some of the molecules rotate the light to the right (dextrorotary), some to the left (levorotary); so the solution is optically neutral. However, in proteins of living organisms, the amino acids are always levorotary, with the exception of antibodies and some toxins, proteins in the cell walls of some micro-organisms. Does this exclusive rotational property not suggest that a first, ancient cell, possessing levorotary amino acids, was the origin of all that lives? Besides this, molecular biologists have determined that in all living organisms, DNA molecules function as the carriers of the hereditary information when cells divide, in meiosis or mitosis. Doesn't the universal genetic code of DNA, that all living organisms share, suggest their common origin?

I admit that not one category of evidence has, in itself, enough weight to prove the thesis that all biological species have developed from a common origin. Taken together, however, the evidence in favor of one evolutionary mega-development is exceedingly strong. Life on earth forms one impressive original whole.

However, with that conclusion the philosophical problems only begin! What is not proven is that this unitary origin can naturalistically be ascribed to purely mechanistic processes of "random variation" and "differential survival." For community in origin does not contradict uniqueness in design. For example, a log cabin is built up of pine or other logs; yet the design of the cabin cannot be brought back to the properties of the pine trees. A Volvo is assembled from steel and aluminum; yet the concept of the car cannot be inferred from the properties of iron ore and bauxite.[2]

To put it more strongly, the naturalistic explanation of the communal origin of life is untenable. It results in logical inconsistencies, which include category mistakes, tautologies, and performative self-contradictions. That was the essence of the previous chapter. In the present chapter I want to make clear that the notion of a continuous and gradual change of species based on purely

---

[2] Michael Polanyi makes a similar point in his two well-known articles: "Life Transcending Physics and Chemistry," *Chemical & Engineering News*, August 21, 1967, 54–66; "Life's Irreducible Structure," *Science* 160 (1968), 1308–12.

mechanical variation and selection also does not agree with the empirical facts. Species manifest themselves as durable reproductive communities (section 1). Diverse theories circulate about this, also on the bio-molecular level (section 2). Where the species do change, naturalistic explanations, insofar as they appear to be correct, often prove to be incomplete (section 3). The most problematic appear to be those factors that have given rise to new biological kingdoms and to the becoming of the human species (section 4).

I THE DURABILITY OF BIOLOGICAL SPECIES

Natural selection is not only, or in the first place, a process of change, as Darwin thought. On the contrary, before Wallace and Darwin it was already understood that selection in nature doesn't usually lead to change but to consolidation. Only with a change in the environment – such as climate change or deforestation – do organisms with diverging traits gain opportunities to develop, and natural selection begins to work in favor of change.

This last point has been empirically confirmed in, among others, the well-known case of the peppered moth, *Biston betularia*. A dark (melanic) form of this nocturnal moth, first described in England in 1848, made up 1 percent of this species at that time. A half-century later, 90 percent of the moths were of the dark form. What was the explanation? The environmental pollution that accompanied the Industrial Revolution had given the tinted specimens a razor-thin but effective selective advantage. On sooty birch trees bird predators noticed them less easily than their light-colored conspecifics.

In a stable environment with adapted life forms and ecological balance, the situation is decidedly different. Deviating variants usually appear to be at a disadvantage. The selection process assures that types around the mean maintain themselves and that mutants with disproportional traits are penalized. Thus, infant death is highest in babies with above- and below-average birth weights. And the survival chances of starlings caught in a snowstorm prove to be highest in specimens with a normal body type and average wing length. For that reason, many present-day ants still remarkably resemble the animals that were trapped in amber millions of years ago. Furthermore, living fossils such as the lobe-finned coelacanth, caught in ocean trenches off the coasts of Madagascar and New Guinea, contradict the necessity of regular species change. In short, in normal circumstances natural selection conserves the medium and the mean. It cherishes biological species as reproductive communities with historically balanced durable patterns, and it tends to discourage species change. Thus one could speak here of stabilizing selection as a favored type of selection.

This striving for stability can be interrupted by ecological incidents when, for example, the movement of tectonic plates, the shift of the earth's axis, the impact of a meteor, or another calamity causes the dawn of a new geological era. When, in the late Cretaceous period, a meteorite of approximately ten kilometers in diameter gave the earth such a jolt that the sun was darkened for a protracted period, half of all animal species disappeared, including the dinosaurs. What was the result? The abandoned terrain was occupied in a rapid tempo by birds, heirs of the dinosaurs, and by mammals which until then had been small, primitive, nocturnal animals. Similarly, the Ice Age gave life on earth an entirely new look. It spurred the primates on to radical modifications. Hominids enlarged their cranial capacities. Human consciousness awoke. Consciousness arises from suffering, the great Russian writer Dostoyevsky once suggested. Indeed, for a real jump ahead one needs a catastrophe, a shattering cause for adaptation.

I think that no person will ever be able to come close to determining the degree to which selection was a factor of stability or a motor for change. For this one would have to be able to specify all the selective forces in every era, in all populations of plants, animals, and micro-organisms. However, much evidence suggests that conservation was the rule, and progression the exception. Species present themselves as reproductive communities with buffered, historically balanced patterns of durability, while changes in species occur as relatively short interruptions occasioned by circumstances.

Seen from a macro-evolutionary perspective, it now becomes clear how precisely the mentioned principles of competition, variation, selection, and transmission are attuned to each other. In regard to the varieties that originate spontaneously in the genetic transmission in a new generation of living organisms, competition within a species ensures in normal circumstances that nature selects for durability; it ensures in turbulent times that nature selects for novel adaptive forms. How incisive these novelties are in the light of the naturalistic continuity claim we shall have to examine in the chapters that follow.

2 GRADUALISM AND PUNCTUATED EQUILIBRIA

With my emphasis on the stabilizing effects of natural selection I come close to the well-known position of the paleobiologists Niles Eldredge and Stephen J. Gould. They remind us that biological species do not fluctuate constantly or progress gradually but are, by their very nature, static systems. As such, species display great periods of constancy and even present themselves within the horizon of our experience as durable and clearly distinguishable entities: "Species are real entities, not just a passing stage in a continuous evolutionary stream."[3] As early as 1972 Eldredge and Gould suggested that current theories about the phylogeny of species as a gradual and progressive development in the direction of extant species do not agree with the capricious nature of the evolution process and with the breaks in the succession found in the fossil record.[4] Thus they state: "Indeed, it is the chief frustration of the fossil record that we do not have empirical evidence for sustained trends in the evolution of most complex morphological adaptations."[5]

In contrast to the classic taxonomic opinions of Linnaeus, i.e. the theory of the constancy of discrete species, and also to modern "gradualism" as it was postulated by Darwin and his followers, Eldredge and Gould depict the species as groups of individuals with varying traits; nevertheless, the profile of the group does not change, or hardly changes. In nature a rigorous rule reigns: that species are static and as homeostatic systems resist phenotypic change. On the

---

[3] N. Eldredge, *Time Frames: The Rethinking of Darwinian Evolution and the Theory of Punctuated Equilibria* (New York: Simon and Schuster, 1985), p. 34.

[4] N. Eldredge and S. J. Gould, "Punctuated Equilibria: An Alternative to Phyletic Gradualism," in T. J. M. Schopf (ed.), *Models in Paleobiology* (San Francisco: Freeman, Cooper & Company, 1972), pp. 82–115. According to Darwin and "phyletic gradualism" the "breaks" in the succession of phylogenetically related fossils can be explained as the fortuitous incompleteness of the known fossil material.

[5] S. J. Gould and N. Eldredge, "Species Selection: Its Range and Power," *Nature* 334 (1988), 19. Gould calls the puzzling absence of authentic transitional forms the "trade secret of paleontology." See "Evolution's Erratic Pace," *Natural History* 86:5 (1977), 12–16.

micro-level, characteristics of plants and animals can oscillate, but the strict necessity of equilibrium in nature usually prevents changes in species and macro-evolutionary or supra-specific changes. Changes of this type only get a chance in isolated ecosystems, or under exceptional circumstances, when earthquakes or other natural disasters disrupt the ecological equilibrium.

The message of Eldredge and Gould, often indicated as "punctuated equilibrium" or colloquially as "punk eek," is clear.[6] Considering the evolutionary changes that have indeed occurred on earth periodically, there must have been some rather profound circumstances that led to them; it is difficult to imagine that these changes can be explained by the minimal adaptations that are postulated for natural selection in the Darwinian model. Only the supposed occurrence of catastrophic, violent eruptions and the theory of punctuated equilibria can make clear to us why the fossil record in sedimental layers exhibits so many hiatuses and shifts. It must have been a spectacular coincidence of fortuitous circumstances that led, in former times, to fundamental evolutionary transitions. However, these evolutionary transitions are so exceptional that it is almost impossible for paleontologists to recount the exact circumstances under which they took place. They have to be reconstructed. In other words, a cloud of uncertainty and elusiveness surrounds the origin of truly new life forms.

From the above, we can conclude the following. Evolutionary science is not as rectilinear and objective a scientific approach as it would seem at first. Theoretical assumptions and ideological preoccupations inevitably play a role. Not surprisingly, Eldredge and Gould could cite the statement of the English immunologist Peter B. Medawar with approval: "Innocent, unbiased observation is a myth."[7] A second conclusion also forces itself upon us. That what

---

[6] Before Eldredge and Gould, G. G. Simpson had already outlined the essentials. Structural changes in families, orders, and classes occurred, in his opinion, in unstable situations that had to be overcome as quickly as possible. They were too short in duration to have left wide evidence in the fossil archives. G. G. Simpson, *Tempo and Mode of Evolution* (New York: Columbia University Press, 1944).

[7] P. B. Medawar, *Induction and Intuition in Scientific Thought* (Philadelphia: American Philosophical Society, 1969), p. 28. Well-known is Gould's abhorrence of genetic determinism, partly motivated by left-wing sympathies; these sympathies prompted him to refer, in Marxist fashion, to dialectical turning points in the earth's history.

we have called "the durability of biological species," and what
Eldredge describes as "stasis alternating with rapid changes," does
not imply a justification or affirmation of the traditional dogma of
species constancy, as creationists often suggest.[8] We do not have to
ask ourselves if the development of life has been subject to evolutionary change; we have to attempt to reconstruct how this development took place.

3 THE ANCIENT LITHOGRAPHIC BIRD

Speaking of evolutionary change, a notable transitional creature was
discovered in 1861: the petrified ancient bird *Archaeopteryx lithographica*. The animal had claws on fore- and hind-limbs, jaws with
teeth, a body covered with scales, and a long tail. Like a reptile. It
also possessed feathers and wings. Like a bird. Taxonomically the
animal is known in literature as a transitional type between reptiles
and birds. Is it a transitional animal? Hardly. This ancient bird
presents itself as a complete system. Organs in a nascent state are
not to be found. All limbs are fully functional. A genuine missing
link should show pre-functional characteristics, such as wing
stumps. But *Archaeopteryx* – as far as I know approximately a dozen
specimens have been found – flew with broad wing strokes.

Archaeopteryx has to make us think. How, solely on the basis of
mechanical selection procedures, could intermediary life forms with
rudimentary organs ever maintain themselves in nature? What is the
selective advantage of an eyeball that cannot see or a wing stump
that cannot fly?[9] It is plausible that in the struggle for existence,
non- or badly functioning organs are quickly discarded as superfluous baggage via negative selection.[10] From Darwin to Dawkins,

[8] See N. Eldredge, *The Triumph of Evolution and the Failure of Creationism* (New York: Macmillan, 2000).
[9] R. Dawkins, *Climbing Mount Improbable* (New York: W. W. Norton & Co., 1996). In chapter 4 Dawkins describes how flightless birds were previously seen as transitions to flying birds. Wrong; it is now known that flightless birds such as the emu, cassowary, and kiwi had flying ancestors. Just as the blind cave fish of Postonia had ancestors that could see. The environment causes atrophy of organs that are no longer useful.
[10] Stephen Gould writes: "can we invent a reasonable sequence of intermediate forms – that is, viable, functioning organisms – between ancestors and descendants in major structural transitions? I submit, although it may only reflect my lack of imagination, that the answer

experts on evolution have therefore attempted with the aid of fictional notions or virtual computer simulations to think of transitional organs that are, at the same time, functional. It is clear that explorations of this kind always demand empirical confirmation, precisely because here the wish can so easily become the mother of invention.[11]

An important topic of attention here is the eye, one of the most complicated organs in the animal body. Darwin was very conscious of this complexity. In a letter to his friend the American botanist Asa Gray he wrote: "The eye, to this day, gives me a cold shudder, but when I think of the fine known gradations, my reason tells I ought to conquer the cold shudder."[12] And I get a cold shudder when I read in my newspaper: "The human brain contains one hundred billion neurons, twice as many glia cells and at least a thousand times as many synapses, places where neurons make contact."[13]

The structure of the eye is interesting. It must have evolved, over the last hundreds of millions of years, along many different routes in flatworms, mollusks, insects, and vertebrates. Nevertheless, these developments did not progress entirely separately, so it appears from a comparison of phylogenetic data with current insights from molecular developmental biology by the Swiss biologist Walter Gehring. Gehring has suggested that, at one time, more than five hundred million years ago, during the explosion of life forms in the Cambrium, a common ancestor already possessed a light sensitive

is no." S. J. Gould, *The Panda's Thumb: More Reflections in Natural History* (New York: W. W. Norton, 1980), p. 189.

[11] Nowadays computer simulations are the order of the day. Richard Dawkins describes such a study that attempts to establish the transitional stages in the development of the eye in "The Eye in a Twinkling," *Nature* 368 (1994), 690–91 and in ch. 4 of *Climbing Mount Improbable*.

[12] F. Darwin (ed.), *The Life and Letters of Charles Darwin*, vol. 11, pp. 66–67. Many evolutionary thinkers have taken up Darwin's challenge; they have attempted to describe functional intermediate stages in the development of the mammalian eye. See, for example, Simpson, *The Meaning of Evolution*, ch. 4.

[13] D. F. Swaab, "Wij zijn onze hersenen" (We are our brains), in newspaper *Trouw*, September 30, 2000, 49. In this article, a prime example of reductionism, the neurobiologist Dick Swaab concludes: "Of course we shall return to dust, for we are, even during our lives, nothing more than our shroud of dust" (trans. H. Cook). The statement is contradictory. How can we "return to dust" when we are nothing but dust? How can we be a "shroud of dust" if there is nothing to shroud?

organ.[14] In view of such recent observations the explanatory power of selectionism appears to be limited. The search for intermediate stages we should make subordinate to the question of how the original life forms came into being. How did the first light sensitive skin cell originate or, to formulate it more precisely (for a skin cell is only a vehicle), how did the phenomenon of light sensitivity get its opportunity to originate? Not the increasing complexity but the origin of new articulations of life challenges thought.

Before the Cambrian explosion there were – in the endless crawl of the Pre-Cambrium – all kinds of unicellular organisms such as blue-green algae and bacteria; in addition to protozoa there were also coelomate and segmented animals, etc. In the Cambrium a myriad of new biotic forms appeared in surprisingly short order.[15] Besides a multiplicity of metaphytes (plants), animal-like and animal forms came to light: a great variety of sponges, molluscs, arthropods, and other invertebrates. Traces of mutual descent or signs of transition between all these bizarre life forms are difficult to discern, even if we employ modern, molecular rather than traditional, anatomical comparisons. Only in the vertebrates, which appeared after the Cambrium, do we find a clear, although not totally rectilinear, succession of classes: cyclostomes, cartilaginous and bony fishes, amphibians, reptiles, birds, and mammals.

Earlier, I stated that three and a half billion years ago the first life on earth began to stir, and it did so in an unimaginably short time. However, not only in the Cambrium but also later, after the Cretaceous period, and at the origin of hominids in the late Pleistocene, similar eruptions of vital energy occurred. Were they all the result of micro-evolutionary species changes, originated in

[14] W. J. Gehring, *Master Control Genes in Development and Evolution: The Homeobox* (New Haven: Yale University Press, 1998); W. J. Gehring and K. Ikeo, "Pax 6: Mastering Eye Morphogenesis and Eye Evolution," *Trends in Genetics* 15 (1999), 371–77.

[15] The beginning of the Cambrium is now dated at about 543 million years ago. The Cambrian explosion took place, chiefly, between 530 and 525 years ago. Taxonomically speaking, there were then about thirty-five living animal phyla, each with its own design or body plan. In one of his best books, S. J. Gould describes the discovery of the results of the Cambrian explosion as they were found in a shale deposit in the Rocky Mountains of Canada. He also describes the erroneous classification of these animals, in *Wonderful Life: The Burgess Shale and the Nature of History* (New York: W. W. Norton, 1989). See also H. Cook, "Wonderful Life: Burgess Shale and the History of Biology," *Perspectives on Science and Christian Faith* 47 (1995), 159–63.

endless series of minute mutations, because nature happens to select genes, as R. Dawkins and G. C. Williams, in a renewed plea for gradualism, assert? Whence this sudden manifestation of original life forms? Whence, in particular, the origin of the multifaceted ingenuity of *Homo sapiens* that must have developed, on the geological time scale in the blinking of an eye, yesterday, right where we live?

Nowadays questions such as these bring the idea to researchers from all kinds of disciplines that the gradualist view of evolution – supported, or not, by the gene selectionism of Dawkins and Williams – is perhaps lacking in explanatory power, especially where it concerns originating formations.[16] The thought asserts itself: isn't evolution more than the strictly fortuitous launching of material processes with the aid of brute selection mechanisms? Are there not reasons to assume that organic nature has indeed developed fortuitously, but has done so within specific boundary conditions, boundary conditions that we still have to describe in more detail?

For this reason, thinkers such as Stuart Kauffman reject the depiction of evolution as a strictly contingent and purposeless process, one-sidedly determined by the neo-Darwinian principles of chance variation and natural selection. In his book *At Home in the Universe* Kauffman presents biological evolution as an inherently self-organizing process determined by laws of self-organization and complexity. He sees a living organism as a collection of molecules with properties that manifest built-in propensities for interaction. With increased aggregation and interaction these molecules cross a critical boundary; they can then, by spontaneous self-organization, catalyze their mutual formation. Computer simulations of these processes of complexification, interaction, and self-organization demonstrate, in his view, that nature gives evidence of being able to generate a meaningful and purposeful process. In Kauffman's computational complexity theory the human species finally comes on the scene as a possible fulfillment of the catalytic capabilities of nature. Kauffman's conclusion is that life in its physical environment is not a *corpus alienum* – a foreign body – and that we must

---

[16] Darwin was already worried about this; he expressed his concern in chapter 10 of the *Origin* (first edition).

learn to see humans, in particular, as being "at home in the universe."[17]

Whatever we may think of Gould – he often tends to interpret the development of life not as a catalyzing process but as a monocausal chain of natural events – with his punctualism he has put the neo-Darwinian continuity claim up for discussion. In his vision, too, evolution is more than a steady, mechanical process of adaptation. In the complex design of living organisms, there are besides the principle of natural selection constructive-architectural and contingent-historical factors that assert themselves. New properties emerge and Gould refers to specific "biology rules."[18] Finally, he wants to qualify the selection principle further.

In the debate among biologists about natural selection, some postulate that nature selects genes (Dawkins' idea of "selfish genes"). Others suggest that the selection process acts on individual organisms (Darwin's "struggle for life"), or also on populations and species (Gould's idea of "species selection"). For me this discussion is of secondary importance as long as two points are recognized. First, whether we deal with genes, individuals, or larger assemblies, nature's selection acts on living organisms, not dead material. Thus, natural selection is never a strictly mechanical but always a functional, biological process. To be more specific, it is a realization of basal biotic rules or principles such as spontaneous self-organization, homeostasis, DNA transmission, and survival. Second, in organic nature, part and whole are subject to the same biological laws or principles. Thus, no matter where the principle of selection acts, it affects not only genes, but also the organisms which posses them and the communities in which these organisms and their genes thrive.

What I want to say with this is the following. In the debate on selection, Dawkins emphasizes the specific contribution of genes, Gould on the other hand the particular input of individuals and more inclusive categories such as species. These positions would appear to be contradictory, but they do not necessarily exclude each

---

[17] S. A. Kauffman, *At Home in the Universe: The Search for Laws of Self-Organization and Complexity* (New York: Viking, 1995).

[18] N. Eldredge and S. J. Gould, "Biology Rules," *Civilization* 5 (1998), 86–88.

other. The debate has a somewhat ambivalent character because the impression is created that there are various levels of selection at issue, indicated as a "hierarchical structure of selection" (Gould). In most cases, gene selection, individual selection, species selection, and above-species selection occur as an interaction between parts and (smaller or greater) wholes on the same biological level. On such a level, genes as well as individuals and species are fully attuned to each other in their struggle for survival. The selective processes that take place on this level are coordinated processes. The only topic that may give rise to difference of opinion is where the initiative for the selection may originate.

Yet, I would not consider every reference to "higher level selection" to be misplaced. In the world of living creatures selection procedures take place on various levels, thus also on levels that transcend the strictly biotic struggle for selfishness and survival. On the sensitive level of animals one can think of the behavioral rituals of animals in pair formation and mate selection, resulting in sexual selection. On the level of human culture one can think of the entrance procedures of schools and businesses, resulting in educational and economic selection. From an ontological perspective – a perspective that we will make explicit in the chapters to come – these are indeed forms of higher level selection, with their own part/whole relationships. Higher level selections are not exclusively aimed at selfishness and survival but also at well-being and, amongst humans, at values and norms.

The danger is not imaginary that we, as often as we bring the process of evolution to mind, stare ourselves blind at the spectacular formations of peaks that the life sciences can put before our eyes, at the sophisticated structures of ancient birds, hawks' eyes, and human brains. For *Archaeopteryx lithographica* evolutionary biologists may well come up with a convincing explanation of its origin, as they may for the sophisticated eye of the hawk, and, perhaps, for Albert Einstein's super-brain.[19] For whether one deals with fossils,

[19] In regard to the ancient bird, I point to *Protopteryx fengningensis*, a 120-million-year-old fossil recently unearthed in Northern China. The bird probably had two central tail feathers with a quill or shaft but no web (hairs). Were these feathers elongated scales? Apart from that, the animal had normal feathers and down: in other words, it had much in common with birds of today. See F. Zhang and Z. Zhou, "A Primitive Enantiornithine Bird and the Origin of Feathers," *Science* 290 (2000), 1955–59. Also complete is

like *Archaeopteryx*, or living organisms that show connections between phyla, like *Peripatus* or *Neopilina galathea*, they cannot be anything but functional. The vestigial legs in the boa or the wing stumps in flightless birds are also evidence of a functional transition. So we have to assume that some of these organisms indeed lie close to a fork on the evolutionary road.

Does the core of the problem not lie in another realm, in the unobtrusive formations *ex origine*, i.e., original formations of new life? Of course I think, in general, of the jump from lifeless to living reality. But I also think, more concretely, of the additional information that was the impetus for the origin of bacteria, plants, animals and, not to forget, the human mind. The most pressing problems do not concern the genesis of species or the bifurcation of supra-specific taxa. They concern, rather, the origin of novel arrangements of being and novel biological kingdoms. What induced the first microbe? How did the first light-sensitive cells arise in animals? How did the first primates arise that started to attune their grey matter to logical principles of identity and contradiction, and to moral principles of honesty and good faith?

It is the new ontological arrangements at the boundaries of the biological kingdoms that pose the greatest challenge for evolutionary research and that are, at the same time, the most insurmountable barriers. Why don't we know what to do with these original formations? Because we are mortals and we lack what Hillary Putnam has called "God's Eye point of view."[20] We are creatures and have been maneuvered into the virtually impossible position of trying to recover the story of our own origins. It is like losing one's eyeglasses. One looks and looks for them and wonders in despair whether one can ever find them without one's glasses on.

"Evolution is episodic," I heard Ian Tattersall – Curator of the Department of Anthropology of the American Museum of Natural

Microraptor gui, a 125-million-year-old fossil, a dinosaur from the same area with feathers on its fore- and hind limbs and tail. Were they used as wings to glide from the treetops? Gliding as a transition to flying? Regrettably the transition has not been fully worked out: the gliding *Microraptor* was 25 million years younger than the flying *Archaeopteryx*. See R. O. Prum, "Palaeontology: Dinosaurs Take to the Air," *Nature* 421 (2003), 323–24; X. Xu *et al.*, "Four-Winged Dinosaurs from China," *Nature* 421 (2003), 335–40.
[20] H. Putnam, *Reason, Truth and History* (Cambridge: Cambridge University Press, 1981), p. 49.

History, New York City – once say. Suppose that the process of evolution progresses episodically. Suppose it regularly gets stuck in consolidating periods of balance but in exceptional circumstances breaks out in new life forms, does it then have a purpose? Can we sensibly speak of a general direction of life from inanimate material, straight through the kingdoms of Protista, Plantae, and Animalia in the direction of *Homo sapiens*? The more we conclude that a monocausal, mechanistic account of origins is a panacea for naturalistic scientists and does no justice to the mystery of the living world, the more we recognize the need for an alternative. Is there a meaningful alternative?

4 GOD, TIME, AND TAXONOMY

At this point Christians often have the tendency to bring God into this discussion. God would have, at some point of time, brought into being plants, animals, and humans. At some point of time? Doesn't the Bible say explicitly "By the seventh day God had finished the work he had been doing" (Gen. 2:2)? In theology the idea that God as creator continues to work in earthly history is often designated as *creatio continua*, continuous creation. That concept seems to me to be a most unfortunate counterpart to the continuity concept of neo-Darwinian naturalism. Continuous creation is a creationistic formula borne out of perplexity.[21]

The Bible begins with the majestic words, "In the beginning God created." God did not create intermittently in time. "In the beginning," is not a definition of time but of origin. That is clear from the entire Bible. Nowhere does the Bible place God at a distance in time, in a hoary past. In fact, it shows Him to be intimately involved in daily life. God as creator is revealed as the immediate origin of all that was and all that is. God shows himself as the source of all life, not just of the first human beings or the first creatures. Believing parents, therefore, can justifiably call their baby

---

[21] Those who read the creation account of Gen. 1–2:4a as a literal report of God's creating work do not only misinterpret the creation days but must also assume that the animals before the fall, in harmony with Gen. 1:30, were all herbivores. In that case the carnivores could only have been created after the fall, and the idea of *creatio continua* then becomes almost unavoidable, despite Gen. 2:2.

a gift from heaven even though everyone knows that the infant came from normal parents. And David, poet after God's heart, can prayerfully whisper to Him:

> O Lord, you have searched me and you know me.
> You know when I sit and when I rise;
> You perceive my thoughts from afar,
> You discern my going out and my lying down;
> You are familiar with all my ways . . .
> For you created my inmost being;
> You knit me together in my mother's womb.
> I praise you because I am fearfully and wonderfully made.[22]

In short, in biblical perspective God is the creator of everything from the very beginning. He is also creator of time, of the past and the present, thus also of everything that originated or originates in time. Creation or evolution? It is a senseless alternative. Creation is the origin of evolution; evolution is the temporal realization of creation.

God did not create a cosmic commencement with additions afterward, say in the Cambrian, the Mesozoic, or the Cenozoic period. Then He would have had to intervene from above, in an autonomous mechanical order of nature. Such a mechanistic view of nature amounts to deism, and such a supernatural intervention to dualism. But nature is not a machine, and God is not a mechanic who occasionally checks the clock that he has made from the outside. "Do not forsake the work of your hands" is a prayer we often use at the beginning of a worship service. God manifests his faithfulness to the world in the care by which he sustains the world, from moment to moment, and by imprinting His laws upon it. The world "hangs upon" a permanent law to exist. Without this law of creation being in force – natural laws are at best mirroring models of this – the world would burst like a soap bubble.

Creatio continua? Created in the beginning, the world is the object of God's continuing care, not the object of incidental interventions. Created reality reveals itself as the dynamic disclosure process of time and world history. This disclosure process thus has

---

[22] Psalm 139:1–3, 13–14.

cosmic dimensions, and its importance for us is a simple conclusion from Augustine's insight that God, along with everything he created, also called time into being (see ch. 2, section 5).

This view throws new light on the disclosure process of time. With the origin of the biological kingdoms on earth, new ontological arrangements did indeed arise, such as the biotic way of being of bacteria, the vegetative nature of plants, and the sentient character of animals. But these innovations in no way justify an appeal to new creative intervention. God created the world in the beginning, with all the creaturely possibilities that it entails. Naturally, this creaturely potential did not come to full realization at once. At the moment of the Big Bang not a mineral could yet be found, but the Big Bang did initiate the process of cosmic evolution. Protons and electrons began to unite to form the lighter elements such as hydrogen and helium. Heavier atoms, such as carbon, nitrogen and oxygen developed since then, in the fiery smelting-furnaces of early stars. Molecules formed later – perhaps including organic molecules – in interstellar dust storms, shielded against cosmic radiation. Gradually the spattering secret of creation came to light, and fanned out in time. Only then did formations such as the Milky Way and intergalactic spaces group themselves, and galaxies of stars and satellites of suns come to be. And, yes, at a given moment, somewhere in a far corner of the expanding universe, the Earth appeared. And this Earth gave birth to the first stirrings of life, from which, in a process of billions of years, the biological kingdoms developed.

The traditional classification systems in taxonomy initially recognized only two kingdoms of living beings: plants and animals. Haeckel introduced the term "protista" to indicate unicellular systems. He identified three kingdoms: Protista, Plantae, and Animalia, i.e. unicellular organisms, plants, and animals. The further distinction within Protista between protophytes and protozoa (plant-like and animal-like unicellular organisms) proved to be untenable.

Important is the further distinction H. F. Copeland made between prokaryotic unicellular organisms (systems devoid of nuclear and other internal membranes) such as bacteria and blue-green algae, and eukaryotic organisms (protists possessing such internal membranes, including undifferentiated, aggregate multicellular organisms) such as algae and sponges. By uniting the prokaryotes into the new kingdom of the Monera, Copeland came to a total of four kingdoms.[23]

The well-known division of living organisms into five kingdoms by R. H. Whittaker is for our purposes less relevant. Besides the four kingdoms named above, Whittaker introduced the kingdom of Fungi.[24] From a taxonomic point of view this is an obvious way of dividing living things, based on modes of nutrition: plants feed themselves by photosynthesis, fungi by absorption, animals by ingestion. Because our analysis is ontological, not aimed at modes of nutrition but at modes of being, this distinction would seem to be less important for our discussion.

In the footsteps of Carl Woese, Professor of Microbiology at the University of Illinois, taxonomists have since the 1990s distinguished between archaebacteria (Archaea) and true bacteria (Eubacteria) within the kingdom of the Prokaryota. Thus they arrived at six primary biological kingdoms: Bacteria, Archaea, Protista, Plantae, Fungi, and Animalia.[25] However, at this time research in genetic and molecular biology advanced with leaps and bounds. It threw an entirely new light on the evolutionary process and led to what is now called the "phylogenetic revolution."

The result of all these developments is that the systematic position of the six kingdoms that have been distinguished has come into question. Thus, molecular biologists have suggested that the pro-karyotic Bacteria are, in evolutionary perspective, of older date than the much smaller Archaea; the relationship between both kingdoms has still not been clarified. Furthermore, they have opened for discussion the unity of the kingdom of protists, a kingdom that probably includes over 200,000 species ranging from amoebae to unicellular algae. They have made it plausible that, from a phylogenetic point of view, some green algae (sometimes indicated as Streptophyta) show a greater affinity with the plant kingdom than

[23] H. F. Copeland, "The Kingdom of Organisms," *Quarterly Review of Biology* 13 (1938), 383–420.
[24] R. H. Whittaker, "New Concepts of Kingdoms of Organisms," *Science* 163 (1969), 150–60.
[25] C. R. Woese and G. E. Fox, "Phylogenetic Structure of the Prokaryotic Domain: The Primary Kingdoms," *Proceedings of the National Academy of Sciences of the USA* 74 (1977), 5088–90. For a review see V. Morell, "Microbiology's Scarred Revolutionary," *Science* 276 (1997), 699–702; W. F. Doolittle, "Uprooting the Tree of Life," *Scientific American* 282 (February 2000), 90–95.

with most other unicellular eukaryotes. Reasoning of this kind can lead to a redefinition of the plant kingdom; analogical reasoning could result in a redefinition of the animal kingdom. Furthermore, DNA data seem to indicate that the kingdom of protista has a polyphyletic origin. A complicating factor in the discussion is that in some stages of the evolutionary process an exchange of genetic material between micro-organisms cannot be excluded. Finally, the question asserts itself, whether and how far the significant differences between the archaea and bacteria are ontologically relevant. For what I said earlier in regard to the fungi is also valid in a more general sense: a taxonomic classification does not, by definition, coincide with a categorization into ontological domains.

I will draw some provisional conclusions. To answer the principal question of this book – the question whether the evolution process proceeds purely by chance or whether it also gives expression to purposes – we cannot appeal to creative ideas or designs with which the divine Logos would have enriched living reality from time to time. We need insight into the specific character and genealogical succession of the distinctive ontological arrangements that are unique to living nature. Do these arrangements offer an evolutionary perspective of purpose and meaning? We have to conclude that systematic biology is, at present, in such a state of flux that it presents few taxonomic points of contact for acquiring such a perspective. In the chapters that follow we will have to be satisfied with an onto-logical exploration of the living world that focusses on the most principal points. I shall, in first instance, join in with the intuitively and widely accepted differences between unicellular organisms, plants, animals, and human beings: I want to pose the question by which ontological profiles these groups can be distinguished from one another. But at the end of my argument (see ch. 13, sections 1–3) I wish to return to some of the more detailed taxonomic distinctions that we have touched upon.

I would like to add a few clarifications. I see unicellular organisms as systems with a biotic function, i.e., as beings that regulate themselves, divide and reproduce, but lack a morphological speci-fication into organs. There is differentiation in the cell but no specialization of the cells into tissues and organs. Plants possess an organic or vegetative structure. They are, in the full sense of the word, organisms, for growth, reproduction, and nutrition take place by means of tools (organon = tool) in the form of specialized cells, tissues, and organs. Thus they display intercellular interactions that supersede the intracellular interactions (of organelles such as ribosomes and chloroplasts) in unicellular organisms. Of still higher order are the animals, understood as organisms in which, on the basis of sense organs and nerve paths, internal functions have developed in the sense of perception and feeling. Finally I hold to the unique ontological identity of human beings. In human beings, as we shall see, mental competencies and spiritual depth have developed. It does not make sense, however, to claim a separate kingdom for humans because *Homo sapiens* does not represent a kingdom of species but a single species.

In the evolutionary disclosure of temporal reality, the origin of the kingdoms and the manifestation of increasingly higher ontological competencies must have occurred in an orderly sequence. Higher functions could only realize themselves in lower life forms, and the most elementary life forms had to realize themselves in the world of matter and radiation, of inorganic and organic matter (probably supplied from outer space). However this process took place, from the most primitive bacteria the species developed haphazardly, but still – no biologist will deny it – in a way that they proved to be carriers of increasingly complex designs. We shall try to give account of the question of how the phylogenetic development of the species and the appearance of the kingdoms are related to the new ontological profiles that emerged at crucial junctures of the history of the earth. I consider the English philosophers Lloyd Morgan and Samuel Alexander to be the first thinkers who have reflected on the phenomenon of emergence, a topic I will discuss in the next chapter.

CHAPTER 6

The emergence theory of Morgan and Alexander

The theory of emergence is inseparably connected with the names of two philosophers of the early twentieth century: Conwy Lloyd Morgan (1852–1936) and Samuel Alexander (1859–1938). Morgan and Alexander were proponents of evolution in the spirit of Darwin. However, they introduced the concept of emergent evolution in order to oppose the reductive tendencies that were already becoming apparent in evolutionistic circles of their time.

Since the time of Morgan and Alexander the topic of emergence has been put on the agenda repeatedly not only by philosophers of science, systems theorists, and process thinkers but also by biologists, physiologists, and paleontologists. In the first group are authors such as R. Woltereck, B. Bavink, L. von Bertalanffy, M. Polanyi, A. N. Whitehead, K. R. Popper, J. R. Searle, and P. Checkland. In the second category I include scholars such as J. S. Haldane, L. J. Henderson, W. B. Cannon, J. C. Eccles, F. Jacob, T. Dobzhansky, G. L. Stebbins, S. A. Kauffman, W. H. Thorpe, S. J. Gould, and N. Eldredge.

Following in the footsteps of Morgan and Alexander all these people have argued, from various angles and with different arguments, for the notion of emergent evolution and they have made evolutionary naturalism with the accompanying reductionism an object of their criticism. They have raised such questions as these: is reductive naturalism in agreement with the complicated nature of the living world? Is the fundamental continuity that we see in the process of evolution between inanimate and animate nature not often paired with elements of radical novelty? Do we not see in the evolutionary process, besides very explainable causal developments, at times also developments that follow a completely new set of principles, such as the principle of cellular organization and genetic transmission? In short, the proponents of emergent evolution have come to the conclusion that in organic nature specific arrangements of being have arisen with totally new functions and properties, not reducible to the order of physical nature.

From the viewpoint of evolutionary naturalism the objection is often made that the theory of emergent evolution is internally inconsistent. In it, physical reality would turn into non-physical reality. This is a tendentious representation of affairs. Physical reality is and remains physical. The only question is whether in the physical world more-than-physical phenomena could come to realization. Emergence theory wants to keep open the possibility that evolution was, at times, paired with revolution, i.e. changes that are so radical that they are not directly reducible to preceding developments. Not the recognition of novelty but the forced reduction of all the new to the old brings about contradictions (see ch. 4, section 3).

In this chapter we first want to examine the emergence theory of its founders, the views of Morgan and Alexander (section 1). We will then pay attention to the intentionality of human self-consciousness as a specific example of the phenomenon of emergence (section 2). Finally, we will point out some negative and positive aspects of current emergence theories (section 3).

I EMERGENCE ACCORDING TO MORGAN AND ALEXANDER

In this section I want to concentrate on the views of C. Lloyd Morgan and Samuel Alexander. I would add here that their theory of emergent evolution was shaped further by the ideas of C. D. Broad, J. C. Smuts, and J. H. Woodger, but I shall not discuss these authors explicitly.[1]

---

[1] C. D. Broad formulates, in *The Mind and Its Place in Nature* (New York: Routledge and Kegan Paul, 1925), a refined or "emergent" vitalism over against the "one-level ontology" of the then current biological mechanism and over against the less refined or "substantial" vitalism of Hans Driesch. In opposition to both mechanism and vitalism, J. C. Smuts, in *Holism and Evolution* (London: Macmillan, 1926), introduces a "holistic" view of nature, in

Morgan and his younger friend and colleague Alexander assume that natural reality is involved in a process of progressive evolutionary change. They object, however, to the scientistic idea that this process is completely explainable in the language of the physical sciences. Both find untenable the so-called mechanicism in biology, the view that all phenomena of life are, basically, nothing but purely mechanistic processes. They have no difficulty with the fact that evolution theory leaves room for mechanistic explanatory components, but they emphasize that this approach is not complete. It does not supply an adequate explanation for what occurs in the evolutionary process as a whole. Mechanistic thought cannot explain how in living organisms characteristics and behaviors manifest themselves that are fully unknown in material things.

Alexander was Professor of Philosophy at the University of Manchester. He outlined his ideas on emergence in his Gifford Lectures, delivered between 1916 and 1918 and published under the title, *Space, Time, and Deity*.[2] Morgan, originally a graduate student of Thomas H. Huxley, was a zoologist and Professor of Psychology in Bristol. He followed in the footsteps of Alexander with his Gifford Lectures of 1921 to 1922; they were given the title *Emergent Evolution*.[3] In this work, Morgan insists on a broader framework of the world. He has in view "a consistent scheme which is conceived at a level of reflective thought that supplements, though it does not supersede, science. There must be nothing in this scheme which is discrepant with science; but, on this understanding, there may be constitutive features which complete the otherwise incomplete delivery of strictly scientific thought."[4]

Evolution is not always a uniform and continuous process of development. From time to time it gives evidence of major "discontinuities" and critical "turning points" by the abrupt appearance of

---

which the "organized complexity" of living organisms is a pivotal concept. In *Biological Principles: A Critical Study* (New York: Harcourt, 1929), J. H. Woodger makes a plea for the methodological recognition of a hierarchy of "levels of complexity" as a distinct characteristic of living systems.

[2] S. Alexander, *Space, Time and Deity: The Gifford Lectures at Glasgow 1916–1918* (London: Macmillan, 1920; repr. Kila, MT: Kessinger Publishing, 2004).

[3] C. L. Morgan, *Emergent Evolution* (London: Williams and Norgate, 1923; repr. New York: AMS Press, 1977).

[4] *Ibid.*, § x.

"emergents." Emergents are phenomena that supervene existing causal systems, that are truly new and that cannot be explained or predicted from general laws of nature. Evolution is "jumpy," Morgan states defiantly. Occasionally it gives evidence of a progressive, saltatory change from a lower to a higher level of reality.

While Morgan and Alexander reject mechanism, they also reject the opposite option, the so-called neo-vitalism of Hans Driesch and his followers. The vital force to which Driesch appeals, "entelechy," present in living systems, they dismiss as an explanatory factor. They do recognize the unique nature of living organisms, but they see the vitalistic appeal to a special power active in living entities as an unscientific loophole, even as a metaphysical speculation. Though material reality in living organisms demonstrates a qualitative surplus value and entirely new properties, they see no reason to ascribe these properties to a scientifically nontestable principle of life. These properties can be made understandable by an explanation that lies closer at hand, namely from the complex organizational structure that living organisms display on a higher level of reality.[5]

Morgan and Alexander thus arrive at an alternative, more inclusive, theory of evolution, a theory necessary to explain the organic variety, increasing diversity, and structural complexity that present themselves in the genealogical development of living systems. To this end, they employ three key concepts. The first of these is the idea of *emergence*. Although variety, diversity, and complexity occur widely in living nature, in certain crucial situations emergence could manifest itself in the sense that functions and properties came

---

[5] Vitalism is of Aristotelian origin. It opposes mechanism, which views living organisms as complex machines, determined by causal natural laws. Vitalism posits that organic systems, by virtue of processes of homeostasis, regeneration, reproduction, and heredity, have a purposeful principle of life all their own, so that their activities are primarily determined not by causality but by finality or purpose. When biochemists discovered that organic substances could be synthesized from inorganic reagents, Hans Driesch formulated the theory of "neo-vitalism." This theory has a strongly holistic perspective. Observing that half a sea urchin egg still has the potency to develop a complete sea urchin, he defined the vitality of organisms as their entelechy: their innate directedness to the system as a whole. Living beings would posses, from the embryo stage onward, this idea of the whole as the purpose (telos) of development. The "entelechy" postulated by Driesch is related to the *élan vital* of Bergson and the driving *dedans* of Teilhard de Chardin. Cf. E. Nordenskiöld, *The History of Biology: A Survey* (New York: Alfred A. Knopf, 1932), pp. 606–12.

to the fore that are not reducible to previous functions and properties. Next is the concept of *level*. With emergence the functional change brings the organism involved to a higher level of organization, a level that will distinguish itself by properties all its own from the level of reality upon which it rests. Finally, they mention the concept of *novelty*. The emergence of a higher level of organization implies a qualitative renewal that (a) is more than a reorganization of the properties that are characteristic of the previous level of being; that (b) does not offer just an additional functionality but structural renewal of the organism as a whole; and that (c) is so radical that a scientific explanation in the form of a total reduction to a previous level of being is excluded.

2 THE INTENTIONALITY OF HUMAN CONSCIOUSNESS

The emergence philosophy of Morgan and Alexander can be criticized on several counts but their point of departure must give us reason for thought. Even if the entire world is caught in a process of transformational change, it does not follow by definition that all that is later can be fully explained in terms of what came before. To put it another way, one cannot exclude, a priori, the possibility that in the evolutionary dynamic of time new structures and characteristics have come to light. Neither is it obvious or self-evident that these new structures and characteristics can be fully reduced to more basic structures and qualities, and ultimately to the structural features that are characteristic of inanimate nature.

To elucidate the significance of this position, I take as an example human self-consciousness, a topic to which I shall return more extensively later. Neurophysiologists have determined that the structure of the human brain strongly resembles that of primates, in particular that of the chimpanzees, even if human brains are three times as large. This affinity does not exclude that in the human brain a new mode of being crystallized out at a given moment, in such a way that one can speak here, and nowhere else, of mind or mental self-consciousness. Is this mode of being entirely new? Upon closer examination it appears that mental self-consciousness is an ability that transcends the cerebral ability of primates in at least two crucial ways: in regards to intentionality and normativity.

Human consciousness is, in the first place, intentional in nature. That is to say, mental images, lingual expressions, and moral opinions have an intention; they are in relation to a real or ideal object. Human images, exclamations, and actions are not just expressions of subjective experience, as they would be in animals. To the contrary, in human consciousness they articulate themselves as object-related, i.e. as exosomatic functions. They deal with something that is not just given with human bodily functions. Mental images, language, and morals are concerned with matters that transcend the immediacy of our corporeal existence. For in word, deed, and gesture, we communicate with each other about scientific theories, political topics, and moral questions, even if there are, for ourselves, no immediate concerns or interests involved.

Human consciousness has, furthermore, a normative nature. It is directed toward normative criteria, standards by which it measures itself. I do not mean to say that the opinions we hold dear, about ourselves or the world around us, can always be characterized as normatively correct, but that they are normatively determined. Our ideas may be wrong, our statements misleading, our acts objectionable, but this does not alter the fact that we, as people, address each other, also in regard to our failures, on the basis of norms such as truth, accuracy, solidarity, and the like. In short, as mental and spiritual beings, human individuals give evidence of responsibility on the basis of norms and values that they share with others. We do not hold animals accountable. We can train them and drill them, but it makes no sense to appeal to their sense of responsibility, in the way we do in the case of human persons. The reason for this is that we experience human consciousness as emergent, that is, of a higher order than the level of experience of animals.

Emergence theory focusses on the novelty, unpredictability, and irreducibility, to use the words of C. D. Broad, of higher level phenomena.[6] Mental consciousness is only one example of this. To all higher-level phenomena there is this aspect of novelty, unpredictability, and irreducibility, not as an additional but a fundamental characteristic. Irreducible novelty is, in the emergence school of Morgan, Alexander, and others, characteristic of all possible forms of

---

[6] See Broad, *The Mind and Its Place in Nature*.

life; it affects these forms in their entirety. In opposition to the reductionism of today the theory of emergence often speaks of holism, to emphasize that higher-level phenomena put a stamp on the whole system. The new level does not layer itself upon the previous levels as a geological layer; on the contrary, it encloses them as in concentric circles or in a set of nested bowls. System A is enclosed by system AB, system AB by system ABC, etc. Thus, in a biological organism inorganic reality is enclosed by life. The material components become an integral part of a living reality. In other words, where a biological structure appears as a new mode of being, it also has innovating side effects on the physical infrastructure.

Once again, I give an example here: the organism of the plant. The plant, compared with the physico-chemical structure of an inanimate thing, has an additional ontological function: its self-regulating ability as an organically and morphogenetically differentiated system. This new ontological level of the plant necessarily brings with it a reorganization of the molecular, physico-chemical substrate. For the plant can only function as a self-regulating system because, in all its cells and tissues, molecules have arranged themselves into a new sort of complex molecules: biomolecules such as proteins, lipids, carbohydrates, and nucleic acids. The newness of the plant as a morphogenetic system is able to control the underlying level of the plant as a molecular system.[7]

Something similar occurs in the even more highly developed sensitive structure of an animal. The animal has the ability to receive sensory impressions, an ability that is lacking in vegetable systems. Yet, this new, sensitive level of being – think of sight, hearing, smell, and echo-location – has a feedback effect on the total body plan of the animal. For, compared to the plant, the morphogenetic structure of the animal body has been changed in such a way that it provides for the nerve pathways that are essential for

---

[7] Also in the work of H. Dooyeweerd, whose ideas will be discussed later, the levels are not *Stufen*, i.e., separated layers that are stacked on top of each other. He sees them as aspects of a concrete thing or phenomenon. In *A New Critique of Theoretical Thought*, vol. III (Amsterdam: H. J. Paris, 1957), pp. 84, 729–33, 762–63, and in "Het substantiebegrip in de moderne natuurphilosophie," *Philosophia Reformata* 15 (1950), 66–139, Dooyeweerd criticizes emergence theory. His criticism is determined to a large degree by a one-sided orientation on Woltereck, who is indeed a proponent of a "theory of *Stufen*." R. Woltereck, *Ontologie des Lebendigen* (Stuttgart: F. Enke, 1940).

feeling and sensory observation. The sensory nerves, afferent, give messages to the central nervous system, and the motor nerves, efferent, coming from the central nervous system, move our limbs, eyes, and activate our glands, etc. Also the physico-chemical function has, in its turn, been reorganized, for the animal body is dependent, for example, on the hormones secreted by the endocrine glands that regulate the metabolism, growth, body temperature, and reproduction of animal systems. In other words, in animals the novelty of the emergent, sensitive level has a feedback effect on all the underlying levels.

3 METAPHYSICS AND THE STANDPOINT OF EXPERIENCE

The comments that I made above about the organizational levels that can be distinguished in the biosystem of plants, of animals, and also in human beings form, in fact, the beginning of my critique of Morgan and Alexander. The number of levels that they distinguish is minimal and, as I see it, not specified adequately (1). Furthermore, the distinctions that both of them utilize are not free of metaphysical speculation (2).

(1) First of all, the number of functional levels that would have been produced by emergent evolution appears to be rather minimal and in my view articulated with insufficient precision. Thus there is lacking a clearly defined distinction between the level on which bacterial systems present themselves, the level that has become characteristic of plants, and the level that is peculiar to animals, although distinctive characteristics become noticeable on all these levels (I will soon return to this topic).

Morgan and Alexander do recognize the unique position and significance of the human person as center of contemplation and reflection. But they avoid the bothersome question of whether the human mind – taking note, for example, of its logical, moral, and esthetic capacities – would not have differentiated into a variety of mental functions of an emergent character. Morgan distinguishes only four levels of being: the psycho-physical, life, the spirit, and God. Alexander discerns five: space–time, matter, life, spirit, and God. Of course, neither of them denies that qualitative differences among levels occur, also within the realm of culture, for instance among art, science, and morals. In their view, however, this difference in cultural values has nothing to do with a continuing process of emergent evolution. It can be explained from nature, i.e. from the various needs that are part and parcel of human nature.

Let me clarify this point by examining the ideas of Alexander, who searched, from an early stage in his career, for the correlations between ethics, biology, and psychology. In his book, *Beauty and the Other Forms of Value*, Alexander bases the values of beauty, truth, and goodness on bodily instincts and psychological impulses, i.e. on the impulse of the human being to construct, on curiosity, and on sympathy, respectively. These impulses have, by their very nature, a particular and practical intention. But the human spirit can alter their character; mental reflection and contemplation cause disengagement and generalization. The feelings of engagement in the surrounding world become less direct; the natural impulses begin to spread to larger and larger circles of people. In this way beauty, truth, and goodness have extended themselves into general cultural values, according to Alexander. For cultural values are those competencies and qualities in the human being that serve to satisfy impulses that have loosened themselves from particular interests. Take the value of moral goodness. Humans began to call good those impulses and behaviors in which they had learned to adapt themselves to others through a general sympathetic sentiment. They began, conversely, to call bad those impulses and behaviors that they had learned to reject because they did not agree with the general sentiment of sympathy.[8]

No doubt, there are intrinsic connections that can be determined to exist between natural impulses and cultural values. But the attempt of Alexander to reduce the general values and norms of human society to natural sentiments extends further and is anything but an innocent exercise. For it has as a consequence that incisive philosophical questions, of whether culture contains irreducible elements of novelty, and whether, at crucial turning-points, the process of emergent evolution perhaps continues itself from the realm of nature into the realm of culture, are prematurely cast aside.

---

[8] S. Alexander, *Beauty and the Other Forms of Value* (London: Macmillan, 1933).

Even after Morgan and Alexander, the problem of possible implications of emergence theory for our view of human culture and society remained systematically under-examined, with a few exceptions in general systems theory and the philosophy of mind (see ch. 8, section 2 and ch. 9, section 6). Emergence thinkers appear to have great difficulty doing justice to the unique characteristics of human beings and of the institutional spheres in society. In the 1950s, Paul Oppenheim and Hilary Putnam began to distinguish between six levels of being: elementary particles, atoms, molecules, unicellular systems, multicellular organisms, and social groups.[9] Here, the question again asserts itself – just as in the case of Alexander – whether the qualitative diversity of institutions in a human society is not the possible result of a continued emergent evolution. Yes, even today, emergence theory lacks a fundamental reflection upon the relation between the notion of emergence and the differentiation process that characterizes modern societies. Adherents usually restrict themselves to a global distinction between five ontological or explanatory levels: the physical, the chemical, the biotic, the mental, and the social level.[10]

(2) Furthermore, the opinions of Alexander and Morgan on emergence are not devoid of metaphysical speculation. In the first instance both base themselves on the standpoint of experience; they plead for an "empirical method." In this framework they pay much attention to the differential complexity of evolutionary phenomena. They also point out the logical inconsistencies that stick to mechanistic naturalism. But in their opposition against mechanicism, a metaphysical way of thinking that is not always distinguishable from vitalism gradually gains the upper hand. Peculiar to nature as a whole would be a creative life force: the tendency to produce new syntheses with emergent qualities. In the evolution of the cosmos, and even more so in the development of life on earth, a *nisus* would reveal itself, a creative inclination that would bring forth ever higher levels of being, proceeding in the direction of the divine.

[9] P. Oppenheim and H. Putnam, "Unity of Science as a Working Hypothesis," in H. Feigl and M. Scriven (eds.), *Minnesota Studies in the Philosophy of Science* 2 (1958), 3–36.
[10] See J. Kim, *Supervenience and Mind: Selected Philosophical Ideas* (Cambridge and New York: Cambridge University Press, 2002), pp. 336–57.

Thus a speculative process philosophy develops in the spirit of Hegel, especially in the thought of Alexander. God is assumed to be the final end of the evolutionary process, the ultimate result of what Henri Bergson earlier called the *élan vital* of nature. The theory of emergence becomes emergentism here, a metaphysical worldview with mystical and pantheistic features. According to Morgan and Alexander the world is on its way to becoming divine. And God is, conversely, busy to manifest himself amongst us as the highest level of emergence. He is, Alexander suggests, the most encompassing apotheosis of being, announcing his coming in people with spiritual qualities: visionary carriers of the divine mystery. This is why investigators should accept their existence in the world with an attitude of humility or "natural piety," Alexander states, inspired by the romantic poet Wordsworth.[11]

I should add here that since Morgan and Alexander a large majority of emergence thinkers have distanced themselves from such uncontrollable pronouncements, which bring discredit to the theory of emergent evolution. Just like Hilary Putnam, they place great emphasis on the application of professional, strictly empirical methods in the life sciences. These thinkers are committed to the sciences with the proviso that the identification of rational thinking with scientific thinking should be dismissed. They reject the exclusivistic idea that science alone provides true descriptions of reality. They emphasize in particular that the physical method, no matter how indispensable, is an abstract form of thought and thus, per definition, represents a limited and one-sided form of knowledge. For this reason they want to make room for other types of knowledge in order to do justice to the differences in levels that force themselves upon us as we experience the world.

In the development toward an empirically oriented emergence philosophy, one could consider Alfred North Whitehead a transitional figure. Whitehead, who with Bertrand Russell became of seminal importance for modern mathematics, seeks a connection with the evolutionary process philosophy of Alexander. He shares his metaphysical aspirations with Alexander but seeks to limit speculative thinking about God. In Whitehead's process philosophy, God

---

[11] Alexander, *Space, Time and Deity*, p. 47.

cannot be ignored; He is the point of departure of all evolutionary developments. He designates Him as the "principle of limitation." The world, as we experience it concretely, is caught in an all-encompassing process of becoming, a process in which, once and again, new spheres of reality emerge. God is the principle that determines, limits, and discloses the dynamic of this becoming reality from its very beginning. But God cannot be presented, in a Hegelian sense, as the philosophical conclusion or logical product of this process.

Even if we reject the speculative, dialectical arguments of Hegelianism, there is still the temptation to develop a "metaphysics of emergence" (Timothy O'Connor). In recent discussions too, many theorists attempt to give a fully reasoned explanation of how the mind has emerged from the brain.[12] Or they expound the relations between higher and lower level phenomena in terms of bottom-up causation, top-down causation, causal interaction, etc., as we shall see later. In most cases such a metaphysical theory of emergence contains a *petitio principii*. For it tries to explain the process of emergent evolution in conformity with general logical principles, but, in doing so, it ignores that these principles only come forward in this process itself. In other words, the authors presuppose what they try to explain. The phenomenon of emergence cannot be built on metaphysical reasoning, but only on experience in the broad sense of the word.

I want to conclude this chapter with a reference to an emergence thinker of more recent date, the eminent French molecular biologist and Nobel Prize winner François Jacob. Jacob, too, emphatically contradicts the viewpoint that biology is merely an annex or extension of the physical sciences. In his view this is excluded, for new limitations and possibilities come to light at higher and more complex levels of being, i.e. at the levels of living organisms and populations. The principle that guides him is that, when reality emerges and integrates on a higher level, the rules of the game that

---

[12] See, e.g., T. O'Connor and H. Y. Wong, "The Metaphysics of Emergence," *Noûs* 39 (2005), 658–78, and J. Kim, "Multiple Realization and the Metaphysics of Reduction," *Philosophy and Phenomenological Research* 52 (1992), 1–26. Much recent literature on metaphysics and emergence can be found in T. O'Connor and H. Y. Wong, "Emergent properties," http://plato.stanford.edu/entries/properties–emergent/.

is played on this level also change. Each level has its own constitutive rules. But note! Despite his connection with the theory of
emergence Jacob strongly rejects the speculative view that a divine
actor or a metaphysical force of life would continually pull the
strings of organic nature. Thus he writes:

> Biology has demonstrated that there is no metaphysical entity hidden
> behind the word "life" . . . From particles to man, there is a whole series of
> integrations, of levels, of discontinuities . . . Investigation of molecules and
> cellular organelles has now become the concern of physicists . . . This does
> not at all mean that biology has become an annex of physics, that it
> represents, as it were, a junior branch concerned with complex systems. At
> each level of organization, novelties appear in both properties and logic.
> To reproduce is not within the power of any single molecule by itself. This
> faculty appears only with the simplest integron deserving to be called a
> living organism, that is, the cell. But thereafter the rules of the game
> change. At the higher-level integron, the cell population, natural selection
> imposes new constraints and offers new possibilities. In this way, and
> without ceasing to obey the principles that govern inanimate systems,
> living systems become subject to phenomena that have no meaning at the
> lower level. Biology can neither be reduced to physics, nor do without it.[13]

The time has come to explore in a more systematic manner the
notion of emergence and its meaning for the life sciences and
evolution theory. But we are committed to the standpoint of
experience. That is to say, in the following chapters we choose
consistently an empirical, non-metaphysical approach.

---

[13] F. Jacob, *The Logic of Living Systems* (London: Allen Lane, 1974), translation of *La logique du vivant* (Paris: Gallimard, 1970). Jacob understands an "integron" to be a "holon," a living whole. Cited from P. Checkland, *Systems Thinking, Systems Practice* (Chichester: John Wiley, 1981), p. 82.

CHAPTER 7

Luctor et emergo: *what is emergent evolution?*

Zeeland, a province in the southwest of The Netherlands, carries a beautiful motto on its coat of arms: *Luctor et Emergo* (I struggle and rise up). In its struggle with water – a challenge to the people of that province through the centuries – Zeeland's new reality has arisen: a world of islands with protective dikes, and fertile fields that have been wrestled from the sea. The motto shows that the people of Zeeland are open to what is new and unknown. Evolutionary biologists should be able to recognize the image. *Luctor* parallels the necessary struggle for survival of the species. *Emergo* mirrors the possibility, small though it may be, that in this struggle something entirely new may come to the fore: a higher form of being with new functional properties.

I MOZART AND "TWINKLE, TWINKLE, LITTLE STAR"

Emergence is like a melody that comes into being at a concert. One sits in the auditorium, full of background noise. But when the conductor climbs the podium, noise gives way to applause, and then – silence. And in that silence the orchestra begins to play a melody. How do the listeners experience that melody? A physicist in the audience has one answer: for him or her the melody is a combination of air vibrations that cause sound waves which resonate in the eardrum. The physicist is right, but is that all? Is the melody not more than sympathetic vibrations of the eardrum? Doesn't music also have characteristics and meanings that make it different from all other sounds? Background noise and applause go in one ear and out the other, but music can touch us in a very personal way. The melody can continue to replay in our mind for days. Whether we are concert aficionados or pop-lovers, people experience music as a new dimension of reality, a world with a character all its own. Music has its own peculiar structure and power of expression. We sense it is bound to rules of harmony and disharmony, and to standards for melody. It is not primarily determined by physical laws but by esthetic laws.

Long ago the incomparable Mozart was struck by the melody we now know as "Twinkle, Twinkle, Little Star." What was it that intrigued him? Not the changes of frequency in the sound waves. No, what he listened to transcended every physical description: a moment of esthetic beauty. Of course, Mozart's variations upon the theme can be described in physical terms, and translated into bits and bytes. At the same time, they have a surplus of meaning that cannot be explained by physical laws. The variations represent a reality of their own, a reality that is governed by laws of harmony, tonalities, principles of form, and rules of composition; yes, by an ultimate standard of artistic conviction. The musical range of meaning leaves the physical range of meaning intact but transcends it at the same time. How? By making it subordinate to esthetic laws and rules of play.

Emergence has to do with this phenomenon of self-transcendence or, as G. L. Stebbins states, "transcendental novelty."[1] Emergence implies that in the process of evolutionary change things transcend themselves in such a manner that a completely new cosmic ordering comes to light. Thus the concept of emergent evolution is more than an epistemological distinction; it has an ontological status. It implies a fundamental innovation not only in the order of knowing but also of being. I define emergent evolution as the coming to the fore of a new arrangement of being in such a way that new functions and properties arise, based on the functions and properties that were already present at preceding levels of being but not reducible to them, because they respond to laws of their own. Thus emergent evolution is innovative evolution. Yet, it is clearly not without continuity. In it continuity and discontinuity are intertwined. In the dynamic process of time reality evolved repeatedly to such a point that it became the permanent infrastructure for a higher or

---

[1] G. L. Stebbins, *Darwin to DNA, Molecules to Humanity* (San Francisco: Freeman, 1982), p. 167.

transcendental mode of existence structured by new, non-reductive organizational principles.

Emergence, or self-transcendence, does not manifest itself exclusively in the areas of art and culture, say, in Mozart's music. It lies at the root of all our basic experiences of reality. Emergence is presupposed in our experiences of nature, for example in the distinction we make spontaneously between inanimate and animate nature, between minerals and living organisms, between plants, animals, and humans, etc. In all those distinctions we recognize that there are various kinds of reality, even though it remains a challenge to account for them all in our descriptions. We, human beings, are, for some reason, deeply familiar with the fact that our earthly reality has disclosed itself into a structural diversity of arrangements, in which we, ourselves, participate by virtue of a diversity of bodily and mental competencies.

In the sciences, too, the realization has gained ground that in empirical reality we are dealing with an ontological diversity of phenomena. It is true, all kinds of empiricistic currents in philosophy – think of the logical positivism of Rudolf Carnap and the Vienna Circle – have tried to ignore this diversity. They cherished the ideal of the "unification of science," as if there is only one uniform reality and one type of science to describe it. But that is not how things are. The world is dynamic and irresistibly innovative. Although it originated as a purely physical reality, it opened its doors to new formulas of existence, to worlds of organic life, sensory perception, logical comprehension, moral action, etc. That is to say, it reorganized itself into more and more complicated above-physical arrangements of being, into a "hierarchy of complex systems." And modern science reflects this diversity and complexity. In the nineteenth and twentieth centuries, it unfolded into a broad scale of theoretical disciplines. Nowadays it presents itself, in the terminology of Nancey Murphy, as "a hierarchy of sciences."[2]

Especially the life sciences have discovered the phenomenon of emergence. The different disciplines are witness to the fact that in living organisms we encounter a fundamental diversity of organizational

---

[2] N. Murphy, "A Hierarchy of Sciences," http://www.counterbalance.net/evp-mind/ahier-frame.html.

forms. Thus many scholars realize that the future of their particular discipline doesn't lie in reduction and unification but in interdisciplinary cooperation, for example, among molecular biology, genetics, physiology, and population biology. In fact, the whole edifice of the modern sciences is attuned to the phenomenon of emergence and ontological differences. For the organizational levels of the world constitute, in rough outline, the research domains of the principal areas into which the phenomenon of science has been differentiated in modern times.

2 ORGANIZATIONAL LEVELS IN NATURE

In *The Origin of Species* Darwin preferred to describe evolution as "descent with modification." I would like to describe emergent evolution as "descent with innovative modification." With these words I wish to say that evolution is not merely a process of change; it is also a process of irreducible renewal. Just as in culture music has developed into a world in itself, determined by laws of sound, harmony, beat, and rhythm that are not deducible from physical laws, so also in living nature particular worlds have emerged determined by laws that are not deducible from laws of physics. As I continue, I will bring these worlds into the discussion as ontological domains, i.e. as organizational levels of reality.

Recent discussions about emergence primarily refer to the ontological domains that we can distinguish in nature. They usually do not touch culture. I will also focus my comments in this chapter on nature. The organizational levels of culture will be discussed later. To facilitate clarity I limit myself to four levels, even though the current state of affairs in the natural and life sciences probably gives rise to more detailed distinctions (see ch. 13, sections 1–2). My exploration of the terrain in this chapter is therefore no more than a provisional sketch. I distinguish between the following four domains in nature:

(1) The physical domain. This domain is of a basic nature. One can see all things that happen and all processes that occur in the earthly and cosmic reality as physical phenomena. Even if some things are more than that – think of living organisms – they do have their roots in the physical world and also always display, for this

reason, physical or physico-chemical characteristics. On the basis of this fundamental physical function we can say: all phenomena in the earthly and cosmic reality make up part of the physical domain.

The physical domain and all material and energetic processes that take place in this domain are determined by universal natural laws. These can be universal physical laws, such as the laws of Maxwell or Einstein's famous formula, $E = mc^2$, but also applied chemical rules such as that an acid and a base yield a salt and water.

On earth the physical domain is not limited to inanimate nature. It also extends into the living world. For living organisms also have a material basis. Bacteria, plants, animals, and human beings are living creatures but at the same time they exhibit a physical function and physical properties. (This is the grain of truth in reductive physicalism.) But in living systems the physical function has become subordinate to higher functions. Thus in every organism metabolic processes take place, a transformation of physical substances in such a way that the supply of energy meets the needs of life. Energy has become especially significant in the form of adenosine triphosphate (ATP), a molecule that plays a central role in the energy exchange of all living cells.

(2) The biotic domain. This is the level upon which life manifests itself to us. Life emerged under the very special circumstances that had arisen here after the cooling down of the earth. Thanks to a moderate climate, the availability of water, etc., complex physical entities reorganized themselves in such a way that a new, biotic function was brought about. This new arrangement of being characterized itself through cellular self-organization. Cell formation came to light in bacteria and other unicellular organisms. Perhaps it initially arose in only one prokaryotic ancestor and then spread to other individuals. Thus, unicellular (and aggregated multicellular) organisms have a physical infrastructure and an additional biotic superstructure. The highest function in a concrete entity is the prevailing function; that's to say here, the biotic function characterizes or qualifies the unicellular organism as a whole. Unicellular organisms can therefore be designated as biotically qualified or, briefly, as biotic systems. They distinguish themselves by a spontaneous self-regulation of the cell that is paired with DNA-replication and reproduction.

Afterward, this biotic domain broadened. For not only bacteria and eukaryotic algae but also plants and animals have a biotic function, with this proviso, that cellular self-organization takes place here in subordination to functions that are still higher.[3]

The biotic function is determined by laws of spontaneous self-organization. In these I do not only include the rules of cellular organization, self-regulation, replication, and reproduction, but also the Darwinian algorithm of competition, variation, selection, and genetic transmission that I mentioned in an earlier context.

Biotic laws are nomologically universal. But they differ from physical laws because they are not nomologically uniform; usually they do not allow exact predictions. The reason is that biotic laws have attuned themselves to the particular circumstances in which they operate and are oriented toward the self-preservation of species in their habitat. Therefore I prefer to indicate biotic laws as "principles," i.e. laws that have a universal character and a specified elaboration (see ch. 4, section 2). Let me take reproduction as an example. Reproduction can be seen as a biotic principle in the sense of a universal law with specific applications. All living organisms, from the most primitive unicellular bacteria to the most highly developed vertebrates, have a natural urge to propagate themselves. But they do so in diverse manners dependent on the species, its habitat, and its position in the phylogenetic process. There is reproduction by fission, budding, parthenogenesis, and mating.

(3) The vegetative domain. This is the level upon which, in the evolutionary process, the particular character of plants has developed. Also the vegetative function can only manifest itself under very specific circumstances. The probability of emergence is always based on the actual fulfillment of prior life conditions, says the Canadian philosopher Bernard Lonergan.[4] Indeed, the vegetative mode of being emerged when the world of biotic systems had evolved to the extent that vegetative life became possible. Plants are

---

[3] Unicellular organisms do not only include the kingdoms of Bacteria and Archaea but also a great diversity of eukaryotes (protists). Given this taxonomic diversity it may be necessary to introduce more specific ontological distinctions in regard to the biotic mode of being (see ch. 13, section 1).

[4] B. J. F. Lonergan, *Insight: A Study of Human Understanding*, Collected Works (20 vols.), vol. III (1958) (Toronto: University of Toronto Press, 1992), p. 145.

complex multicellular systems; they probably derived from a special type of green algae. A plant has a physical and a biotic infrastructure for it is a molecular system with supplies of energies and simultaneously a cellular system with spontaneous self-regulation. But the peculiar character of plants lies in something else, in the emergent properties of growth and organic differentiation. The plant developes specialized body forms, a diversity of cells, tissues, and organs for the purpose of nutrition, reproduction, photosynthesis, etc. This morphogenetic ability I will indicate in what follows as the vegetative function. It is a prevailing function. The plant is thus a vegetatively qualified or vegetative system.

Often the term "vegetative" is exclusively applied to plants but this is incorrect. The word has an Aristotelian background and originally means "able to grow." Thus one should not identify it with photosynthesis and other plant-like phenomena. This ability to grow is inherent in multicellular organisms in general, animals and people included. For instance, we speak of the vegetative state of a patient. We say of some people that they simply vegetate. And we distinguish the vegetative (sympathetic) nervous system of human beings and animals. In short, from an ontological point of view all multicellular organisms have a vegetative function, i.e. the ability to differentiate from an amorphous beginning and to grow into an adult specimen with an articulated pattern of forms. But we have to take into account that the vegetative function in animals and people is subordinate to yet higher functions. Organs such as the eye and the brain are vegetatively developed tools but they are in the service of sensitive and mental functions.

There are vegetative principles, i.e. morphogenetic rules on the basis of which organisms grow into a multicellular system, and their cells, tissues, and organs specialize according to a set pattern. Vegetative principles are, like biotic principles, universal laws, but not in a nomological sense of the word. They are particularized and attuned to the morphogenesis of the species concerned.[5] I mention as an example the heritability laws of Gregor Mendel, which he formulated a century and a half ago on the basis of seven crosses of the common garden pea. These laws, rediscovered in 1900 by Hugo

---

[5] Instead of "vegetative" I therefore use the word "morphogenetic" at times.

de Vries, would become of fundamental importance for the modern theory of genetics. Nevertheless, Mendel's laws, no matter how general their formulation, had a specialized application; they were principles. When, later, he investigated these principles, on the advice of Karl W. von Nägeli, in hawkweed (genus *Hieracium*) he obtained practically no results. Small wonder; specialists discovered afterward that the flowers of hawkweed, unlike the flowers of the garden pea, can also form seed without pollination. In other words, there is a great variety of applied vegetative principles![6]

(4) The sensitive domain. This is the level upon which the specific character of animals came to light. Although derived from a different type of protist than plants, animals also have physical properties (volume and weight), biotic characteristics (cellular make-up), and vegetative traits (bodily specialization). Distinctive for animals is that in the evolutionary process they obtained access to sensory perception and inner (psychic) feeling. I designate these characteristics as the sensitive function. It is based on the preceding functions. The sensitive function is an inner ability that manifests itself in outward behavior, in mating, hunting, socializing, etc. Sensitivity expresses itself in complex patterns of behavior that are in part instinctive and innate, in part prompted by immediate observation, and in part mediated by learning processes that are peculiar to the species.

The sensitive domain, too, is governed by universal but non-uniform laws or organizational principles. They are particularized in animal species and manifest themselves as rules of behavior. These sensitive principles determine how animals through external adaptations react to stimuli from their environment and how they associate and communicate with each other. Depending on various patterns of behavior, as established by animal psychology and by modern ethology in the footsteps of Konrad Lorenz and Niko Tinbergen, one can distinguish between organizational principles of imprinting, association, aggression, habituation, courtship, etc.

Later I want to discuss the question of the extent to which the human species takes an exceptional position among all living

---

[6] Of course, there are all kinds of situations in the garden pea where the laws do not apply. Mendel tried twenty-two crosses, seven of which gave him the three to one ratio.

creatures. Here I merely mention that the sensitive domain does not only include animals; humans, too, have a sensitive function. Sensory perceptions and experiences do not only affect animal behaviors but also human behavior. Humans recognize themselves in animal behaviors. The comparability of animal and human behavior is a fact that ethologists often draw attention to, for teaching and amusement. However, human behaviors are largely made subservient to mental and moral principles. This is a fact that ethologists often overlook.

All in all, the process of evolution in the sense of emergent evolution has disclosed a multiplicity of ontological domains in nature. It disclosed them by first originating bacteria in possession of a biotic function, then plants provided with a vegetative capacity, and, subsequently, animals equipped with sensitive abilities. It should be clear that we could not interpret this process dualistically, as the addition of animated powers to inanimate matter, as if incommensurate realities had been piled on top of one another like ontological layers. Such a dualism is at odds with the unity and coherence of nature, and with the unity that manifests itself in living organisms. The biotic, vegetative, and sensitive are not capabilities that were simply added to an already existing physical reality by means of a supernatural intervention at a given moment in a hoary past. In my judgment one can best describe them as emergent abilities, i.e. abilities that came to be in and on the basis of material reality by spontaneous self-organization. How this was possible we shall have to examine in more detail later. Our provisional conclusion shall be that on earth a diversity of ontological arrangements came into being by virtue of a series of reorderings of an already existing order.

Do not interpret my understanding of emergent evolution in terms of organizational levels and ontological domains in the sense of Aristotle, who also distinguished in nature a physical, a vegetative, and a sensitive ordering, but who did not have the faintest notion of emergent evolution. The orderings of nature are not determined, as Aristotle's metaphysics suggests, by "formal causes" that he supposes to be inherent in the structure of the cosmos and oriented to divinity, the all-determining form of all forms. That is a speculative train of thought. No, what I have in mind are orderings that acquired, after hundreds of millions of years, a different configuration because they proved to be receptive to new, above-physical ordering principles.

In short, on earth has arisen a multiform nature with a scale of ordering principles and organizational levels. The physical level is foundational: it is as wide as the cosmic universe. It does not only encompass energy fields and mineral substances, it is also the material basis of all living organisms. On this basis the biotic level elevates itself. The biotic mode of being manifests itself in the entire living world because cellular organization, metabolism, and reproduction are not only characteristic of the unicellular system of bacterial entities but also occur in plants and animals, in fact in all the multicellular organisms that subsequently originated. The vegetative level is a yet higher step. It is characteristic of the plant kingdom, but it is not lacking in the animal kingdom, for morphogenetic specification is not only found in the bodies of plants but also in those of animals. Finally, the highest in nature – we do not discuss humans and their culture here – is the sensitive level. One encounters it exclusively in the animal kingdom for it is only in animals that an inner life, in the sense of sensory experiences and instinctive feelings, has developed. An animal is a sensitive system.

In regard to the biotic domain a warning comment is warranted. We now know that the bacterial world consists of an immense variety of unicellular organisms. In chapters 4 and 5 we made acquaintance with pre-biotic and biotic forms of life, prokaryotic and eukaryotic systems, and archae- and eubacteria. Thus, further investigations could demonstrate that "the biotic" is a collective name for diverse levels of being (see ch. 13, section 1). But for now I discuss the biotic mode of being as one level (see Figure 7.1).

Biologists often describe the domains in nature as levels of increasing complexity. Correctly so. The organizational pattern of biotic phenomena, as present in even the most primitive bacteria and archaea, is far more complex than the organizational pattern of physical things. Even more complicated is the organizational pattern of plants, and plant-like organisms such as fungi and lichens. And these, in turn, cannot equal the sophistication that we encounter in the sentient structures that determine animal behavior, even in the simplest flatworm.

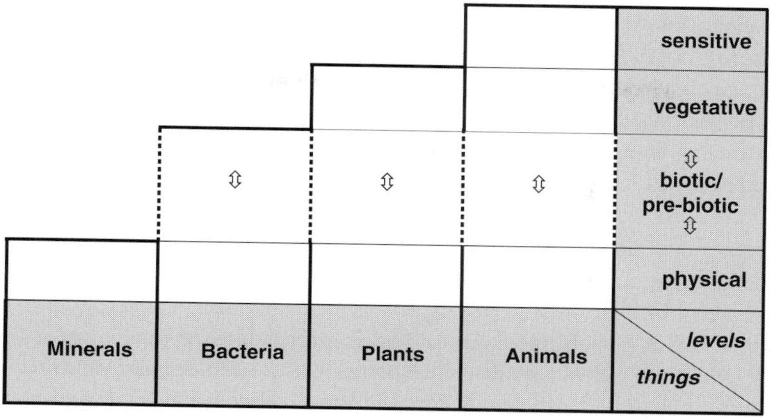

Figure 7.1 Schematic model of "things" and their organizational levels

However, speaking of "levels of complexity" can lead us to the wrong conclusion that the various organizational levels distinguish themselves by quantitative differences: the higher, the more complex! This false impression is reinforced when we distinguish lower and higher levels as parts and wholes or as micro- and macro-domains: the higher, the more inclusive! Indeed, the differences between simple and complex, micro and macro, or part and whole, are widespread but they are not of decisive significance. For upon close examination one encounters the difference between elementary and complex, part and whole, single and inclusive, also at every separate level of being. Just think of the distinction between particle physics and astrophysics, or between microbiology and population biology.

What I intend to say is this: the real differences in levels of complexity are not quantitative but qualitative in nature. The biotic structure of unicellular microbes is more complex than the physical structure of minerals, but what is essential is that it is of a different nature: it is a source of self-regulating life. Different again is the vegetative structure of plants: it manifests morphological specification. The sensitive structure of animals, too, is a category all its own: it is able to sensitively react to external stimuli. What I recall here has always been a key message of Broad, Morgan, and Alexander: the development of life on earth is a process that has brought forth unpredictable and irreducible novelties.

In these non-quantitative but qualitative innovations we also find the reason why, in a living organism, higher level properties can go hand in hand with lower level properties, an observation that is difficult to explain with a purely quantitative approach in terms of increasing complexity. In living organisms the different levels of reality are present simultaneously. A bacterium is a self-regulating cell, but it is, at the same time, a molecular system, like a mineral. A plant is a multicellular organism, but it is also a self-regulating entity, like a bacterium. An animal is a senso-motor unity, but it is, at the same time, a multicellular organism, a self-regulating entity, and a physico-chemical system. In living things unity of design and diversity of levels go hand in hand.

There is still one point I would like to note here. Among the various ontological levels there exist not only qualitative differences but also intrinsic coherences. The higher levels with the corresponding functions rest upon the lower levels. Take an animal: it would not have sensitive abilities if its body were not equipped with sensory organs, i.e. vegetatively developed tools that make sensitive behavior possible. The morphogenetic ordering of these sense organs would in turn not be able to function without the self-regulating ability of the biotic or cellular systems that make up these organs. In turn, these cellular systems would not be able to work without the energy fields of physical systems, i.e. without receptivity for chemical stimuli and electric impulses. Indeed, higher levels are often more complex, but this is largely the case because they have the lower echelons as their indispensable infrastructure.

My conclusion is this. There are good arguments to support the thesis that the organizational levels in nature are ontological domains, anchored in reality itself. They are not mental fabrications; witness the multiplicity and diversity of empirical disciplines that represent modern science and that only jointly can give account of this multifaceted reality. Also the pre-theoretical or daily life experience orients itself on ontological differences in levels as often as we distinguish between matter and life, minerals and microbes, plants and animals, etc. In fact, these differences in levels force themselves so overwhelmingly upon us that they not only determine our individual actions but also the public behavior of politicians, environmental organizations, medical professionals, disaster relief services, vegetarian societies, etc. Since these qualitative differences have come to light on earth, we can do nothing but experience them in their fundamental diversity. In what follows I wish to designate this diversity of arrangements of being and possibilities of experience, in common with Ernst Cassirer and Herman Dooyeweerd, as "modes of being" or "modes of experience."[7]

3 ENTITIES AND MODALITIES

One can capture emergent evolution ontologically in terms of organizational levels and domains. One can also conceive of emergent evolution functionally, in terms of entities and modalities. In this section I will choose the latter approach. I understand *entities* to be phenomena that appear to us as concrete things. I think of a stone, a cactus, and a leopard; I also think of inclusive or collective phenomena such as an earthquake, a cornfield, or a grasshopper plague. I understand *modalities* to be the functions or functional dispositions that can be noticed about things or entities. Thus modalities are never concrete things. They are modes of being that we experience with respect to things, or, to put it differently, they are functional characteristics of things on any level of reality.

Many entities, in particular living organisms, are multifunctional. They have a diversity of modal dispositions and therefore they function on various organizational levels of the world, i.e. in a diversity of ontological domains. Material things, such as minerals, only have a physical function; they are carriers of physical properties. One could call them physical subjects, for they function actively and exclusively in the physical domain. Other entities, like bacteria, plants, and animals, also possess above-physical functions and properties. For this reason one could designate them from a

---

[7] In his *Philosophie der symbolischen Formen*, English: *The Philosophy of Symbolic Forms*, 3 vols. (New Haven: Yale University Press, 1955–57) E. Cassirer speaks of "Erfahrungsmodalitäten." In *A New Critique of Theoretical Thought*, Dooyeweerd speaks of "modes of being." In the view of both, the modes of being are simultaneously modes of experience; there is just a change in perspective. Things present themselves in a variety of ways and thus we experience them in different manners.

functionalistic perspective as biotic, vegetative, and sensitive subjects, respectively, for they also function actively in higher and for them more characteristic domains.

In a functionalistic frame of reference, we can now define emergent evolution as such a process of development that novelty comes to the fore as an ontological array of the world that was not yet present at a preceding organizational level of the world. That is to say, in the evolutionary process, some things have elevated themselves at a critical moment above physical reality and gained a profile or design as entities with above-physical modal functions, yet based on the physical infrastructure. Thus, in the first instance, bacterial systems originated with an additional biotic modality. Afterward, higher organisms came into existence with modal functions that manifested themselves on a successively higher level. It is this amazing hierarchy of organizational levels that has come to light in the disclosure process of time.

This hierarchical order proves to be determinative of the ontological profile of all things and phenomena that we find in the world, humans included.[8] For, while minerals have only physical properties, bacteria also display biotic characteristics; plants, moreover, vegetative characteristics; animals sensitive characteristics; and the human profile is, finally, also characterized by mental properties. The coming chapters will make clear that human beings even manifest a fundamental diversity of mental properties (see Figure 7.2).

It would be folly to assume that the process of emergent evolution has brought forth novelties in the sense of entirely new entities or beings. What came to be were additional modal arrangements. Entities already in existence underwent such a reprogramming – I speak of course in metaphors – that new functions arose. One can compare this renewal to a computer that acquires new functions through an added software program. But this comparison is not entirely successful. The functioning of the software continues to be explainable from the original binary functions of the computer; the above-physical functions of living entities, however, are an irreducible

---

[8] U. Zylstra, "Living Things as Hierarchically Organized Structures," *Synthese* 91 (1992), 111–33.

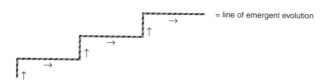

Figure 7.2 Schematic model of emergent evolution

novelty. The biotic function began when molecular aggregates rearranged into self-regulating unicellular micro-organisms. New abilities also developed in plants, animals, and people, thanks to the reallocation of the underlying abilities. They underwent *modi*-fication in such a way that new modal functions were realized on the basis of the old. Indeed, Darwin was right: evolution is "descent with modification."

Here, then, is the reason that physicists can analyze not only minerals, but also micro-organisms, plants, animals, and people, with all their specific character traits as components of the physical domain. Living entities are physical systems. They can be subjected to physical and chemical research because they continue to be part of the physical domain of meaning. On this hard fact the universality of the method of physical science is based. The physical method can explain all concrete phenomena, including the characteristics of living things. The question is again and again: can it explain these phenomena *entirely*? Is the essence of living creatures exhausted in the physico-chemical domain? That is questionable indeed. For besides the physicists and chemists, attention is also demanded by microbiologists, botanists, zoologists, and researchers in the humanities, attention to the supra-physical significances that are part and parcel of living systems. These significances do not gain their rightful places in physical research.

How the world ever began to participate in these new modal arrangements of reality is an event that we, in all probability, will never be able to fathom fully. Rather than an explanatory theory, is "emergence" then a magic formula? A provisional answer could be as follows. The idea of emergence is not an explanatory theory. It is a theoretical framework in which the explanatory theories of physicists, microbiologists, botanists etc. have a better chance of success.

The theory of emergence is receptive to all physical explanations that can be posited for the origin and expansion of life. At the same time it keeps open the possibility that in living nature developments took place that crossed the boundaries of physical research. For this reason it refuses to ignore the possible indications of irreducible novelty. This is the reason, too, why it views with suspicion the naturalistic claim that evolutionary science can explain the unexplainable, that it has, in fact, solved the riddle of life. This suspicion is more realistic than the evolutionistic story that at a time, long ago, matter, all by itself, started to clump together into swarming bacteria or, stronger yet, that causally determined natural motions gradually changed into deeds of human freedom. What actually did happen remains to be seen.

4 SUPERVENIENCE, CORRELATION, AND IDIONOMY

The key concept of emergence is often clarified today by the notion of "supervenience," a term that the English language philosopher Richard Hare introduced to distinguish between natural and moral properties.[9] Partly, phenomena at a higher structural level can be explained by infrastructural processes, but they can only be fully understood in terms of properties that surpass or supervene the properties at preceding levels of existence. Therefore they are called supervenient. Supervenient properties are properties at a higher level and with a surplus of meaning. Thus, cell division in bacteria is a supervenient property compared with the possibilities for division that manifest themselves, also in bacterial systems, at the underlying physical or molecular level. Thus, the reproductive methods of plants are supervenient in regard to the cell division pattern that one finds, also in plants, at the underlying biotic or cellular level. Thus, the complicated reproductive behavior of animals, with all the sexual feelings that it raises, is supervenient to the processes of union that assures the reproduction, also in animals, at the strictly vegetative level. And this vegetative union of animals supervenes, in turn, the cellular and physical unification, i.e. the union of sperm and egg cells and the junction of DNA molecules.

Supervenience implies correlation. In an organism supervient properties are higher-order properties that always correlate with subjacent properties; that is, they are attended by properties that are present in the organism at an underlying level. Think, once again, of the cell division of bacteria. Although cell division is a higher-order characteristic of bacteria, and is lacking in physical systems, it does not occur independently. Given the intrinsic coherence between the biotic and physical domains, cellular processes in bacteria always occur in conjunction with processes at the subjacent, physical, level. Correlation means, in this case, that the cell division of bacteria realizes itself by division processes in their internal molecular affairs.

In the life sciences the words "emergence" and "supervenience" are used with great ease, even by proponents of a reductive naturalism, as soon as phenomena with new characteristics manifest themselves. It is to be recommended, in my opinion, to use the terms "emergence" and "supervenience" in a well-defined manner. To use an example: when oxygen and hydrogen combine to form water, new properties such as freezing and liquidity appear.

[9] R. M. Hare, *The Language of Morals* (Oxford: Clarendon Press, 1952), p. 145.

Nevertheless, there is no reason to call these properties supervenient. For even if they are new, they can be explained by the structural traits of the underlying atoms. The supervenient properties of emergent life forms, on the contrary, are characteristics that cannot be completely explained from the structural properties of more elementary constellations and that are, therefore, to be recognized as non-reductive in nature.

A central characteristic of the emergence concept is the element of autonomy or, as I prefer to say, of idionomy.[10] The domains that emerge are idionomic, i.e. they are governed by laws or principles with an independent character. In earlier emergence theories this point has not received the attention it deserves, not even by the aforementioned Charles Broad. For what else could lie at the basis of the characteristics of novelty, irreducibility, and unpredictability, to which Broad appealed, than the sovereignty of laws that are determinative of emerging phenomena? Often novelty is reducible. It can then be explained causally as a heretofore unknown result of a known state of affairs. However, this does not obtain in the case of emergent phenomena such as the origin of life on earth. One can only do justice to such exceptional situations by assuming that a completely new state of affairs announces itself here. This state of affairs is new because – as François Jacob puts it (see ch. 6, section 3) – the "rules of the game" have changed. With emergence not only new phenomena come to the fore. New, sovereign laws of causation manifest themselves that are constitutive of the phenomena mentioned, as Uko Zylstra has convincingly suggested in a recent article in *Zygon*.[11]

I take the biotic domain as an example, in particular the reproductive characteristics in bacteria. Why is the biotic way of being of

---

[10] I distinguish between idionomy (having laws of its own) and autonomy (setting its own laws). The idea of autonomy is connected to the philosophical misconception that the laws of nature are based on the selfsufficiency of reason. The idea of rational self-grounding is as contradictory as the image of Baron von Münchhausen who pulled himself out of a swamp by his hair. Reason cannot set its own laws, for every rational act already presupposes the validity of laws. In their ultimate unexplainability, laws point above themselves to a mystery of being. Christian faith sees God as the ultimate lawgiver, but this is not a rational argument (see ch. 10, section 2).

[11] U. Zylstra, "Intelligent-Design Theory: An Argument for Biotic Laws," *Zygon* 39 (2004), 175–91.

bacteria irreducibly new and why can its ability for cell division be characterized as supervenient? The answer must be: because, in the final analysis, the vitality of bacteria is not determined by physical but by biotic laws such as self-regulation and reproduction, that in the physical domain are not only absent but totally meaningless. Having become operative in bacterial systems, these principles do hold for the whole biotic domain. Indirectly they even control the material substrate, for in bacteria protein molecules, enzymes, DNA strands, etc. are continuously produced for the maintenance of life.

In phylogenetic history the emergence of a new idionomic principle, no matter in which living thing, is correlated with a rearrangement of the whole thing right into its molecular foundations. The principle that comes to the fore is manifested in what is commonly designated in chaos theory as "self-organization of nature." That is to say, nature reorganizes itself over its full width, in all modalities of the organism concerned.

Idionomy and self-organization thus understood are two sides of the same coin. They are an unmistakable indication of emergence. The idionomy of biological laws expresses itself in the spontaneous self-organization of living organisms. This self-organization manifests itself in an abundant diversity of cell structures, body profiles, behavior patterns, etc. All these organic structures have a specific or typical complexity, that is to say, they are specified in each type of organism. One can indicate these specific structures as the "design" of an organism. To be clear, I use "design" here in the empirical sense of the word.

In recent decades it has become increasingly clear how, also on the cellular level, the design of organisms has evolved. Design can be regarded as the product of natural processes regulated by laws, according to Del Ratzsch.[12] The physical world already displays designs as the physical product of law-governed processes. Think of a stellar system, an atomic nucleus, or a crystal structure. No matter how complex these designs sometimes are, we are used to explaining their origin by laws of physical nature. Thus, it is reasonable that the designs we encounter in the living world are also the result of

[12] D. L. Ratzsch, *Nature, Design, and Science: The Status of Design in Natural Science* (Albany: State University of New York Press, 2001), ch. 11.

natural processes determined by biological laws, explainable by evolutionary theories.

I am always puzzled by the confident assertion by some that a given design in the living world cannot have an empirical basis or an evolutionary origin; it must be due to an intelligent intervention from outside. Why must an extraterrestrial intervention have occurred? How would empirical science be able to ascertain a supra-empirical intervention? Along which route would such an intervention in the regular order have taken place? The usual answer to all these questions is that the alleged design must have an alternative origin because it is infinitely more complex and specific than in physical systems. This may be correct but it does not constitute a counter-argument. Remember that the laws which govern living systems are also much more complex and specific than the basal laws of physical nature; they manifest themselves as "germinative principles" or laws with differentiated applications, suited to a concrete situation (see ch. 4, section 2). Thus it is likely that, rather than an extraterrestrial author, such specified principles have put a stamp upon the body plan of living things.

A notable trait of living organisms is that the highest modal function has control over the entire system. All underlying functions are attuned to this controlling or qualifying function; they find in the latter their meaning or destination. Thus matter, in itself, has no self-regulating and reproductive faculty, but in bacteria the molecular machine contributes to the controlling biotic function, i.e. homeostatic and reproductive objectives, of the unicellular system. Thus bacteria as unicellular entities have no vegetative faculty, but in the plant the cellular tissues and organs contribute to the growth and morphogenetic differentiation of the vegetatively qualified system. Thus an organically developed body is in itself nothing more than a vegetative system, but in an animal it contributes to the sensitive system by forming sense organs and nerves. On the modal scale the leading function is in control of the other functions; it determines the identity of the organism as a whole. For this reason one can consider a bacterium as a biotically qualified or biotic subject, a plant as a vegetative subject, and an animal as a sensitive subject, even though these entities also posses other functions (see Figure 2).

Because living organisms are equipped with idionomic functions and faculties, they have developed causal powers of their own. "To be real is to have causal powers," according to the well-known dictum of Alexander.[13] Causal powers were for Alexander not exclusively physical powers. Not only falling stones are causally determined. That bacteria propel themselves with flagella toward an object, that bulrushes send their roots into the soggy soil, that birds of prey pounce on their quarry, these are all peculiar forms of causality that are connected to the specific purposes that organisms strive after. That is to say, in living nature not only mechanical forces but also purposes can be seen as causes. For in all biosystems the deliberate or unconscious pursuing of goals is a necessary condition for initiating specific movements or changes.

Thus not all causes are mechanical causes; to the contrary, there are also final causes. On all levels above the physical we find these final causes. In fact, I know of no scientists who, in the explanation of empirical phenomena, appeal as often to final causes as biologists do, even though many have the tendency, afterward, to reinterpret these final causes as the fortuitous outcomes of mechanical impulses. This appeal to final causes is not a covert continuation of Aristotelian teleology. It is, rather, the conscious or subconscious admission that final causes are of indispensable significance in the explanation of behavior of all living organisms. And because this finality presents itself in different idionomic spheres, we have to take final causes of different kinds into account. A final cause does not only determine a flagellated bacterium that is in search of food but it is also, in another manner, determinative of a lotus that opens its flowers to the light of the sun. It does not only determine the behavior of a bull that mates with a heifer in heat but it also determines the behavior of a businessman who consults his agenda.

Thus, the mechanical or non-directional causality of inanimate nature has a full-fledged counterpart in the directionality of living nature, i.e., in the functional *efficiency* of bacterial systems, in the differential *effectiveness* of vegetative systems, in the instinctive *directedness* of animal systems, and, finally, in the intentional *purposefulness* of human and societal actors. It is not easy to understand

[13] See Jaegwon Kim, *Supervenience and Mind*, p. 348.

how all these types of directional causality go hand in hand. The intentions that play an important role in the acts of human beings even demand, in the humanities, a causal method that is, at the same time, interpretative. I cannot discuss this further here, but it is clear that in the life sciences causal explanations that are strictly mechanical will not suffice.

In short, every living organism can be seen as participating in a hierarchy of ontological domains, domains that cannot be reduced to each other because they give evidence of different laws and causalities. At the basic level mechanical laws are operational, while in higher echelons supra-mechanical principles function, the highest of which are in control. All life scientists are confronted by this ontological hierarchy. Ontological orders are often called explanatory levels, and rightly so. The differences between them are so fundamental that one science to explain all of life's phenomena appears to be impossible.

For this reason biology and the other sciences of life can never become an annex of physics. Even molecular biology and biochemistry, which study the physical substrate of emergent life, and thus employ physical methods, nevertheless occupy a place of their own in the spectrum of the sciences. In their investigations of molecular processes in the cell they need to keep in mind the tight correlation between molecular and cellular processes. John Henry Woodger, the eminent precursor of emergence thought, expressed this situation well in his *Biological Principles*: "An entity having the hierarchical type such as we find in the organism requires investigation at all levels, and investigation of one level cannot replace the necessity of investigations of levels higher up in the hierarchy."[14]

The attempt by some theoreticians to reduce the emergence phenomenon to a "long series of minimal emergences" is, therefore, a late attempt to accommodate to the continuity claim of evolutionary naturalism.[15] It is a vain attempt. From a philosophical standpoint the discontinuities that result from emergence can only be adequately accounted for by a theory of ontological stratification.

[14] Woodger, *Biological Principles*, p. 316.
[15] T. A. Goudge, "Emergent Evolutionism," in *The Encyclopedia of Philosophy*, vol. III (New York: Macmillan and Free Press, 1972), p. 475.

And from the viewpoint of the special sciences they can only be met by a program of interdisciplinary cooperation in which mechanical, functional and (as far as the human realm is concerned) interpretative explanations complement each other.[16]

5 CHIMPANZEES AND THE HIV VIRUS

I want to elucidate the fundamental necessity of interdisciplinary cooperation between the sciences – in practice this necessity has been obvious for a long time – on the basis of the phenomenon of immunity. At first sight immunity seems to be nothing else than a physical phenomenon, a process of molecular chain reactions that fights infections and toxins. Still, this physical (biochemical) analysis does not explain everything. It does not account for the fact that living systems, particularly in the chordates, possess such an immunological defense pattern while inanimate systems do not. Immunity appears to be a feature that coincides exclusively with a basic characteristic of life, i.e. homeostasis. Immunity is a supervenient property of higher animals that is determined by the general biological principle of self-regulation.

The quotation from Woodger does not suggest that lower level explanations are without benefit. To the contrary: they make it possible to bring supervenient phenomena within reach of exact data analysis. Lower level explanations take advantage of the fact that processes at a higher or controlling level bring infrastructural processes along, at times incorrectly labeled as "top-down causation." In many cases it is possible to determine what is happening at the top level by studying the lower levels. Think of the blood tests in the medical laboratory to diagnose a person's illness. Think of the lie detector that measures blood pressure, pulse,

---

[16] For the coherence between a theory of ontological stratification and the various explanatory levels in the sciences see H. Looren de Jong, *Naturalism and Psychology: A Theoretical Study* (Kampen: J. H. Kok, 1992), pp. 57–81. Looren de Jong, a theoretical psychologist, chooses a functional explanation of mental processes, even if human beings themselves experience these processes in terms of interpretable intentions. There are good reasons for his approach, but it is restricted. All intentional processes are functional; not all functional processes are intentional. The emergence perspective prevents the extrapolation of interpretative-intentional explanations to a dualism or mentalism in the line of Descartes.

respiratory rate, and perspiration to determine someone's honesty. And think especially of the DNA tests that can reveal someone's personal identity, kinship relations, risks of hereditary illness, and so much more. It is these correlating processes between infrastructure and superstructure that can make basic research so valuable and rewarding.

Speaking of immunity, there is at present a specialized research project that investigates the question of why chimpanzees are immune to the HIV virus, at least for the human variant, even though 99.4 percent of chimp DNA conforms to that of humans. I assume that the investigators will find a suitable answer to this question in the coming years. They will only find an answer, not the answer. Biochemists will never be able to make the immune system of these animals completely transparent. For, why do chimpanzees have this defense system and not people, although both groups possess a similar genome? Scientists have proposed the not unlikely hypothesis of a large-scale AIDS epidemic a few million years ago, where, in the battle for survival, a group of chimpanzees survived by virtue of an accidental gene mutation. (That group would be comparable to a well-known group of prostitutes in Kenya that were recently found to escape HIV infection through a fortuitous genetic variant.) The problem of *how* the immune system of chimpanzees reacts to HIV is basic; it can be described in physico-chemical formulas. The question of *why* these animals are immune while people are not demands a different approach, a higher level description in the aforementioned terms of competition, variation, selection, and transmission. In short, it demands a biological analysis.

We encounter a general rule here. Low level explanations are correlative explanations, and are, therefore, partial and circumstantial. They lay bare the basic conditions for events that occur at a higher level. They show the correlative relationships between high and low, but they do not, however, lay bare the essence of events that occur at higher levels. They do not explain how a living organism functions as a total system. The lie detector tells us that a person is lying, but does not tell us why the suspect lies.

Of course, a physicist can tell us in detail how the lens of the fish-eye corrects for the refractive index of the water; why the fish-eye lens is not suitable for human observation (except for some photographers); and why the eyes of the hawk can make triangular measurements. Of course, the molecular biologist can tell us what the effects on the retina are of color vision, and what neural effects occur afterward in the sense of brain signals at a particular wavelength. What these scientists cannot make clear to us is how all these processes that are externally measurable bring about something internal in animal and person: the inner and extremely individual experience of seeing. Whoever explains the molecular or physiological workings of the sensory organs does not yet explain the act of observing. To put it more strongly, the physical and physiological (or vegetative) explanations of the senses *presuppose* the sensitive mode of being, for without seeing there would be no eye and without hearing there would be no ear.

In the theory of science it is not unusual to name the explanation of higher level phenomena with the help of scientific data a "naturalistic method." This is an interesting point. In this case we are not dealing with ontological naturalism, a view that we discussed earlier (see ch.3, section 3), but with methodological naturalism. I want to explicitly discuss this topic later (see ch. 9, section 5), but I have no problems with such a view of naturalism. Taken in itself, methodological naturalism is non-reductive. Neuroscientists who just wish to elucidate the complex correlations between processes of consciousness and brain activities, without denying the subjective orientation of consciousness to cognitive contents and norms, represent a non-reductive position.[17] For the demonstration of these correlations implies, in fact, the acknowledgment that consciousness is different from and more than the brain. This also becomes apparent from their research. For no matter how much knowledge neurologists may have of the cerebral activities upon which consciousness depends, they bypass the intentional content of consciousness. And they totally ignore the normative principles of consciousness, for example the logical principles of identity and contradiction, which consciousness must obey if its content is to be meaningful.[18]

---

[17] The rejection of the subjective side of consciousness is illustrated in the disputable book by D. C. Dennett: *Consciousness Explained* (Boston: Little, Brown & Co., 1991).

[18] We encounter here the difference between natural laws and norms: determinative laws and normative laws. Natural laws compel, normative principles do not compel but oblige. The laws of nature are universal and they cannot be broken. Norms, decisive for culture and

One thing the correlative explanations of methodological naturalism make clear to us: there is no transcendence without
dependence! Even the earliest life on earth could only germinate
when – probably in the hydrothermal cauldron of superheated ocean
water at fault-lines in the earth's crust – organic macro-molecules
came into existence that, once they were aggregated, provided the
necessary basis for the emergence of the first unicellular systems. And
conversely, there is no dependence without transcendence! For on
the question of how these molecular assemblages could form, biochemists provide more and more clarity, but their formulas remain
lower-level formulas. They explain the assemblages but they do not
explain the correlate of those assemblages: the singularity of life.
They do not explain how molecular building blocks could be taken
over under the aegis of life principles and how they began to
rearrange into the extremely complex but stable order of the biological cell.

6 MICHAEL BEHE AND HIS MOUSETRAP

With the discussion of the complex order of the cell we return to
the topic of the Intelligent Design theory. It is especially the
aforementioned biochemist, Michael Behe, who, in the popular and
much-quoted book *Darwin's Black Box*, calls our attention to the
complex systems that are to be found in the biological cell.[19] In his
view these systems are so complex that they could not have arisen
from random developments, and they, rather, need to be regarded
as an expression of a conscious and purposeful design. What is to be
thought of this?

Behe does not reject Darwin's opinions about selection and
evolution; to the contrary, he assumes that natural selection acts on

---

society, can be broken. This happens, e.g., when someone makes a logical mistake, i.e.,
transgresses a logical norm. For this reason natural laws can, and norms cannot, provide
sufficient causal explanations. For normative principles do not offer compelling causes, only
urgent reasons. Consider the premises in a logical argument or the motives in an ethical
decision; normative principles demand but do not guarantee that the person who is
involved draws the correct conclusions from them.

[19] Michael Behe, *Darwin's Black Box* (New York: The Free Press, 1996).

populations to change gene frequencies, and that mutation in amino acid sequences of proteins can indeed result in species change.

Yet, in *Darwin's Black Box* he comes to the conclusion that Darwin's theory does not offer an adequate explanation for the origin of life on its most elementary level, that is, of the biological cell. Behe is prepared to excuse Darwin for this. After all, in Darwin's time the intricate molecular mechanism of the cell was not known; for Darwin the cell was a "black box." Today's biochemists and molecular biologists know much more. With sophisticated equipment they have succeeded in opening the black box. And what have they found? The cell is a composite of extremely complicated molecular systems. In the cells of plants and animals, and also in unicellular micro-organisms, we encounter "irreducible complexities." The cell confronts us with systems that are so intricately put together that they cannot be evolutionarily derived from preceding systems. I designate this as Behe's irreducibility thesis. It requires some explanation. A cellular system is a molecular network in the cell that carries out a specific function. Such a system can be regarded as "irreducibly complex" when it includes a collection of interactive components that are all necessary for the function of the whole, and when the lack of one component would frustrate the system as a whole. As examples, Behe describes the bacterial flagellar motor and the working of cellular cilia, the metabolic process and the defense system of body cells, the blood clotting system of mammalian cells, and the signal transport in optic nerve cells. No matter how diverse these mechanisms are, in his view they are irreducible, for their manner of functioning depends on such a cooperation of proteins and enzymes that each component has a specific task and is, at the same time, an indispensable link in a causal chain of activities. Such a mechanism cannot have evolved from a simpler one for in that case one or more elements would have been lacking and the system would not have been able to function.

Above, I defended the opinion that the cell is an entity in which diverse modal functions are interwoven. The cell is, first of all, a physical system; it functions as an extremely complex and inter-active network of physical processes. But in the cell this physical function is made subservient to biotic and perhaps even higher functions; one can also say that the molecular substrate correlates with emergent modes of being. How the cell has been able to articulate itself as a multimodal entity is difficult to reconstruct. But we must conclude that at a crucial moment in the evolutionary history, perhaps in the "black smokers" of an overheated arch-ocean, conglomerates of physical particles came in the grip of new modal laws, laws of life, and in this way got a chance of rearranging themselves into biotic systems. By spontaneous self-organization and without losing their physical characteristics, they began to obey above-physical principles such as DNA-replication and reproduction, and thus they developed in their milieu an appropriate body design and behavior pattern.

Behe ignores this multimodal approach to living cells and organisms. His eyes are fixed on the physical system, i.e. on the cell as a "black box" supplied with an assortment of mechanisms. On the basis of this mechanistic approach he simply presents the causal systems in the cell as "molecular machines." His line of reasoning now proceeds as follows. In the complex mini-machinery of the cell the components interact so precisely that they are all necessary, and not one can be missing or the whole machinery would come to a stop. An evolutionary precursor phase of such a system cannot exist, for the system would not be able to operate in an incomplete condition. Thus the molecular machine could not have developed from something else. In its non-reductive complexity it must have arisen by a conscious intervention from outside: an intelligent design.[20]

As I said, one of Behe's examples is the propelling flagellum of bacteria. This structure resembles a rotary motor with a shaft and a propeller; the bacterium can move itself with these elements. Upon closer examination, the flagellum is a complicated motor system with scores of components that faultlessly interact with each other. Why can this system be designated as irreducible? Because all components were indispensable, right from the start, to enable the motor to function. Thus the system cannot have developed by natural selection from a simpler system with fewer components.

As a demonstrative example for his argument, Behe uses the common mousetrap. This contraption, too, is a combination of

---

[20] Behe, *Darwin's Black Box*, ch. 2, and "Molecular Machines: Experimental Support for the Design Inference", http://www.arn.org/docs/behe/mb_mm92496.htm.

interactive components, an irreducibly complex system. Behe lists five parts of the mousetrap.[21] I would distinguish six: a platform, on the platform a striking spring, over the spring a hook, in the platform a trapdoor, on the trapdoor a metal eye connected with the hook over the spring, and on top of the trapdoor the bait. When the mouse touches the bait, the trapdoor falls into the platform, the hook slips from the metal ring, the tightened spring is released, and the mouse receives a deadly blow. In Behe's view the mousetrap is so constructed that all these components work together, and not one is dispensable. Therefore, the mousetrap cannot have been developed from a simpler system; it must have been designed all at one time. It is an irreducible complex system. This is also the case with the small molecular machines of the cell. They cannot have developed from previous cellular constellations by natural selection because these would have been, by definition, incomplete and dysfunctional. Thus, they must have been intentionally introduced and are, therefore, dependent on an intelligent design.

Against this presentation of affairs I want to make five kinds of objections, respectively of a theological, methodological, technological, biological, and philosophical nature.

(1) Theological objections. I can be brief about my theological objections to Behe. They are comparable to those I mentioned in an earlier context in connection with Dembski. I share with Dembski and Behe the biblical view that life on earth refers to an untraceable creation mystery. However, in Dembski's thought living things bring their creaturely mystery only to expression in incidental cases. His filter theory concludes intelligent design only in exceptional cases, namely where rational explanations fall short. I spoke about Dembski's incidentalism. This incidentalism is also characteristic of Behe. He only speaks of design where a complex molecular system in a biological cell cannot be explained from preceding systems. Behe's position therefore leads, just as Dembski's does, to the questionable paradigm of a "God of the gaps" and to the equally questionable dogma of a *creatio continua*. In short, where do we find God's omnipresence in the world? The incidentalistic interpretation is simultaneously a minimalistic interpretation.

---

[21] Behe, *Darwin's Black Box*, p. 42.

(2) Methodological reservations. It is the task of science to explain complex phenomena in more elementary data by logical analysis. I consider it to be incorrect to put a priori bounds on this method by an irreducibility thesis such as the one postulated by Behe. Science cannot anticipate what is still unknown, precisely because it is still unknown. The science of today cannot determine what the science of the future can or cannot explain. A definitive rejection of explanatory possibilities in science is only justified after convincing alternatives have suggested themselves. In regard to so-called "irreducible complexities" in the cell, too, one cannot limit the explanatory power of science in advance. A lack of proof is not a proof of lack.

Behe could object that his irreducibility thesis refers to basic mechanisms in the cell, where we encounter no black box, no non-transparent situations that can yet be cleared up in due time. Are the complex mechanisms in the cell indeed non-reductive and fully transparent? Remember that this concerns bio-molecular processes. These lend themselves indeed to mechanistic explanations; however, with this not everything has been said. Bio-mechanical operations are mechanical but indirectly they refer to life. They presuppose the self-regulating power of life that holds together the cell and its mechanisms as a biotic system.

Behe commits here a hysteron-proteron fallacy, i.e., a reversal of concepts in an argument. He does not realize that *in vivo*, i.e. in a living system, not the molecular but the biotic function has acquired primacy. That is not a vitalistic creed but an empirical fact. Life governs the molecular economy in which it has realized itself. Bio-molecular mechanisms are mechanisms, but simultaneously they are subjacent to the purposes of life. Take the flagellated bacterium. As long as it is alive, the flagellum functions. If it dies, the flagellum apparatus disintegrates. Thus the comparison with the mousetrap fails. The trap always works as long as it is complete. Molecular mechanisms in the cell, no matter how complete, in the last resort only work under the regimen of life.

(3) Technological reflections. Cell and mousetrap are incomparable, even if it were true that the mousetrap is designed all at one time. And, for that matter, is that true? Not really, for the invention of the mousetrap went through several intermediate stages; it was

the culmination of a technological evolution. Long before modern citizens equipped their well-constructed dwellings with mousetraps, they attempted to catch animals with mechanisms like a trapdoor, bait, a set spring (in a leg trap), a hook and eye, applied in various combinations. Apart from the platform, needed as the basis element for the other parts, the mousetrap is an assembly of five technological components that, throughout the centuries, were used to catch animals and that go back, in part, to the Stone Age. The mousetrap is a complex system, but certainly not an irreducibly complex system.

It is more apt to compare the origin of life to one of humankind's greatest discoveries, the wheel, 5,500 years ago in Mesopotamia (Kish, Susa). The concept of the wheel would also seem to be irreducible and unique, originated in one step in an intelligent (human) design. But appearances deceive, even in this case. The principle of the wheel goes back to two other technological discoveries: the invention of the spool, used for spinning wool, and the use of the sled, pulled over rolling logs. In short, there are strong indications for the general thesis that the clever solutions in organic nature, as much as the clever inventions in technology, all have a history of development.

(4) Biological criticisms. From the biological side, too, objections have been registered against Behe's thesis that molecular complexes in the cell are evolutionarily irreducible. I recount three of them.

(a) The thesis of irreducibility is premature. Somewhere Behe claims that for the system of the flagellum more than 240 protein components are required. But this does not hold for Helicobacter pylori. This bacterium (known among the wider public as the ulcer bacterium) only requires thirty-three proteins for the propulsion of its flagellum. In fact, when in some mutants of this species some protein components of the flagellum were disabled, the propulsion ability remained more or less intact. Thus even the flagellum of Helicobacter may be reducible to a still simpler structure.[22]

---

[22] B. H. Weber, "Irreducible Complexity and the Problem of Biochemical Emergence," *Biology and Philosophy* 14 (1999), 593–605; F. M. Harold, "Biochemical Topology: From Vectorial Metabolism to Morphogenesis," *Bioscience Reports* 11, 347–85.

(b) The dilemma of natural selection or conscious design falls short. The evolutionary process was not caused exclusively by natural selection and gradual adaptations. Other factors have also played a role. One can think of genetic aberrations, lateral genetic transmissions (via a virus for example), climate changes, and natural disasters. Early in history exaptation probably also took place. Exaptation (i.e getting attached to) means that an existing structure is incorporated into another, more complex, structure and gains a new function there.[23] Thus there are indications that the motor system of the bacterial flagellum developed by the assembly of proteins from the more elementary system of secretion.[24]

(c) Following the footsteps of E. Jantsch, in *The Self-Organizing Universe*,[25] some have brought forward the paradigm of the "self-organization of nature" as a plausible alternative to the Darwinian theory of natural selection and its counterpart, the theory of an intelligent design. Investigators such as P. Cilliers and S. A. Kauffman[26] suggest that molecular complexes aggregate spontaneously into constellations of increasing complexity until they reach a critical turning-point. They then crystallize by the spontaneous self-organization of nature into complex life forms, yes, even into increasingly complex organisms with emergent properties. Thus Stuart Kauffman, with his autocatalytic theory based on computer calculations, has formulated a clear, although in my opinion not altogether convincing, alternative to Darwin's selection theory and its opposite, the design theory.[27]

---

[23] Mitochondrial DNA in eukaryotic cells may well be an exaptation of DNA that originated in earlier, prokaryotic organisms. Maybe mitochondria themselves, and also chloroplasts in plants, as Lynn Margulis has suggested, have arisen by the inclusion of organisms in others. Her theory, brought forward in *Origin of Eukaryotic Cells* (New Haven: Yale University Press, 1970) and implying that the eukaryotic cell is a symbiotic union of primitive prokaryotic cells, is now widely accepted.

[24] N. Shanks and K. H. Joplin, "Redundant Complexity: A Critical Analysis of Intelligent Design in Biochemistry," *Philosophy of Science* 66 (1999), 275.

[25] E. Jantsch, *The Self-Organizing Universe: Scientific and Human Implications of the Emerging Paradigm of Evolution* (New York: Pergamon Press, 1980).

[26] P. Cilliers, *Complexity and Postmodernism: Understanding Complex Systems* (London, New York: Routledge, 1998); S. A. Kauffman, *The Origins of Order: Self Organization and Selection in Evolution* (New York: Oxford University Press, 1993).

[27] With his search for "laws of self-organization" Kauffman (see ch. 5, section 3) creates the impression that the phenomenon of emergence would be an explainable and almost predictable fact. Kauffman, *At Home in the Universe*, p. 61: "emergence of autocatalytic sets is almost

(5) Finally some philosophical considerations. Doesn't the theory of emergent evolution, as it has been defended in this book, imply an element of irreducible novelty that Intelligent Design in its own language describes as irreducible complexity? Where, actually, does the difference lie?

I admit there is a similarity and even a certain affinity between what the design theory designates as irreducibly complex and the emergence theory as irreducibly novel. In living nature we encounter phenomena with characteristics that are simultaneously extremely complex and irreducibly new. And in the light of these phenomena both views call attention to the incompleteness of all naturalistic explanations of the evolutionary process.

There is, however, also a basic difference between the concept of irreducible complexity in the Intelligent Design theory and the notion of irreducible novelty in the theory of emergence. I will express this difference in the words "incidentalism versus levelism."

Behe's opinion attests to incidentalism. He orients himself toward the mechanisms that occur in the living cell. He states that in incidental cases these mechanisms display such an original complexity that they cannot be explained evolutionarily. Behe's analysis betrays a mechanistic way of thinking: a one-sided fixation upon the so-called "molecular machinery" of the cell, i.e. the physical domain of reality. His arguments resemble, as peas in a pod, the mechanistic approach of his naturalistic opponents, with this difference, that the difficulties that adhere to the mechanistic paradigm are for the latter a scientific challenge and for Behe the basis for incidental references to a metaphysical constructor.

The theory of emergence as we have presented it is based on "levelism" (I borrow this term from John Searle). This theory is not just a correction of mechanicism; it offers a real alternative. It assumes levels in reality that are, on the one hand, idionomic, and are, on the other hand, rooted in a basic physical level. Because of this rootedness, all evolutionary developments, also as they first

inevitable." But facts are only explainable on the basis of laws that hold *within* idionomic realms. Emerging phenomena are by definition not explainable from an underlying domain. P. P. Kirschenmann, "On Self-Organization, Design, and the Almost-Inevitableness of Complex Order: Some Critical Assessments," *Studies in Science and Theology* 8 (2001–2), 17–42. We have to reconsider the idionomy of these domains.

occurred in the amoeba, in the plant body, in animal sensitivity, and in the human mind, remain a challenge for physics and the other natural sciences. The appeal of emergence theory to irreducible novelty is therefore of an entirely different order than the straight-forward appeal to complexity. It is based on the insight that all life phenomena are expressions of a material reality that is, at the same time, a more-than-material reality. Life phenomena are subject to physical laws and mechanical processes but they are simultaneously open to above-physical explanations, explanations that are based on higher ordering principles such as the laws of cellular organization and genetic transmission. These are laws that presuppose but also supersede the laws of mechanical causation.

Thus I do not deny that molecular mechanisms lie at the basis of life in the cell. The genesis of unicellular and multicellular organisms was paired with complex reorganizations of the physical realm in which life realized itself. Hence we have no reason to put limitations on science or to label the molecular reality in living cells as an area that is only partially accessible for evolutionary explanations. To the contrary, scientific research shows that even in the earliest bacterial systems that flourished on earth, the proteins and other organic substances had a long pre-history behind them, deep into cosmic space. Only the emergent mode of being in the service of which these substances could be recruited manifested itself as totally new.

If we accept that the laws that govern above-physical reality are not derived from the laws of the physical universe, as the naturalists suggest, nor the result of incidental and exceptional interventions by a divine designer, as the proponents of ID suggest, then what is their origin or place in the evolutionary process? How can we account for the idionomy of above-physical laws in the disclosure process of time? This question will be one of the most basic topics that we have to examine in what follows. Whatever the answer may be, it is not necessarily exceptional. It should be comparable to the answer that we would give to the question regarding the origin of the laws of physical nature.

My conclusion is threefold:

(1) Life's irreducibility is not based on the exceptional complexity of a number of mechanical systems in the cell but on the idionomic sovereignty of the biotic domain as a whole.

(2) The irreducible character of this domain and the analysis of the biological rules that determine this domain, is not a limitation but rather a specific challenge for the life sciences.

(3) One can assume that the biophysical search for the molecular mechanisms in the cell and the specific analyses of cytology and the other life sciences support each other. Bruce Weber states: "The self-organizing tendencies of biochemical systems may help guide the formation of complex, patterned structures that can subsequently acquire functional value for which improvements can be selected."[28] I agree with this, assuming that emergence and self-organization go hand in hand.

In closing I note the following. For many the self-multiplication of living things via the genetic code that cells carry in them in the form of the DNA molecule forms the proof, par excellence, that neither a design theory as brought to us by Behe nor an emergence theory as I have formulated can have the last word. The molecular nature of DNA would suggest a consistent mechanistic explanation of life. How shall we judge this?

The transmission of genetic traits is indeed a molecular and mechanical process that lies at the basis of life. At the same time we have to realize that the semantics of the encoded information, the message enclosed in the DNA, is not understandable in molecular sequences. In the language of physics and chemistry the message contained in the genetic code is meaningless. Scientists do speak of "information molecules" but everything depends on their message: the significance of the content that the code has for the transmission of traits to a following generation of living beings. Information molecules are just carriers of this message. They do not explain life; they presuppose life.

In discussions about DNA mechanistic explanations appear to fall short. Michael Polanyi and Marjorie Grene have elucidated this beautifully.[29] They start from the thesis that a one-level ontology that views the world as a molecular network, exclusively governed by the laws of physics and chemistry, contradicts itself. For every

---

[28] Weber, "Irreducible Complexity," 595.
[29] M. Grene, *The Understanding of Nature* (Dordrecht: D. Reidel, 1974); M. Polanyi, "Life's Irreducible Structure," *Science* 160 (1968), 1308–12.

single-level ontology presupposes molecular processes plus knowledge regarding them. With this knowledge a second, not unimportant structural level is smuggled into a pretended one-dimensional account. Polanyi emphasizes this fundamental difference of ontic levels as follows:

[A] boundary condition which harnesses the principles of a lower level in the service of a new, higher level establishes a semantic relation between the two levels. The higher comprehends the working of the lower and thus forms the meaning of the lower. And as we ascend a hierarchy of boundaries, we reach to ever higher levels of meaning.[30]

Grene and Polanyi apply this difference in levels to the phenomenon of DNA replication. At first sight, the DNA replication in the germ-line cells of living organisms is a molecular process. This process implies such an arrangement of the organic bases in the DNA, however, that the code is formed that makes the self-multiplication of life possible. Now this code is only recognizable on a higher, biological level of meaning; it cannot be translated into physical terms. On this basis we can conclude: DNA replication does not form a ground for justification of strictly mechanistic explanations. To the contrary, its exceptional significance comes to light on the emergent level of living systems.

---

[30] Polanyi, "Life's Irreducible Structure," 1311. The aforementioned information scientist, Werner Gitt, also uses this argument. He states that matter, information, and life conform with "separate levels of observed reality." Gitt, *In 6 Tagen*, p. 156.

CHAPTER 8

Toward a general theory of emergent evolution

Philosophers and evolutionary biologists have developed emergence theory primarily to enable them to give an account of the structural variety, diversity, and complexity that are characteristic of systems that function in living nature. The question must be asked: doesn't the theory of emergence have a greater radius of action? Isn't it also applicable to systems in culture, to the music of Bach and Mozart and to the theories of Newton and Albert Einstein? Don't we have solid arguments to speak of GTEE, i.e. a general theory of emergent evolution? Can GTEE shed light on the unique nature of humankind on the one hand and on the special character of the social institutions that humankind has produced on the other hand?

At stake here is a significant topic that was already being discussed in Darwin's time, in a century that witnessed the Industrial Revolution and momentous changes in society. In England the philosopher and sociologist Herbert Spencer became an eminent advocate of social Darwinism. Spencer compared human behavior to the behavior of animals, and the form of human associations to the structure of living organisms. His conclusion was that humankind is not unique, and that the struggle for life and the survival of the fittest are natural laws that extend themselves fully into human society. Thus society should provide opportunity for the entrepreneurial spirit of the liberal citizenry and should not frustrate this spirit by social measures in favor of the working classes. For evolutionary development may not be impeded; it is the only guarantee for the advancement of the human species. The political economist William Graham Sumner, in the United States, proclaimed the same arch-conservative and elitist message. Sumner stated that society is subject to "social selection." Such selection would automatically favor the population, particularly the commercial top layer, business people who qualify as pioneers of the future on the basis of their societal fitness and excellence.

Social Darwinism was anything but social. And its naturalistic starting-point showed a theoretical shortage. Social Darwinism could not make clear why political and social measures were counterproductive and would hinder the effectiveness of evolutionary principles, assuming that these principles are indeed inviolable laws of nature. To put it another way, it did not know how to do justice to the unique position of humans and their politico-social responsibilities. For this reason social Darwinism became discredited. Its practical investigations and comparative views of human and animal behavior were adopted by Konrad Lorenz and other ethologists. And its theoretical aspirations to regard human society as a mere product of biological rules were revived in the so-called sociobiology of Edward O. Wilson and his colleagues.[1]

All these developments caused the theme of a general theory of emergent evolution to be snowed under. Still, whether the unique position of the human person and the extraordinary status of human civilization can be made transparent within an emergence perspective remains a topical question. This is reason for me to make some supplementary comments in this chapter about the human mind (section 1) and about human society (section 2). I round off these explorations with a sketch for a theory of ontological stratification (section 3).

1 JOHN SEARLE AND THE MYSTERY OF CONSCIOUSNESS

The notion of emergent evolution touches, in the first place, the position of the human person, particularly the significance of human consciousness. It is in this area that the American philosopher John Searle has performed pioneering work. Searle proves

[1] Most attention was focussed on the development of an evolutionary epistemology that follows in the footsteps of K. Lorenz, "Kant's Doctrine of the A Priori in the Light of Contemporary Biology" (German, 1941), in H. C. Plotkin (ed.), *Learning, Development, and Culture: Essays in Evolutionary Epistemology* (New York: Wiley, 1982); G. Vollmer, *Evolutionäre Erkenntnistheorie* (Stuttgart: Hirzel, 1975); M. Ruse, *Taking Darwin Seriously: A Naturalistic Approach to Philosophy* (Oxford: Blackwell, 1986).

himself to be a sharp and perceptive critic of the so-called phil-osophy of mind, a trend in philosophical anthropology that I hope to return to more extensively in a later context (see ch. 9, section 5). In his book *The Mystery of Consciousness*, a collection of essays that appeared previously as book reviews in *The New York Review of Books,* he emphasizes that the philosophy of mind has ended up in naturalistic channels.[2] Mental philosophers and cognitive psych-ologists with this perspective – Searle himself sees no advantage in naturalism – too quickly and easily want to explain the human mind as a function of the brain. "Mental processes are biological functions of the body in general and of the brain in particular in just the same sense that circulation of the blood is a function of the heart or breathing is a function of the lungs," stated the anatomist Charles Judson Herrick as early as 1929.[3]

Naturally, brains and consciousness are closely connected. Nevertheless, according to Searle the particular nature of the human mind, the mystery of consciousness, should be kept in view more adequately. We can only do justice to human consciousness if we consider it to be an irreducible phenomenon with emergent prop-erties, properties that do not occur on underlying levels (e.g. the physical or biotic) and that come to light exclusively in a certain type of brain, that is, the human brain.

Thus, Searle makes a case for a non-reductive view of human consciousness. However, he wants to avoid the early-modern antithesis of mind and matter as expressed by Descartes. Searle is certainly not a proponent of Cartesian dualism or mentalism; he emphasizes the unbreakable coherence between body and mind, brain and consciousness. He even stresses – just as I did in the previous chapter – that there is an intrinsic intertwining of emer-gent phenomena and substrate phenomena. Processes of con-sciousness have a unique and distinctive status, but they can only "realize" themselves in the brain.[4]

Regrettably, a subsequent point on his agenda spoils much of the good he has done, by positing the thesis that consciousness does not

[2] J. R. Searle, *The Mystery of Consciousness* (London: Granta Books, 1997).
[3] C. J. Herrick, *The Thinking Machine* (Chicago: University of Chicago Press, 1929), p. 250.
[4] J. R. Searle, *The Rediscovery of the Mind* (Cambridge, MA: MIT Press, 1992).

only realize itself *in* the brain but that it is also caused *by* the brain: "brains cause minds."[5] In *The Mystery of Consciousness* he applies this view to the central thesis that consciousness is an emergent property of human brains, caused by those brains. Thus he ends up with the concept of "bottom-up causation," a concept that is often referred to as causal emergence.

On this point I have to distance myself from Searle's ideas. The concept of causal emergence is, in my view, a contradictory one.[6] No one will deny that processes of consciousness are connected with brain activities. However, if one declares that these processes are caused by brain activities, then the reason for designating them to be emergent disappears. That, besides physical causation, something like "mental causation" exists is beyond doubt. For the world-changing influence of the human species does not rest on the frail state of its physical and physiological capabilities, but on the exceptional power and effectiveness of its mental abilities. Consciousness is emergent by virtue of the idionomy of these mental abilities.

More detail is needed here. Properly speaking, consciousness should be seen as a multiplicity of mental competencies, a complicated union of modal functions, including analytical, aesthetic, and moral functions.[7] There is a triad of robust reasons that can support the recognition of such a modal diversity of consciousness functions:

(1) The mental functions distinguish themselves from each other by specific characteristics; to put it another way, they have their own ontological identity. For this reason we distinguish a person's logical abilities from his or her artistic gifts, and those, once again, from his or her moral make-up. A person can be strong in one area, and weaker in others.

---

[5] J. R. Searle, *Minds, Brains, and Science* (Cambridge, MA: Harvard University Press, 1984), p. 20.

[6] I have similar reservations in regard to the concept of "top-down causation" (see ch. 7, section 5). Searle defends it in *Intentionality: An Essay in the Philosophy of Mind* (Cambridge: Cambridge University Press, 1983), ch. 10.

[7] It is also true that these modal functions of human beings (also their bodily functions) finally cohere in the deeper unity of the I, that is, the human person (see ch. 9, section 3).

(2) The mental functions distinguish themselves from each other by idionomic causation. In other words, they manifest disparate forms of mental causality. Logical intellect, for example, is demonstrated by the construction of conclusive reasons; musical competence by the harmonization of melodies; moral consciousness by the participation in volunteer projects.

(3) The mental functions distinguish themselves by an orientation to various normative principles. In the above examples they are aimed at logical rules, principles of harmony, and standards of solidarity.[8] This orientation implies that people know themselves to be accountable for conscious behaviors. No one holds them accountable, however, for neurophysiological disorders or brain deficiencies. In short, identity, idionomy, and normativity are hallmarks of the emergent character of the modal functions of consciousness.

Searle, in my view, confuses the multilevel or multimodal complexity of human consciousness with his suggestion of a causal coupling between brain and consciousness. This confusion already occurs in his definitions of concepts. He applies emergence to the change of characteristics that can occur in the relationship of part and whole, of micro- and macro-properties, and of element and system. Thus he says, "An emergent property of a system is one that is causally explained by the behavior of the elements of the system; but it is not a property of any individual elements and it cannot be explained simply as a summation of the properties of those elements."[9]

Further distinctions are needed here. Usually, part and whole, element and system lie on the same level of being. Thus system characteristics can be explained on the basis of the behavior of the elements that make up the system. Emergence, on the contrary, transcends the part–whole relationship. Emergence is present when phenomena with truly new meanings occur: phenomena that cannot be explained on the current level of being, and that get meaning only at a higher level. Given this hierarchical differentiation, every

---

[8] Natural laws and normative laws differ in that one cannot transgress the former but one can transgress the latter.

[9] Searle, *The Mystery of Consciousness*, p. 18.

level is characterized by its own laws and type of causation: every level unfolds its own possibilities for causal explanation. The emergence of a new level of being is, for that reason, not comparable to the appearance of new characteristics on an existing system level. The truly new – in the ontological sense of the word – transcends, by definition, the laws and explanatory possibilities that reveal themselves on a lower level. Note that I do not say that lower-level explanations would be unimportant, superfluous or impossible! No, I would assert that they are not sufficient to do justice to what occurs on a higher level. Brain specialists and cognitive neuroscientists will never be able to give a full account of the logical considerations of a grand master at the chessboard.

Searle does not adequately recognize the ontological difference between level bound (thus horizontal or intramodal) part–whole relations and level-crossing (thus vertical or intermodal) lower–higher level relations. Something can be an emergent property for him, and, at the same time, can be explainable from out of the lower level. Thus, on the one hand, he designates the fluidity of water to be an emergent property compared to the properties of separate water molecules; on the other hand he states that the structure of water molecules causes and explains the fluid character of water.[10] He then draws an analogy with consciousness. He considers consciousness to be an emergent property compared to the properties of brain neurons, but he also asserts that the neurons are the cause of consciousness.

Can the liquid nature of water be compared with the logical character of consciousness? In my view, this liquidity is not an emergent property; it is a physical characteristic that can be explained from the physical structure and properties of H_2O molecules. The insight of the chess master is, on the contrary, an emergent characteristic, for logical considerations cannot be explained, or even named, on the basis of the underlying biophysical and neurophysiological processes.

One must grant Searle that there are close connections "between phenomena at different levels in the very same underlying stuff."[11] Thus correlative relationships can be shown between the physical condition of, say, a chess master and his or her analytical

[10] Searle, *The Rediscovery of the Mind*, p. 218.   [11] Searle, *Intentionality*, p. 266.

performances in chess. But correlative explanations are not causal explanations. Explanations based on correlations, no matter how legitimate, bypass the supervenient character of the mental functions. For example, a medical doctor can uncover why the chess master had a blind spot, or why he could plan his game only three or four moves ahead; perhaps he had hypoglycemia or a shortage of sleep. But these conclusions do not, in any way, make his chess moves logically transparent. Biochemical and neurobiological explanations are not trivial but they are indirect; they ignore the intentional and normative orientation of the mind (see ch. 6, section 2). They depend on what I described earlier as the correlating processes between infra- and superstructure and for this reason they supply only circumstantial evidence.

Searle's description of emergence as "bottom-up causation" I see as a contradictory train of thought. This is especially the case for the observation that causal emergence is physical in nature.[12] It is as though Searle, in spite of his anti-reductionism, cannot let go of a latent ontological naturalism, of modernity's faith in science. To speak here of "non-reductive physicalism" – a nettlesome problem in the philosophy of mind for several decades now[13] – indicates a legitimate rejection of mentalistic dualism as well as of materialistic monism. For the rest "non-reductive physicalism" is, in my judgment, more a pseudo-scientific mantra than a fully considered scientific position.

According to the definition of its founders, the concept of emergence refers to the feature of irreducible novelty. For us this

---

[12] Searle, *The Rediscovery of the Mind*, p. 14: "Consciousness is a mental, and therefore physical, property of the brain." A. W. M. Meijers, "Mental Causation and Searle's Impossible Conception of Unconscious Intentionality," *International Journal of Philosophical Studies* 8 (2000), 155–70.

[13] D. Davidson, "Mental Events," in *Essays on Actions and Events: The Philosophical Essays of Donald Davidson* (New York: Oxford University Press, 1980), pp. 207–25; p. 214. This essay is historically important because Davidson introduces here the concept of "supervenience" in the philosophy of mind in support of the theory of a non-reductive physicalism: "Mental characteristics are in some sense dependent, or supervenient, on physical characteristics." From a Christian point of view, Nancey Murphy demonstrates openness for the hierarchy of levels in the living world. She, too, translates this insight into a non-reductive physicalism. See N. Murphy, "Non-Reductive Physicalism: Philosophical Issues," in W. S. Brown, N. Murphy, and H. Newton Malony (eds.), *Whatever Happened to the Soul? Scientific and Theological Portraits of Human Nature* (Minneapolis, MN: Fortress Press, 1998), ch. 6. But Murphy's concern is legitimate: "no new kinds of metaphysical 'ingredients' need to be added to produce higher-level entities from lower" (p. 129).

can mean nothing else than that the modal functions of consciousness are idionomic, possessing their own forms of causality.
We have to consider the implications of this starting-point for all
levels at which the human mind reveals itself: now as logical
understanding, technical ingenuity, or economic acumen, then,
again, as aesthetic taste or moral conviction, etc. All these modal
functions, which should be distinguished from each other in greater
precision than can be done in this book,[14] are themselves not
physically or physiologically determined but are supervenient. They
are steered by causes that, on the level of human acting, we usually
designate as "reasons" or "intentional considerations."

In summary, every mental level demands recognition as a domain
that distinguishes itself by normative principles, social practices, and
causative connections of its own. This recognition may never be at
the cost of the insight that there are also substrate levels that play a
role, and that mental causes correlate with physical and physiological causes in the brain.

2 PETER CHECKLAND AND THE STRUCTURES OF SOCIETY

A general theory of emergent evolution not only clarifies our view
of the structure of human consciousness, but also of the architecture
of human society. Given the topic of our study, I can only make
some brief comments on the latter. I do this on the basis of
Peter Checkland's book *Systems Thinking, Systems Practice*. Checkland analyzes the question of societal organization using so-called
systems thinking. To give this systems thinking a sharper, ontological profile, he bases it on central insights from emergence
philosophy. He follows the Hungarian-Canadian systems thinker
and biologist Ludwig von Bertalanffy, author of the seminal essay
General System Theory, who as early as the 1950s resisted reductionistic tendencies not only in biology and psychology but also in
the social sciences.[15]

---

[14] See H. Dooyeweerd, *A New Critique of Theoretical Thought*, vol. 11.
[15] L. von Bertalanffy, "General System Theory" (1956), in *General System Theory: Foundations, Development, Applications* (New York: Braziller, 1968), ch. 2. Von Bertalanffy was cofounder of the Society for General Systems Research.

Following the footsteps of von Bertalanffy, Checkland emphasizes that not only biological organisms but also societal organizations should be considered as systems. He considers a system to be a
set of elements connected together to form a whole; this whole
shows emergent characteristics in the sense of properties which are
properties of the whole, rather than properties of its component
parts.[16] For Checkland, systems thinking is a scientific analysis of
"organized complexity" equipped with such emergent properties. In
the case of societal organizations – designated as "human activity
systems" by Checkland – there are in his view important emergent
characteristics at stake such as self-regulation, internal communication, and transmission of values. He presents systems thinking,
therefore, as a necessary supplement to the detailed mechanistic
analyses that are characteristic of the natural sciences. No matter
how useful the natural sciences may be, they are, according to him,
unable to uncover the totality structure and thus the irreducible or
emergent qualities of that reality that meets us in the institutions
and activity systems that, together, constitute society.[17]

In Checkland's analysis of these societal systems – his book deals,
among others, with the family unit, the factory, and the nation-state –
we encounter the phenomenon of emergence time and again.
Checkland wants to demonstrate that human activity systems, no
matter where on earth they took shape, are complex organizations
with features entirely their own. In these systems a distinct new
principle manifests itself, a normative value that is incorporated into
the system, and with which the system stands or falls. Of course, in
the dynamic of history this value is always expressed and worked out
in different ways, but in his view it remains recognizable as an
"irreducible residue," a core value that cannot be reduced to the
physical domain.

Here I am reminded of the words of the Church Father
Augustine. Long ago he commented that a state that disregards the
norm of justice is nothing but a *magnum latrocinium*, a band of
robbers on a larger scale. A state that does not uphold justice arms

[16] Checkland, *Systems Thinking*, p. 3.
[17] For a discussion by Peter Checkland about the relationships between modern biology, the
idea of emergence, and present-day systems thought, see ibid., pp. 74–82.

itself and wages war for the sake of power and gain, thus resembling a gang of robbers. For a gang of robbers, too, accepts leadership, forms a closed community, fights for gain, and divides the spoils as agreed beforehand. In this context Augustine recounts the delightful story of a pirate who was captured by Alexander the Great. The man had a way with words, for when the king asked him how he dared to make the oceans unsafe he answered boldly: "We both make the oceans unsafe. But my ship is small and your navy is large. That is why you are called a king and I am called a pirate."[18]

Augustine knew nothing of theories about evolution or emergence. But he knew full well that when human beings organize themselves in a system of state, then the state represents a different order than the order we encounter in nature. The order of the state transcends the order of nature. In nature the law of the jungle prevails, but not in the state. The state in the true sense of the word, i.e. the state not as it actually may be but as it normatively should be, is a community of justice. Such a state acts according to an intuitive nuclear moment that we can indicate as the principle of justice. Amongst all nations on earth we find this notion of justice as a primary intuition. The principle is universal but the elaboration of this principle in concrete laws, rules, and practices is particular and historically determined. Concrete laws, rules, and practices may be just but they differ from country to country, from people to people, and from one time to another.

I propose that we also apply this normative view of the state to civil society, i.e. to the non-state organizations in human society. For these non-state structures, too, are more than products of nature. They have originated from the competitive powers of nature but within the context of human culture they bring to expression a societal norm that transcends the biological principles of competition and selection. Thus I make a case for a communitarian vision of human society, a vision that not only holds the state in high regard as a community of justice but also the business enterprise as a community of profitable production, the family as a community of love, the church as a community of faith, etc. In this

---

[18] See Augustine, *De civitate Dei* (413–26), 4, 4. The citation of the pirate has been translated freely.

communitarian vision all social activity systems order themselves around normative core values such as justice, profit, love, and ultimate devotion. These nuclear values can be conceived as irreducible residues.[19] They are principles, i.e. universal laws with particular applications. In daily life they must be elaborated more fully, and must be attuned to the natural possibilities, climatographic conditions, and historical circumstances that are peculiar to each people.

Therefore, in spite of these common core values, human societies always have a different appearance. In the course of history they have differentiated into a great variety of social worlds under the guidance of emergent principles. It is difficult to say how this process of emergence occurred since prehistoric times and how these principles could assert their claim on the human mind. Were they bolts of lightning that struck into the mental and spiritual world of the great formative leaders in history such as Confucius, Hammurabi, Jesus, or Gandhi, with a societal revolution as the result? Or was it like water dripping, slowly hollowing out a stone; quiet powers that steadily worked into the consciousness of lowly folk, from the earliest beginnings of civilization? Whatever the case, the long-term effect was spectacular. In the history of humankind the principles of animate nature were overruled by a regime of cultural principals, even if this was a case of two steps forward, one step back.

There is similarity but also difference between cultural principles and biological principles. Earlier we saw that in nature biological principles emerged as initial or germinative laws, i.e. laws that are universal but allow a variety of particular applications. In this way diverse types of life forms originated (see ch. 4, section 2). In a comparable manner cultural principles came to the fore in human societies as initial universal laws that made particular applications possible; these applications became concrete in diverse types of

[19] Human consciousness includes a diversity of modal functions, each with its own normative nucleus. This diversity of functions reflects itself in a diversity of social institutions. These institutions are multimodal entities but in each system one mental function is in control (see ch. 7, section 4). Thus the state has a physical function (state territory), a sensitive function (patriotism), a logical function (*raison d'état*), and an economic function (state finances) etc., but the politico-juridical function takes the lead. Justice is the normative core value for we experience the state primarily as a community of justice.

societal structures. However, this particularization did not proceed in the same manner in culture as in nature. In nature the principles were actualized haphazardly, by trial and error, by the rather messy processes of mutation and selection. But in culture humans intervene between principle and practice. Cultural principles do not seek their way blindly. They appeal to the conscience, i.e. the sensitivity to norms on the part of people who deeply from within realize that in society starting-points for the good life are at issue. Thus choices have to be made. This is a good reason why people always judge social developments critically. Sometimes they embrace them enthusiastically, in other cases they fight them tooth and nail or correct them.

In short, in the process of evolution biological principles find the proper applications by themselves but the applications of cultural principles require human mediation. People are faced with the task to "positivize" the general principles that emerge in culture into concrete rules for practical conduct. That is to say, they have to work out these initial principles in juridical laws, market principles, moral codes, musical styles, religious commands, etc., according to their own insights.[20] No wonder that the differences that we encounter between human civilizations diverge more widely than the differences that we find between populations of another biological species.

Diversification in culture is also advanced by the fact that cultural principles, contrary to biological principles, are norms, i.e. laws that can be transgressed. In each culture we do indeed find antinormative tendencies. Over this whole wide earth, not only the factual behavior of humans but even the positivized laws that are intended to steer behavior in good channels bear witness to injustice. Evil has crept into the rules by favoring those in power and neglecting the poor and oppressed. Or, to put it differently, laws have to implement the normative principle but they often violate it. They can even develop in a totally anti-normative direction, as the Nazi

---

[20] The kernel of each cultural norm is a universally valid principle that has to be elaborated in standards that are historically determined and applicable in a concrete society. See J. Klapwijk, "Pluralism of Norms and Values: On the Claim and Reception of the Universal," *Philosophia Reformata* 59 (1994), 158–92.

state has shown. But note: the abhorrence that the Nazi state and other cruel dictatorships evoke does not contradict but rather affirms the universal validity of the principle of justice as an emergent standard. For we would not experience this abhorrence without an intuitive notion of justice.

We can conclude that world history is not just the monotonous report of random events but also the overwhelming story of emerging worlds, disclosures of meaning, and realizations of new norms. These norms are particular, captured from a historical tradition, adapted to a natural situation, and as such they are tentative expressions of a universal norm principle that we experience intuitively. For there would be no system of state without an intuitive awareness of an all-embracing justice. There would be no ties of family or friendship without a general principle of love and trust. There would be no business life without the universal core value of economic profit. There would be no religions without a shared commitment of people to what they experience as ultimate reality.

Let us return to Peter Checkland. In his book Checkland has convincingly shown that human activity systems display an emergent character. But he wrestles with the question of how the normative, and at the same time historical, character of social systems must be justified: "we have no adequate account of systemic complexity."[21] In large measure he agrees with the systems analyst Kenneth Ewart Boulding. Boulding suggests that a hierarchy of levels of increasing complexity characterizes our world. As these levels increase in complexity, emergent properties manifest themselves. When we come to the typical human level then we would, in his view, have to make a further distinction. The level of social systems would surpass the level of human consciousness.[22]

I do not share the opinion of Checkland and Boulding that the social level is emergent over the human level. This is a view that one encounters more often among emergence thinkers (see ch. 6,

---

[21] Checkland, *Systems Thinking*, p. 106.
[22] Ibid., pp. 103–6. K. E. Boulding, "General Systems Theory – the Skeleton of Science," *Management Science* 2 (1956), 197–208. In this famous article Boulding provides the skeleton of science: "a framework or structure of systems on which to hang the flesh and blood of particular disciplines and particular subject matters in an orderly and coherent corpus of knowledge" (208).

section 3). As if being human and humane could be taken in itself and would not, in first instance, imply solidarity and social cohesion! In my view, humanness and sociality cannot be dissociated. The various forms of human consciousness as we have distinguished them in the previous section are subject to the same normative principles that apply to the forms of community in which consciousness institutionalizes itself. Not only in human society but among all types of organisms and on all levels of being, life has, at the same time, an individual and a social side. Living organisms can only function in groups.

In Checkland's argument the widespread misconception that social systems represent a higher level than human individuals, because they manifest increasing complexity, now wreaks havoc.[23] I reiterate here, complexity is not the decisive criterion of emergence but idionomy is. Naturally, the system of justice of the state is much more complex than the sense of justice of an individual citizen, but this does not place the state on a higher level. The state is a general embodiment of its citizenry's idionomic consciousness of justice, and the state's laws bind government and its subjects equally. Similarly, the economic acts of an industrial concern are much more complicated than the share of the individual employees. Yet, the industrial firm as a production unit is, in the end, nothing else than the institutionalized result of the economic actions of all the workers of the firm.

I conclude, even if it is on the basis of summary considerations, that the theory of emergence sheds light not only on the building-scheme of organic nature but also on the architecture of human society; but not in the sense that there is a social or institutional level that would surpass the level of human individuals. An institution should be seen as the collective embodiment of individual competencies on the same level of organization, for the same idionomic principle determines the collective structure and the individual competencies. Thus justice is a guideline for the state and

---

[23] Checkland is not consistent. At times his systems theory is the "application of systems ideas to real world situations" where the systems, in hierarchical perspective, manifest a higher degree of complexity. At other times he makes a distinction between natural and social systems and typifies the latter, in a nominalist way, as "intellectual constructs" without reality value or ontological meaning. See *Systems Thinking*, pp. 7–11, 245–50.

for the state's citizens individually. Truth is a standard for a university and for the variety of academic investigators. Profit directs the policy of the corporation and the efforts of the individual employees. Artistic beauty guides the performance of a symphonic orchestra and the playing of the different musicians. Moral love binds a family but also each member. Devotion marks the religious community but also the individual believers.

All in all, the theory of emergent evolution makes clear that wherever the human species established itself on earth, the process of evolution received new opportunities through the emergence of specific cultural competencies and specific social institutions. One can imagine that settlements were established that were fully determined, initially, by natural factors such as climate, soil, interest, and brute force. But, sooner or later, new laws came into force. The laws of the jungle were restrained by cultural standards, even though the threat of barbarism remains to this very day. The standards of culture are of a different order than the laws of nature. Cultural laws are norms. They are not coercive but obligatory because they appeal to freedom and responsibility. They can be obeyed but they can also be criticized or transgressed. They are not uniform but particularized, adapted to the circumstances of time and place in which people live. However relative and time-bound these normative standards may be, they do not lead to a cultural relativism or an anarchy of values. For in the peculiar we humans recognize the ubiquitous; in the foreign we recognize the familiar. In exotic cultures we sometimes discover values and standards that touch our conscience. Cultural norms are particular in the sense that they are particularized expressions of nuclear principles and core values that we cherish deep in our hearts as a common legacy of humanity, ultimate standards of *Homo sapiens*.[24]

3 ONTOLOGICAL STRATIFICATION

The theory of emergence, taken as a general theory of emergent evolution, draws our attention to significant differences in level that occur not only in nature but also in human beings and human

---

[24] Klapwijk, "Pluralism of Norms and Values," 158–92.

society. It can be seen as an ontological vision of the differences in level that have, through evolution, delineated themselves in the world of our experience. In this sense "levelism" is a theory not only of emergent evolution but also of ontological stratification. It implies that the world has gradually disclosed itself in an all-embracing hierarchy of lower and higher levels that reach from the physical and biotic domains up to the complex spheres of human society. With this description I have a double proviso. A theory of ontological stratification should be modally articulated and empirically grounded.

(1) A theory of ontological stratification should be articulated modally. Levels of being are not concrete entities but ways of being, i.e. arrangements that in the process of evolution have manifested themselves in things and phenomena. Thus, in a bacterial "thing," in addition to physical characteristics, a biological function has also become evident; nevertheless, the organism itself is one concrete entity, not the sum of a physical and a biotic entity. In the same way, a human being is not a body plus a soul, not a corporeal and a mental entity, but in the one real person different modal (physical and above-physical) dispositions have come to light. They are incorporated in the unbreakable unity of the human person.[25]

Thus I repudiate the dualistic constructions that are known from ancient and modern philosophy. For example, when we represent a living organism, in the spirit of Aristotle, as a material body to which *vis vitalis* (a form- or life-giving spirit) has been added, we break the one organism in two. Or when we imagine the human person, in the tradition of Descartes, as a union of a bodily substance and a thinking substance, we create, here also, a dichotomy. In both cases the question arises as to how the components cooperate. Are we dealing with top-down causation, with bottom-up causation, or with causal interaction? No matter what answer is given, the question incorrectly suggests that two separate entities are involved. I call this suggestion a form of reification or, as the Germans say, *Verdinglichung*.

---

[25] For a discussion of the deeper unity of the human person as soul or as spiritual person, see ch. 9, section 3.

In a multimodal stratification theory of the world there is an intrinsic coherence between the distinct levels and functions. Consider the chess player once again. The mental exertions of the chess player (logical function) coincide with phenomena of fatigue (sensitive function), cerebral processes (vegetative function), cellular processes (biotic function), and molecular reactions in the brain (physical function). Do not separate these functions! Don't ask: do the brain cells set the thought process going, or does the thought process activate the brain cells? Nor should one ask: do the adenosine triphosphate molecules mobilize the brain cells or do the brain cells stimulate the supply of ATP? All these processes are to be seen as correlating configurations of a concrete phenomenon that functions *simultaneously* on diverse, scientifically abstractable levels of being.[26] Whoever thinks of causation, whether it be in a top-down or bottom-up direction, sooner or later runs into one of the fundamental laws of physics: the law of conservation of energy.

(2) A theory of ontological stratification should be empirically founded. It should keep away from that type of ontology that bases itself not on experience but on metaphysical arguments or intuitions. Levels of being are not shadows or emanations of eternal ideas into time in the way that Platonism suggests. Nor are they representations of metaphysical forms directed toward the deity as the highest final cause in the way that Aristotelianism suggests. They are ontological structures that we can only discover in experience. Thus we have to avoid all metaphysical arguments. For it is obvious that we never can explain or reconstruct emergent structures on the basis of principles that are, in themselves, the fruit of emergent evolution.

Empirical investigations indicate that evolution is not only a gradual and continuous process in which later forms arose from earlier types but also a saltatory or discontinuous process that, in crucial moments, brought to light totally new, idionomic functions. Yet, there is an element of truth in the classical adage *natura non facit saltus*, nature makes no leaps. The emergent functions that are the regalia of

---

[26] Because the physical and the sensitive-psychic are modalities, not entities, they form correlating series in the human being, without there being reason to speak of psychophysical parallelism, in the spirit of Gustav T. Fechner. Psychophysical parallelism, too, is based on reification of modes of being.

new biological kingdoms could only come into being in organisms thanks to the continuous adaptations that took place at the lower levels of their existence. No discontinuity without continuity!

The phenomenon of emergence is so prominently present in the phylogenetic process that the naturalistic notion of a one-dimensional world seems implausible. A less dogmatic conception is obvious. This conception suggests that not only in the beginning – say by way of the Big Bang – the world took shape as an idionomic domain, a world of physical things, but that also afterward, once and again, idionomic realities arose, now of a supra-physical kind. All in all, I argue for a stratification theory that is based on our experiences of a multidimensional reality, originated from emergent evolution. Such a stratification theory is, on the one hand, a clear alternative for the classical philosophies of nature of Platonism and Aristotelianism that I mentioned before and that were based on emanation or teleology. On the other hand, it is a recognizable alternative for the modern worldviews of mechanistic naturalism and vitalism.

Current mechanistic theory states that all phenomena can be explained as mechanical processes determined by the universal laws of nature. It assumes that even biological and higher phenomena are nothing but complex assemblages of molecular processes and therefore reducible to the one-dimensional domain of physical nature. In our discussions we have been able to conclude that higher phenomena do indeed always have a molecular basis and thus provide room for mechanistic explanations. However, these explanations are not sufficient. They do not take into account the special laws and causalities that govern processes at higher levels. Neither do they take into account the correlative constraints, i.e. the limiting boundary conditions, that the higher levels (especially the leading level) place on the movements at the basic level.

Thus movements of calcium and potassium in nerve cells are underdetermined by chemical laws, because chemical laws are not sufficient to give insight into the specific meaning of those movements for the nervous system.[27] Or, to give an example of an

---

[27] See S. E. Toulmin, "The Mentality of Man's Brain," in A. G. Karczmar and J. C. Eccles (eds.), *Brain and Human Behavior* (New York: Springer, 1972); Looren de Jong, *Naturalism and Psychology*, pp. 57–59.

entirely different order, Rembrandt's *Night Watch* does indeed lend itself to unlimited physical and chemical investigations; yet, here too we encounter the problem of underdetermination. For all the data that the well-known Rembrandt Research Project managed to gather have not led to an explanation of how *Night Watch* originated as an artistic product. My conclusion is: mechanistic explanations are relevant, and in the detection of questionable Rembrandts they may even be invaluable, but with respect to multimodal phenomena they can never be complete.

In contrast to the mechanistic view, the theory of vitalism states that living organisms are not the result of mechanical processes, but have arisen from a metaphysical principle of being, a mysterious and goal-oriented *élan vital*. Thus biological phenomena would, in their essence, not be determined by mechanical but by final causes. Hans Driesch, who suggests that organisms strive to realize themselves as total systems, follows a similar line of argument (see ch. 6, section 1).

Indeed, biological organisms manifest themselves as unique and goal-oriented total systems. Therefore the theory of emergence has often been associated with vitalism. But there is an incisive difference. The vitalistic thesis that biological organisms have originated from a metaphysical principle of creative life force and, for this reason, represent a reality completely of their own, is a speculative idea. For experience teaches us that life is based on material reality and that all living systems realize the final order of their biotic mode of being in the mechanical order of the physical mode of being. This is also the starting-point of the general theory of emergent evolution. GTEE is a theory of ontological hierarchy and stratification. It emphasizes not only the ontological differences but also the ontological coherence between the various modal levels. In consequence it does not exclude the mechanistic explanation of living things, but integrates it into a multidisciplinary concept of scientific theory.

Perhaps some readers will pose the question: are explanations on the basis of functionality and finality really derived from experience? Biologists may say that organisms adapt functionally to their environment and that survival is their purpose, but are these expressions not a shorthand summary of what in the final analysis has to be considered as an exclusively mechanical procedure? Are the so-called "functional" explanations not a subjective interpretation of factual experience? I must deny the latter. Experience itself confronts us with the hard fact of multifunctional diversity. Already in daily life we would be hopelessly disoriented if we did not have a clear realization of the qualitative differences in levels between the things that we observe. We would feel completely lost if we did not notice fundamental differences between a thirsty soil and a thirsty plant; or between the modes of life of plants, animals, and people; or, in human society, between the nature of a school, a church, a state, and a family unit.

I admit these fundamental differences in levels are not *given* in experience. They are not empirical data, not individual objects or particular contents of experience. We cannot point to them with a finger, such as to the differences between a crow and a raven. Rather, these differences are *presupposed* in experience. They are – I hope to discuss this in more detail later – general and intuitive principles of orientation that we employ from childhood on to find our way in life. Scientists, too, fall subconsciously back on such preconceived intuitions, the chemist and biologist as much as the legal expert and theologian, in the demarcation of their disciplinary domains.[28] Even in the naturalistic thesis that the living world can be completely reduced to the physical world, the difference between both worlds is the hidden point of departure, its denial a theoretical amendment after the fact!

Why do scientists prefer a reductive naturalism above a multi-leveled view of reality? In our secularized society this reductionism meets an existential and perhaps even religious need for certainty.[29] This certainty is often hard to find. It seems that this certainty is not granted to us in any place other than in the solid methodology of the sciences. Already in elementary school we are raised with scientific certainties; we use these, in first instance, as practical tools in our dealing with things. But we take some liberties with these certainties in subsequent years. We make the physical world picture

---

[28] Here we speak of general intuitions. In the delineation of scientific boundaries, further corrections and definitions are, of course, not excluded.

[29] M. Ruse, "Is Evolution a Secular Religion?," *Science* 299 (2003), 1523–24.

into a philosophical worldview. And we make that philosophical worldview into a religion by absolutizing the physical method and by swearing by a one-level physicalism.

Once maneuvered into that position we lack the means to come to the formulation of an alternative, anti-reductive worldview, even if we feel that this should really happen in order to cope with the complexities of life. No one has expressed the embarrassment or lack of a non-reductive worldview better than Marjorie Grene in her book *The Understanding of Nature*. She writes here:

The anti-reducibility position is, for many people, impossible to accept. Why? Because it breaks through the defences of a simple, one-level physicalism without providing an alternative metaphysics to take its place. To think anti-reductively demands thinking in terms of hierarchical systems, of levels of reality and the like; but we don't know any longer how to think in that way – and to be told, even to *know*, that the contrary position is absurd does not in itself allow us to embrace wholeheartedly what ought to be the more reasonable alternative. For anti-reductivism is "reasonable" only in the perverse sense that its negation is self-contradictory, not in the more substantive sense of fitting smoothly into a *Weltanschauung* in which, as people educated in the ideal of a "scientific" world view, we can feel at home.[30]

If reductionism is absurd, why is it so difficult to gain support for the alternative vision of a multifaceted reality? Probably the answer has to be: because in the scientistic climate of thought of our age we have lost the inspiration of a non-reductive worldview or philosophy. We need a conceptual framework in which emergent phenomena can regain their rightful place. More on this in the following chapter.

[30] M. Grene, *The Understanding of Nature*, p. 59.

CHAPTER 9

Hominization and the philosophy of mind

In the previous two chapters we have examined the theoretical implications that are enclosed in the concept of emergent evolution, in chapter 7 with respect to the levels in living nature and in chapter 8 with respect to the spheres in human society. In the present chapter we concentrate on the uniqueness of the human person. What makes human beings, intertwined as they are with all other living creatures on earth, so exceptional? Is it merely the emergence of mental competencies? Or is there more at play when we speak about "the infinite value of the human person?"

First we consider the frame of reference in which we want to capture the human species in its singularity (section 1). Then we will consider how *Homo sapiens* became human, and the evolutionary process that led to personhood (section 2). All kinds of questions arise here. Has the physical universe, from its very origin, anticipated the arrival on the scene of the human species (section 3)? Can one say about animate nature, too, that it is predisposed to the origin of human beings (section 4)? What must we think of methodological naturalism; is it applicable to living creatures, and particularly to human creatures, considering their supervenient characteristics (section 5)? All these questions lead to a critical encounter with the philosophy of mind (section 6).

I EMERGENT EVOLUTION AS A CONCEPTUAL SCHEME

I can imagine that not every reader finds the idea of emergent evolution presented in this book transparent. Nowhere do I give a ready-to-go definition of this concept. There are reasons for that. Suppose that emergent evolution is a development of such a nature that a level of being appears that is irreducibly new; then it is logically impossible to define this new domain fully in terms of the level that has been transcended. Our insights remain stuck between ship and shore, between the categories of the transcended domain and the domain in question. The transition can only be caught by an approximating concept, an *idea* that explores the boundary-transcending development.

We encounter here the mutual relationship between "concept" and "idea." In everyday life we experience little or no difference between these two words. An idea is, just as a concept, a mental image, i.e. a logical or conceptual representation of things in or around us. However, in philosophical literature the word has gained a more specific meaning. Since Plato and Kant, "idea" stands for a logical representation of something that in our knowledge of the world is of fundamental importance and that the thinking person has some insight into – the original meaning of "idea" is sight – but that the person can nevertheless not fully grasp. An idea is a limiting concept, a representation of affairs that are of foundational importance for humans – for Plato these were the ideas of the true, the good, and the beautiful, and for Kant the ideas of God, the soul, and the world as a whole – but that transcend the ability of the objectifying mind for that very reason. Such founding affairs can only be grasped by approximation and intuition. Thus "idea" came to have the status of a limiting concept, suitable for gaining an approximating image of a phenomenon that escapes precise and objective conceptual determination.

In philosophy "idea" often resembles what Hilary Putnam calls a "conceptual scheme," i.e. a philosophical framework.[1] In this book I use these words in respect to the process of emergent evolution. For this process, too, is a founding phenomenon that drastically exceeds the measure of traditional knowledge of an object. The evolution process confronts us with inanimate matter in which life comes to reveal itself, with life in which thinking begins to occur, and with thought that attempts to define what it meditates on, including the evolutionary process that gave the impetus for this

---

[1] For the term "conceptual scheme" see H. Putnam, *Reason, Truth and History*. In Putnam's thought this term is related to and partially inspired by Wittgenstein's notions of language-games and forms of life.

thought. No wonder, then, that definitions fail on the dynamics of the evolutionary process! Human thought will never be able to understand all that occurs in the process that makes this grasp possible. At most, one can only surmise what it is – with the help of an idea, a conceptual scheme.

Thus I see the idea of emergent evolution as a conceptual scheme. Rather than helping us focus on easy-to-understand facts or objects, it helps us to deal with the process of the becoming of life, a path to becoming in which we, ourselves, are included and, yes, in which the miracle of our understanding had to encompass the new reality. *That* in the history of this cosmos, at the Big Bang and in subsequent aeons of time, non-reductive novelties presented themselves, is beyond doubt. *How* they have occurred, we can only grasp by approximation in an open scheme of thought: the conceptual framework of emergent evolution.

I bring these considerations to the fore to shed light on the status of our theory of emergent evolution. Readers of this book would seriously misunderstand this theory if they interpret it to be an alternative biological explanatory theory. The theory of emergence offers no biological explanations of any kind. Instead, it emphasizes that in living nature a plurality of explanatory levels forces itself upon us. The theory would do violence to this plurality if it subsequently appeared on the scene with some sort of overall explanation. No, emergence theory is not a biological explanatory theory; it is a philosophical framework theory. It outlines a theoretical framework, within the bounds of which, *where feasible*, customary explanatory patterns are employed and, *where necessary*, the idionomic novelty of those phenomena that transcend a given level and a standard pattern of explanation is respected.

Whence this double approach? Does the history of science not show that what investigators first described as a specific explanation for newly discovered phenomena later proved to be amenable to integration in a larger explanatory framework? Do we not have to take a lesson from the British mathematician and physicist James Clerk Maxwell? In 1865, after toiling for ten years, he came to the surprising insight that the newer theories of electricity and magnetism, as previously defended by Ampère and Faraday, were reducible to one encompassing theory. With the help of mathematical formulas, he was able to state a unified theory of electromagnetism that could explain all these phenomena. This example is indeed instructive; but it does not imply that every attempt to reduce the number of explanatory theories is a guaranteed success. Those who by definition wish to reduce all that is new entirely to what already exists have lost their empirical impartiality. They have incorporated in advance the unknown into the known and have thus yielded to the pressure of the evolutionistic continuity claim.

It is good to remember that this naturalistic view of continuity also does not represent an objective concept but a philosophical idea, prompted by pre-theoretical premises. Naturalism, too, is a conceptual scheme, a scheme that should serve the facts of experience but cannot be directly derived from the latter. That an evolutionary scientist employs a conceptual scheme is, in itself, okay, for what can a scientist do with isolated facts? Isolated facts do not exist. This way of handling data becomes suspect, however, when the one-dimensional continuity paradigm is promoted as a scientific achievement, dictated by the facts themselves. Then one confuses a philosophical idea with a scientific theory, just to avoid the crucial experience of novelty.[2]

It is as with the birth of a child. Of course, a competent scientist is able to describe the infant biologically, as a particular specimen of a general species, a living organism that developed by cell divisions from a zygote, a fertilized human ovum. No one needs to diminish this description, yet it lacks something very essential. Every mother knows intuitively that what develops in her womb represents infinitely more than what the conceptual determinations of genetics and embryology can tell her. Her baby is a new and inexpressible miracle.

Doesn't something like this also hold true for the human species? Perhaps, at some time, paleontologists and anthropologists will be able to chart the full line of descent of *Homo sapiens* from the pre-hominids. Already, unprecedented progress has been made. Still, a need for an orientation beyond the biological determination remains, especially where it concerns the question of what the phylogenetic

---

[2] The scientistic faith in science as the ultimate basis of truth forces the naturalist to subsume the notion of novelty entirely under standard scientific concepts.

descent implies. Wasn't the becoming of the first human creature on earth also an incomprehensible mystery, particularly the appearance of the awareness of accountability? Where such novelty forces itself upon us, the scientific explanation falters, the philosophical wonder begins, and emergence thought falls into place.

Evolutionary naturalism is a one-dimensional scheme of thought. Emergence philosophy offers a multidimensional alternative. It is a scheme of thought that frees science from the compulsive thinking that in the history of the earth all expressions of life – unicellular, vegetative, sensitive, and mental – cannot have been anything but the accidental results of mechanical causes. Emergence philosophy invites us to let go of this tunnel vision, to view the world with greater openness, and to consider the ontological possibility that by a reconfiguration of reality new dimensions have been disclosed.

New dimensions also began to delineate themselves the moment that humankind appeared on the world stage. Until now we have given a functional analysis of human beings. We have asked for attention to a number of new, mental functions that distinguish humans from animals in spite of their bodily affinity. However, this functionalistic approach, no matter how necessary, is not sufficient in regard to human beings. In the section that follows I wish to demonstrate that humans also surpass animals in an entirely different manner.

2 THE HUMAN PERSON AND THE MASK

Modern humans have descended from *Homo sapiens*, a human species that originated 195,000 years ago in East Africa. At least, that is how old two skulls, excavated in 1967 in the Omo River valley in the vicinity of Kibish, Ethiopia, are estimated to be.[3] I refrain from judgment about the hominids in the millions of years previous to these *Homo sapiens*, beings that shared their earliest ancestors with chimpanzees. In the 1960s it was assumed that there was a direct line of descent between *Australopithecus*, *Homo habilis*, *Homo erectus*, and *Homo sapiens*, even if side-branches that have disappeared were

---

[3] I. McDougall *et al.*, "Stratigraphic Placement and Age of Modern Humans from Kibish, Ethiopia," *Nature* 433 (2005), 733–36.

taken into account.[4] These relations of descent are a topic of vigorous discussion at present.[5] Excavations in Ethiopia and Kenya that started in the 1990s indicate that *Australopithecus afarensis* – representative "Lucy" was 3.5 million years old – was preceded by many species of hominids. These include *Ardipithecus ramidus* (Ethiopia, 4.4 to 5.8 million years ago), *Ororin tugenensis* ("Millennium man," Kenya, 6 million years ago), and, perhaps, *Sahelanthropus tchadensis* (Chad, 2001, 7 million years ago).

Can one conclude on the basis of tools for chopping or scraping and other implements, and fossil characteristics such as posture and brain volume, that hominids were real people? Paleoanthropologists often assume this, not without evolutionistic prejudices, however. What makes a hominid human is the crucial question. That the Australopithecinae used primitive tools does not say much, for this occurs among animals as well. The fact that *Homo erectus* began to use fire at a certain moment is also not conclusive. The question is whether accidentally discovered skills were followed instinctively and imitatively, or whether they were deliberately passed on to the offspring in a tradition that treasured the wisdom it had acquired. A conclusion by Ian Tattersall is significant. *Homo erectus* – a species that departed from Africa two million years ago for Asia, and that remained there, probably until 18,000 years ago[6] – was not found to possess more modern tools than it took along from Africa. According to Tattersall the species took them along but did not improve on them at all.[7] Can one consider a creature with such

[4] C. L. Brace and M. F. Ashley Montagu, *An Introduction to Physical Anthropology* (New York: Macmillan, 1965); C. L. Brace, *The Stages Of Human Evolution: Human And Cultural Origins* (Englewood Cliffs, NJ: Prentice-Hall, 1967).
[5] Stephen Gould, in an oft-cited and telling comment, revealed that whenever he teaches human evolution "I simply open my old folder and dump the contents into the nearest circular file to start from scratch." S. J. Gould, *Ever Since Darwin: Reflections in Natural History* (New York: W. W. Norton, 1977), p. 56.
[6] Two articles in the same issue of *Nature* report the discovery of *Homo floriensis*, a possible descendant of *Homo erectus*. Small in stature and brain size, it is postulated to have lived on an Indonesian island from about 38,000 to 18,000 years ago. P. Brown *et al.*, "A New Small-Bodied Hominin from the Late Pleistocene of Flores, Indonesia," *Nature* 431 (2004), 1055–61; M. J. Morwood *et al.*, "Archaeology and Age of a New Hominin from Flores in Eastern Indonesia," *Nature* 431 (2004), 1087–91.
[7] I. Tattersall, "Out of Africa Again . . . and Again?," *Scientific American* 276 (April 1997), 60–67.

fixed behavior patterns and such limited capacity to learn to be human? To pose the question is easier than to answer it.

Is *Homo sapiens* an original entity? Its area of distribution was world-wide. For this reason a theory of multiregional origination was in vogue for many years. On the basis of mitochondrial DNA determinations, current views have changed. Strong homogeneity in the human genome all over the world and the greater diversity of mitochondrial DNA among Africans than in other human populations speak in favor of the unity of human origins and of the "out of Africa" theory.[8]

Nowhere in the history of the living world does the moment of emergence force itself upon us more impressively than in the process of hominization, i.e. the evolutionary development of human characteristics. The origin of human beings was more than the accidental rearrangement of animal brain functions in some arbitrary ape ancestor, with reason as the result. Human beings arose from late-Pleistocene hominids that had already distinguished themselves by specific neurological and instinctive adaptations. They possessed more brains, more sensitivity, and more dexterity than did their pre-hominid ancestors.[9] These adaptations proved to be an announcement of things to come: the moment when out of a chaos of sensorial stimuli and instinctive feelings, human self-consciousness emerged.

It must have been an overwhelming turning-point when, from among all the hominids that had wandered on earth, the first human being elevated itself, staggering under the weight of newly felt responsibility and answerability. Made answerable and responsible by whom? The neo-cortex, already enlarged in *Homo erectus*, appears to have grown out into a receiver dish tuned in to signals from the Eternal. In the depths of his consciousness the earth creature hears a voice, a voice calling him to respond and to take responsibility: "Adam, where are you?"[10]

---

[8] *Homo neanderthalensis*, a human species that went extinct in the Gibraltar area 25,000 years ago, should probably be considered to be an independent adjoining species.

[9] *Australopithecus* had an approximate brain volume of 650 cc, *Homo erectus* (including Peking man) 1000 cc, Neanderthals 1700 cc, and the average modern human approximately 1400 cc.

[10] "When God said, 'Adam, where art thou?' he did not mean 'Adam, which bush are you hiding behind?,'" H. Evan Runner (Calvin College, Grand Rapids, MI) commented in one of his lectures.

I refer here to the monumental words of Martin Buber: "Ich werde am Du." That is to say: I become in the encounter with the Thou.[11] In the mysterious meeting with a divine Thou, the I dawns. Over against the Other and in the eyes of others, the human becomes aware of the self, turns inward to the self, overcomes the horde mentality, and discovers the right to be there and the freedom for self-realization, no matter in what area. The birth of the person also proves to be the birth of human culture and religion. Do I assert anything new or unheard of? No, I assume any biologist will agree with me: not anatomy and brain volume, but freedom and responsibility, language and technology, art and religion, make this primate a human being in the sense of what we understand human beings to be.

From the point of view of philosophical anthropology, two features are noteworthy in the process of humanization: functional plurality and pre-functional self-consciousness. Humans developed, in the first place, a diversity of modal functions, greater than what one would encounter with any other creature. They already had at their disposal bodily functions that are comparable, from a modal perspective, with what one encounters in the animal kingdom. But they began to distinguish themselves from all animal species by additional mental functions, such as logical thought, economic acumen, esthetic taste, ethical awareness, and religious experience. *Homo sapiens* metamorphosed into *homo rationalis, homo economicus, homo estheticus, homo moralis,* and so on.

But this expansion with mental functions and competencies was not the only hallmark of human beings. More striking is that humankind internalized and began a dialogue with itself. Human consciousness gained a totally new dimension; it deepened into self-consciousness. Behind the multiplicity of modal functions, the individual began to look for the "I," the "self." He groped for the pre-functional root of humankind's own functional dispositions, the center of its being which enables the individual to say: *I* live, *I* think, *I* belief, etc. And this "I" did not only appear to be the

[11] M. Buber, *Ich und Du* (1923); in *Das dialogische Prinzip* (Heidelberg: Lambert Schneider, 1974), p. 18.

center of human existence, it also revealed itself as a sounding board, the center of relations with others and with the Other.

Compare it with a toddler who, on some auspicious day, in the intensive contact with its parents, hesitantly and for the first time uses the word "I." This awareness of the I, this authentic awareness of self-worth over against others, is an indelible sign of human identity. It is not comparable to any signal or function in the animal kingdom. We, in modern times, like to express this identity in a signature, as did our prehistoric ancestors. From Europe to the remotest parts of Australia one encounters in caves, among the drawings of goats, bears, and bison, real signatures: the enigmatic contours of a human hand, outlined by ochre. As if someone wanted to say: "Look, I was here!"

Human self-consciousness has been localized in the prefrontal cortex. But when, in 1848, in an accident, an iron rod was rammed through the cerebral cortex of the American railway worker Phineas Gage – a famous neurological incident – it became clear that the prefrontal cortex was not the part of the brain that must be removed to wipe out consciousness entirely. Gage regained consciousness. According to the Portuguese-American neurobiologist Antonio R. Damasio, consciousness is, naturally, located in the brain and produced by the brain, but it is difficult to locate more precisely.[12] Damasio doubts whether neurologists will ever find a well-demarcated center of consciousness; the cerebral nuclei are multi-functional, employable for diverse activities. In fact, this is an implicit recognition that brain and self-consciousness are hetero-geneous phenomena.

Earlier I already remarked that the consciousness of the "I" was coupled with the awareness of the divine "Thou." The oldest human beings that we know more than superficially are the Cro-Magnon cave dwellers from the late Paleolithic age (35,000–10,000 BC). These people survived by hunting and fishing; they manufactured combs, ornaments, and decorated rods made from bone. Cro-Magnon artifacts from the Middle East and southern Europe suggest that from prehistoric times *Homo sapiens* was

---

[12] A. R. Damasio, *The Feeling of What Happens: Body and Emotion in the Making of Consciousness* (New York: Harcourt Brace, 1999).

fascinated by the mystery of the divine. World-famous are the cave paintings from Altamira (12,000 BC), Lascaux (18,000–15,000 BC), and Pont d'Arc (32,000 BC). These caves were difficult to enter; they impress themselves upon us as sacred domains, furnished for ritual dances and magical practices. This is also indicated by so-called Venus figures: ivory, stone, and bone fertility symbols that were unearthed in excavations from Western Europe into the deepest parts of Russia. Intriguing is a high relief sculpture, possibly representing a mother Venus figure, found in a hiding place in the rocks of Laussel, near Lascaux.

Specific mourning rites were employed as the dead were buried, as discoveries in some very old caves in the Near East clearly indicate. The caves of Pont d'Arc were a spectacular discovery, made in 1994 by Jean-Marie Chauvet and two colleagues. In the central part, surrounded by hundreds of images of mammoths, bison, butterflies, bears, and cats, there is actually a stone altar on which lies the skull of a bear. In the back of the cave one may see the image of a magician, reminiscent of the Sorcerer of Les Trois Frères. (In a cave near Ariège, this sorcerer is depicted as a man, with the antlers of a deer, the beak of a hawk, the eyes of an owl, the tail of a horse, front legs with bear claws; it is, perhaps, a dancing shaman.)

In short, the artifacts and fossils from prehistoric times tell an incoherent yet impressive narrative of evolutionary self-disclosure, in the sense that in early humans new functional abilities emerged but also the awareness of a reality that transcends their functional existence. If we consider the functional structure, a human being is no more than a vegetative, sensitive, and mental system, the latest link in an evolutionary chain over millions of years. When we consider the vestiges left behind in prehistoric caves, then, in the dawn of their history, the early humans crossed a colossal threshold when they, in the depths of their consciousness, received signals from the unsuspected Other. For the first time on earth a creature bowed down in speechless adoration before the unseen source of power of the universe. A spark of mystical longing occurred. A hominid became human. This human being was not only equipped with mental competencies; it revealed itself as a spiritual being in the pregnant sense of the word, quickened with new life, vivified by the breath (*spiritus*) of God's mouth. Here a person began a dialogue with him or herself and with the ground of his being. Here someone responded to the call to be human.

Modern evolution theory measures out the time required for hominization with a generous hand. But doing so has not solved the puzzle of this turning-point in world history nor the human spiritual depth dimension. And I, too, do not have an answer at hand. But that at a crucial moment human beings appeared on the world stage, knowing themselves to be responsible for their own actions, and in freedom decided to cease the struggle for naked self-interest in favor of mutual respect and humanity, no one can deny. Since that time, this freedom and this responsibility – and not just functional skills – have been a necessary condition for every culture and society. They are even the unspoken assumption of every scientific discourse, although there are academics who suggest that freedom and responsibility are nothing but as yet incompletely understood chains of natural causality.

I do not deny that negative aspects accompanied this evolutionary result. Freedom is ambivalent. Responsibility is vulnerable. Brotherhood plummeted to fratricide. In Genesis the question "Adam, where are you?" is followed by the question "Cain, where is your brother, Abel?" In the history of humankind the faint recognition of God often disappeared. In times of the eclipse of God humans began to construct the most bizarre of idols, just to be able to mirror themselves in what is greater than themselves, at times with frightening consequences for themselves and society. Whatever is the case in all of this, neither the capabilities of the human body nor the competencies of the human mind make the human being really unique. A functionalistic view does not do justice to the uniqueness of humankind, for functionalism sees only the exterior and not the interior of human beings. The human being is unique because all the modal (bodily and mental) functions of its being converge and are rooted in the unity of the spirit, to be more specific, in the spiritual I–Thou relation. It is this central relationship that marks what the human being really is: a *person*.

What distinguishes a human being as a person? I would remind the reader here of the actors on stage in ancient Rome. These actors did not wear special costumes or make-up. Once on stage, to distinguish the various actors, they wore only a *persona*, a mask through (per-) which the voice or sound (-sona) came of the figure that they represented and impersonated. Romans soon began to refer not only to the mask, but also to the human being behind the mask, as *persona*. Why? I suspect it is because they wanted to say: not only the personage on the stage but each human being is referring to someone else. There is in every person the voice of another, a higher or divine power that he or she represents and is called to image.

We still refer to a human individual on the world stage, no matter how carefully disguised behind masks and make-up, as a person. On what basis do we do this? Why are there movements such as Amnesty International and Human Rights Watch that, on principle, defend the integrity of the human person? Not on the basis of the functions and competencies in which a human being may exceed an animal, for these are often the functions that have been severely impaired or mutilated in their clients. No, we speak for the integrity and even for the infinite worth of the human person on the basis of the conviction that every person, no matter how battered or diminished in functional capacities, harbors a pre-functional or spiritual secret. In our speaking of the infinite worth of the human person we bring to expression that human individuals transcend their bodily and mental functions. The deepest knowledge of the human being is not contained in scientific knowledge; it is a spiritual awareness of myself. In biblical language we can say: the person is *imago Dei*, created after the image of God.

The notion of a pre-functional center contradicts the functionalistic views of cognitive psychology. If the "I" or the ego, i.e. the core of human existence, is a person, then it cannot be identified with certain bodily or mental functions. Even the language we use – I move, I live, I feel, I think, etc. – shows that the I is a central reference point that precedes the functions in which that I expresses itself.[13]

The pre-functional reference point is not a thing, an entity or a substance; the I is not a homunculus, a human being in miniature

[13] The Bible often refers to the pre-functional human center as soul or spirit. It is also referred to as the heart. See Prov. 4:23, Matt. 15:18. Take into account that these words have various connotations. In the pre-theoretical language of the Bible one does not find scientific definitions.

within the human being. The I does not exist in itself. It is relational, a central point in a fourfold network of relationships. It is, in the first place, related to the many functions in which it expresses itself, and through which it opens itself to the empirical world in its multimodal diversity. It is, furthermore, related to the I of others, because and to the extent to which we are in intimate and personal relationships with others. It is, moreover, related to our selves because we have a spiritual self-consciousness; we can be open to our deepest selves. It is, finally, if we may believe the Bible, rooted in God, because humans are said to be a reflected image of God: "for in you my soul takes refuge" (Psalm 57:1). In short, the spiritual search to our deepest self seems to be, in the first instance, a concentric effort, but in the final instance it proves to be an eccentric or outward movement. Human beings cannot find the ground of their existence in themselves. The eccentric relationship of the human I to the divine Thou is the basis of all other relationships.

One more point in closing: the spiritual status of the human being as a person does not conflict with the phenomenon of atheism in modern society. Atheism is a fact of life. This fact implies that we are able to ignore the I–Thou relationship. We are able to reinterpret it in strictly innerworldly terms by focussing fully on secular values such as health, wealth, solidarity, or power, often personified in idols. However, this atheistic absolutization of immanent values, too, can, in the last resort, be seen as a spiritual position. It can, to a certain extent, be compared to the worship of innerworldly gods (gods of rain, fertility, and the like) in pagan cultures. Atheism, too, can be considered to be a form of spirituality, a breath that surrounds the human being, a matter of ultimate but introverted trust.

3 THE ANTHROPIC PRINCIPLE

Let us assume that the evolution process at crucial moments indeed emerged into higher modal arrangements and finally resulted in the unique design of the human person. Then the question arises: was this a random process? Or is there a purpose in the living world? In the perspective of emergent evolution, all biosystems, including human ones, are rooted in physical reality; as such they are physically explainable as contingent configurations of particles, fields, rays, and matter. But the emergence perspective offers the add-itional possibility of regarding biosystems as expressions of new orders of being, coming to the fore in the complex diversity of living nature. In this perspective evolution is not a circular course of contingent, physical configurations, but a prestructured route of increasingly higher forms of life that are *sui generis* (one of a kind) and that lend themselves to idionomic, typical biological explan-ations. We, human beings, have joined the journey for the final segment. Our human existence demands its own particular explanations of the kind given in the human sciences. As partici-pants we lack insight into the larger picture. But, reflecting on our phylogenetic past, we discover more and more reasons to regard the macro-evolutionary process as a development that, in spite of the blind indifference of matter, is not without a goal. Don't we have reasons to speak of a directed evolution? We surmise a pathway of meaning in the evolutionary journey.

Are we in the world indeed involved in a development that has meaning? And if we say so, what does that imply? For some people "meaning" is the irreversible *direction of meaning* of the physical universe; they link this to the movement from cause to effects, or to time, which moves inexorably from the past to the present, or to entropy as the measure of the random arrangement of molecules. Others associate "meaning" with the functional *directedness of meaning* in plants and plantlike organisms, as for example in a potato or tulip bulb which always grows upward to the light, no matter how we put them into the ground. Yet others associate the word with the instinctive *experience of meaning* of animals, as in the parental care that even the most voracious crocodiles lavish on their posterity. Most link the word "meaning" to the intentional *orien-tations of meaning* of human beings who have a purpose in living, plan their future, and devote their energies to a better world.

There are not many people that have never noticed any sense in their lives. At the same time, it is certain that the experience of purpose and meaning is disconcertingly fragmentary. Our efforts often come to naught through sickness, accident, or death. Isn't the history of civilization a monotonous narrative of rising, shining, and sinking? Haven't most species of plants and animals permanently disappeared off the face of this earth? Isn't the earth a miniscule dust particle that whirls around in a remote corner of an expanding universe? Are there objective indications that a grand plan lies at the basis of cosmic events? Can science perhaps make it plausible that the physical universe is designed in such a way that it – despite or by virtue of blind laws of nature – laid the basis for all higher levels of being and prepared the way for the advent of human beings?

There are indeed physicists who answer a whole-hearted "yes" to the last question. They no longer accept the stereotype appeal to contingency, i.e. chance, and refer to the "anthropic principle" of the cosmos. The development of the cosmos is not based on pure chance but on intention or, more accurately, design. Everything in the becoming of the world, from the Big Bang on, appears to be so accurately directed to the origin of human life that the conclusion of the fine-tuning of the general laws of nature for the appearance of mankind seems unavoidable.

In support of this conclusion, a number of salient points are brought forward. I mention: the expanding universe that has held itself in balance for billions of years; the distance between sun and earth that is so perfectly regulated that liquid water and a moderate climate are permanently guaranteed; the atmosphere on earth that has created necessary conditions for life; the stability of these conditions that have allowed the origin of higher and higher forms of life, culminating in the appearance of *Homo sapiens*, a being that was able, eventually, to reconstruct its own history. This is all, so it is said, evidence of a well-thought-out design, based on the cosmological constants of physical nature. For if one of these physical constants – the speed of light, gravity, the strong and weak nuclear attractions – had initially had a slightly different value, then the human project would have come to naught.

Supporters of the naturalistic continuity principle should not object here: "If cosmic evolution had not accidentally produced human beings it would, sooner or later, have brought other intelligent beings to life!" This argument can return like a boomerang with deadly force. For without human beings there would be no human consciousness. And, thus, there would be no theoretical human knowledge, thus no theories of origins, as formulated by Dawkins and Darwin, and thus also no possibility to theorize about alternative intelligences as the end product of evolution. If the human mind is a mere toss-up, then so is everything that is hatched by this mind, including the naturalistic model of evolution.

Can the anthropic principle be brought forward as an implicit proof of the existence of God, a scientific indication of something like God's plan for this world? The cosmologist Frank Tipler has argued against this approach, correctly in my opinion.[14] The anthropic principle can be explained in two ways, he suggests. It can be explained as an indication of divine design. This presentation of affairs one encounters, for example, in the views of the physicist and theologian John Polkinghorne.[15] But it is not watertight. It does not offer a deductive proof but, at most, an argument from probability in favor of God. For the possibility that the universe is really a multiverse cannot be excluded. Perhaps there have been billions of Big Bangs or beginnings of universes that have all resulted in nothing, except for that one that continued its development, against all odds. This led to such a favorable outcome for human beings that, once they appeared and saw the result, they reacted by speaking of design. This line of reasoning originated with the atheistic cosmologist Rocky Kolb, and is also defended by such evolutionary philosophers as Daniel Dennett.[16] Tipler is correct: no matter how speculative the postulation of billions of universes is, one cannot simply wipe it from the table. Evolutionists are content with this speculation for it allows them to maintain their principle of one-dimensional continuity.

My conclusion will be clear. The anthropic principle can be understood to mean that idionomic factors in nature elicited such emergent developments that they could lead to the origin of human beings. Thus the principle puts the finger on the possible presence of anticipatory moments in nature. But one cannot manufacture these anticipatory moments into a proof for the existence of God. What I argued earlier in the direction of Intelligent Design is also valid here.

---

[14] J. D. Barrow and F. J. Tipler, *The Anthropic Cosmological Principle* (New York: Oxford University Press, 1986).

[15] J. Polkinghorne, *The Way the World Is: The Christian Perspectives of a Scientist* (Grand Rapids, MI: Eerdmans, 1984), pp. 12–14.

[16] D. C. Dennett, *Darwin's Dangerous Idea: Evolution and the Meanings of Life* (New York: Simon & Schuster, 1995), p. 177: "there has been an evolution of worlds (in the sense of whole universes) and the world we find ourselves in is simply one among countless others that have existed throughout all eternity."

That God exists because He designed the world or conceptualized human beings can never be proven in a scientific sense of the word. The bankruptcy of the scholastic proofs of God has taught us that. Science has been given to us to investigate empirical phenomena. But if God is indeed God, He transcends this world of experience or, to be more precise, He transcends the world of sensitive experiences and logical analyses. Then we only know Him in the experience of faith, an experience receptive to divine revelations. Then we do not ascend to Him, but He descends to us, asking for our faith and trust. For the presence of God one can give good arguments, but these arguments are always on the basis of faith, never logically conclusive grounds.[17] A Christian who sees the world in faith can, at most, see in those grounds an intellectual confirmation of what she or he already believed. Just as in a mirror image, the naturalist can find in counter-arguments such as Kolb's an intellectual confirmation of her or his agnostic or atheistic faith.

In short, in the final analysis the anthropic principle debate confronts us with contrasting faith stances, stances which are engaged in a noble competition. The stakes are high: which framework does most justice to the evolutionary facts, a Christian perspective of purpose and meaning or a materialistic perspective of chance and contingency?

4 BIOLOGICAL CONSTANTS? CONWAY MORRIS

I have asked myself whether the anthropic principle can only be based on constants in the physical domain. Doesn't living nature also give evidence of fine-tuning, an orientation to the human species? There are phylogenetic lines that run from the most primitive bacteria of the Pre-Cambrium to the primates and human beings. In this phylogeny we see a piling up of ontological orderings from the basic laws of physical nature and the organizing principles of living organisms to the most elevated standards of humanity. These patterns fit together so tightly that, in living nature too, one

---

[17] Also the Bible directs us: "By faith we understand that the universe was formed at God's command, so that what is seen was not made out of what was visible," Hebr. 11:3. The Bible knows no other entry route to God for the benefit of an intellectual elite.

can hardly suppress the thought of a structural predisposition or anticipation.

Theorists in the life sciences could attempt to formulate a new anthropic principle based on biological constants. For instance, a point could be made about the informational code or universal grammar-rules laid down billions of years ago in the DNA of the earliest biotic or prebiotic life forms. The design of this code has been elucidated by Crick and Watson, as everyone knows.[18] The design is so astonishingly ingenious. The way it stores instructions for the synthesis of proteins in the cell contains such refined information potential that it suggests it has anticipated, from the very beginning, the genetic code of all higher species, including the human species.[19]

Thus there are good reasons to state that developments in living nature too represent an anticipatory process, an anticipatory process in the sense of a directional or purposeful development but without the implication that the purpose is known. The word "anticipate" has a double meaning. In general it means: to be directed or oriented toward a purpose that is going to come. In particular it means: to be directed or oriented toward a purpose that is known. I call the evolutionary process anticipatory in the general sense of a purposeful movement. In nature we see only anticipatory orientations to what is going to come without specific knowledge of a purpose. Think of the bacterium that is preparing for cell division, of the germinating seed that forms a root, or of birds that build their nest. All these creatures anticipate, but they anticipate only by preparing for what is going to come, not for a well-known purpose. In the same way, emergent evolution is a purposeful process: it anticipates what is "coming" but only in terms of what is "supervenient." Lower levels – in the example above the physical constellation of DNA molecules – disclose themselves for information processing at increasingly higher levels.[20]

---

[18] J. D. Watson and F. H. C. Crick, "Molecular Structure of Nucleic Acids: A Structure for Deoxyribose Nucleic Acid," *Nature* 171 (1953), 737–38.

[19] See also M. Denton, *Nature's Destiny: How the Laws of Biology Reveal Purpose in the Universe* (New York: The Free Press, 1998), pp. 277–82.

[20] Christians can say that the world is created with a purpose, e.g. the kingdom of God. An evolutionary biologist can only conclude that evolution is directional, concerned with

The life sciences can make it acceptable that evolution is more than a mechanical procedure with strictly random results. The evolutionary process gives heed not only to physical directives but also to biological constants. Life conforms to "general principles of biological organization."[21] Thus, emergent evolution is not just an accumulation of fortuitous developments in the world. It is also a pre-structured and level-transcending disclosure of the world. In preceding chapters we encountered ontological orderings so closely aligned to each other that there appeared to be a trail that leads in the direction of human beings. In living nature, too, we can discern anticipating moments, and here they also give us thought even though they cannot prove the presence of a divine author.

Of course, the claim that the genetic code of DNA is a general principle of biological organization can, also in this case, elicit counterclaims *à la* Kolb, claims that suggest that the DNA code, no matter how ingenious it may be, allows a naturalistic explanation. A naturalistic explanation based on a "hypothesis" that one cannot exclude, namely that there have been billions of universes and thus billions of potential breeding grounds for extraterrestrials. Most of them failed, but the genetic formula that developed here on earth had, purely by chance, such a favorable result that it could code even for the diversity of mental functions that are peculiar to the human race. I do not designate such phony assertions as hypotheses; I call them classic examples of metaphysical speculation. They are grasped out of thin air. Like all metaphysics, they are irrefutable but also unprovable.

In his book, *Life's Solution*, with the challenging subtitle *Inevitable Humans in a Lonely Universe*, the paleobiologist Simon Conway Morris from Cambridge University has brought this paradigm of anticipatory evolution to the discussion, in his own way, with the aid of the key concept of evolutionary convergence.[22] Conway

processes yet to come. Compare this with the views of an historian. This person will not easily say that world history has a universal purpose, but will admit that it goes in a certain direction.

[21] For these terms see R. C. Lewontin, "Fallen Angels," *New York Review of Books*, June 14, 1990, 3–7.

[22] S. Conway Morris, *Life's Solution: Inevitable Humans in a Lonely Universe* (Cambridge: Cambridge University Press, 2003).

Morris assumes that "emergent properties" and specific "biological rules" determine organic nature, just as Stephan Gould does.[23] Yet there is a remarkable difference between both of them. For Gould evolution is a random, open-ended process without any inherent predictability. Rewind the tape of life, Gould says in his *Wonderful Life*, and the outcome will be entirely different: no humans, for example. Conway Morris argues the exact reverse. He makes the case that the genesis of human beings must have been more than an endless chain of natural contingencies with a fully uncertain result. Evolutionary history is constrained; not all things are possible. Given certain environmental forces, life shapes itself to adapt. Evolution can begin with divergent anatomical starting-points and different routes, but sooner or later it arrives at convergences, i.e., anatomic structures that are not related and yet resemble each other. That makes the evolution of life far more predictable than is generally thought, perhaps not in terms of genetic details but rather with respect to its general forms and functions, i.e. its phenotypic manifestations.

Standard examples of evolutionary convergence in biology are the likeness of fishes and dolphins, and of birds, bats, and pterosaurs (flying reptiles of dinosaur times). The argument is: dolphins are shaped like fish because there exists an optimal shape for moving through water, etc. For most biologists convergence is an exception but for Conway Morris it is a general characteristic of the living world and its development.

Conway Morris mentions a multitude of examples of convergence. There is, first of all, the convergence of organisms. Thus he brings to mind the example of the kiwi, a bird in New Zealand that more and more has begun to resemble a mammal, an animal group that was absent in that country. There is also the convergence of organs. The author points here to the strong resemblance, for example, that has developed between the squid eye and the chordate eye, which has an entirely different origin. There is even, as biophysicists have worked out, convergence on the cellular level. Thus the DNA-polymerase enzyme system has two different origins in unicellular organisms; yet these have evolved to accomplish the

---

[23] N. Eldredge and S. J. Gould, "Biology Rules," 86–88.

same task, the replication of DNA.[24] All these discoveries make clear that evolution does not occur according to sheer chance but that it is channelized and results in biological constants. Thus there might be a course and a direction to evolution. Conway Morris draws the remarkable conclusion that humans are not the random product of biological caprice. Human intelligence is, rather, an expected and even a "near-inevitable" result of biological principles that lie anchored in nature.[25]

The argument of Conway Morris in favor of evolutionary convergence is not indisputable. In many cases his examples bear more witness to a striking similarity or a remarkable correspondence than to an evolutionary convergence in the strict sense of the words. In my ontological theory this is also what may be expected from an area where above-physical laws hold. As we have seen before, above-physical laws are germinative principles (see ch. 4, section 2). They lead or at least they can lead to a variety of elaborations of what in such a principle is involved, and thus to similar and comparable functional outcomes. Let me mention one example. If the suggestion of molecular biologists like Walter Gehring is true that, during the Cambrium, there was a common ancestor of flatworms, mollusks, insects, and vertebrates, already possessing a light sensitive organ (see ch. 5, section 3), then the corresponding eye structures that we may discover in later periods in different phyla have to be considered as a sign of parallel developments rather than of convergent lines.

The referral of Conway Morris to evolutionary convergencies on the level of bodily properties, sensory modalities, and even of mental and cultural abilities, is a challenging thesis. But the related referral in the Preface of his book to "general principles of biological organization" (R. C. Lewontin) is perhaps even more important. The general features of our bodies and minds are not a freak of nature; they are written into laws of the living world. His words give me reason for a final comment. If a complete explanation of the

[24] For the example of convergence in DNA replication see D. Leipe *et al.*, "Did DNA Replication Evolve Twice Independently?," *Nucleic Acids Research* 27 (1999), 3389.

[25] Conway Morris, *Life's Solution*. For discussions of evolutionary convergence see chs. 6–10, of the kiwi, ch. 8. For biological principles and for the "near-inevitability" of human intelligence see the Preface.

living world in terms of physical laws cannot be achieved, as evolutionary naturalism attempts to do, then we can launch all kinds
of alternatives, such as punctualism, spontaneous self-organization,
exaptation, symbiosis, convergence, etc. But if we really wish to free
ourselves from evolutionistic one-sidedness, then we need to graft
these alternatives upon the notion of above-physical laws of the
universe. That is to say, we are invited to ultimately understand
them in terms of a general theory of emergent evolution and
idionomic domains.

In a chapter to come I shall mention other examples of phenomena in living nature that give expression to above-physical
modes of being and that seem to anticipate the human presence (see
ch. 11, section 2). There appear to be interesting reasons to mark the
development of the cosmos and evolution on earth as events that are
not entirely devoid of purpose and meaning. This meaning would
lie in the fact that the evolutionary process has come to manifest
itself to a progressively stronger extent as favoring the emergence of
higher biosystems and disclosing modes of being that are peculiar to
human nature.

5 METHODOLOGICAL NATURALISM

But first I have to make a methodological excursion. Is not the
theory of emergent evolution, in terms of different modal levels
and an anticipatory development, witness to a lack of scientific
seriousness? Does the possible reference to meaning and purpose
that would manifest itself in the enigmatic self-transcendence of
physical in above-physical domains not quickly become a refuge for
unbridled fantasies? Does it not run the danger of itself becoming a
breeding ground for irrational speculations? This danger is not
imaginary. But the opposite danger is no less real, namely that we
pin ourselves down to a one-dimensional world picture and in
advance ascribe an ultimate explanatory power to the methods of
the natural sciences.

When one asks a physicist what caused the Big Bang, 14 billion
years ago, the answer might be: "What a senseless question! If the Big
Bang is what the name seems to indicate, an originating physical
event, then the question of what went before the origin of physical

reality is as misplaced as asking what preceded time. Even if it became apparent that the Big Bang is not the first origin of the universe, one would still encounter, sooner or later, a boundary, i.e. the scientifically unanswerable question of what is the basis of the deepest origin of physical reality." I would add that it is just as senseless to look for causal explanations for the deepest origin of the above-physical levels of reality, whether we are dealing with bacterial or human systems, assuming that these above-physical levels of reality are idionomic and therefore have their own, irreducible origin.

However, the status of physical ordering differs from above-physical ordering at one cardinal point. Physical ordering seems to have originated from nothing. Above-physical ordering has originated, in a sense, from physical forms of being; that is, they have the physical domain as their inevitable substrate. Monocellular organisms, plants, animals, human beings, and cultural systems are all based on modal rearrangements of molecular conveyers of energy. The molecular system forms, if not a sufficient, then certainly a necessary condition for the existence of the higher systems.

This has implications for the methodology of science. The appeal to emergent novelties and anticipatory moments in the living world should never diminish the universality of the physical domain or the adequacy of physical methods. When the phylogeny of living systems brings forth new configurations that are idionomic and require new explanatory models, these novelties do not leave the physical substrate unchanged. Even at the substrate level innovating processes are brought into being, correlated with what is happening at the above-physical levels. However complicated these processes may become – think of the complex household of the cells – they still lend themselves fully to physical and chemical explanations.

Thus our conclusion must be: the recognition of novelty does not exclude the possibility of lower level explanations. To the contrary, all higher expressions of being take place on a material basis, and remain, for this reason, accessible to physical explanations. The person who describes emergent evolution as a saltatory or discontinuous development may not be far from the truth, but is nevertheless missing the subtlety of the situation. Emergent evolution can be defined as a process of descent with modification in such a way that at crucial moments novelty in the sense of level-transcending change does occur, with the proviso that this change realizes itself in a material substrate that remains explicable in more basal, i.e., physical, terms. The level-transcending change implies a discontinuity that cannot be explained from the preceding situation. The realization on the substrate levels implies a continuity that can be explained from the preceding situation.

For this reason I am a proponent of what in the theory of science is called "methodological naturalism" as opposed to "ontological naturalism." In an earlier context I rejected ontological naturalism. I suggested ontological naturalism is not a result of scientific investigation; rather, it starts from a mechanistic and materialistic ideology. It believes that all things, including biological systems, are, in their deepest being, nothing else but material phenomena. Thus it absolutizes the physical explanation of reality.

It is often said: methodological naturalism is ontological naturalism applied to science. I do not agree with this. Methodological naturalism is more modest in its claims. It considers the method of the natural sciences to be basic but not necessarily exclusive. Because of this methodological modesty it does not pretend that everything is *fully* explainable in physical terms and thus reducible to matter. On the contrary, the ontological claim is absent. Methodological naturalism just looks for natural-scientific explanations, including natural-scientific explanations of living organisms and other phenomena with higher-level properties, on the basis of the correct consideration that also phenomena of life realize themselves in material nature.[26] The argument is that higher-level phenomena correlate with phenomena on lower levels, and therefore leave traces in matter that can be detected, measured, and tested with instruments from physics, chemistry, and the like.[27]

---

[26] A. P. Porter, "Naturalism, Naturalism by Other Means, and Alternatives to Naturalism," *Theology and Science* 1 (2003), 221–37.

[27] William Harvey offers an interesting example. In *Exercitatio anatomica de motu cordis et sanguinis in animalibus* (Frankfurt: Fitzerl, 1628), Harvey describes the heart as a mechanical pump for the circulation of blood, a view that induced Descartes to make a strictly mechanical explanation of the phenomena of life. But Harvey himself sees the mechanical explanation as partial and correlative. In his view living organisms are material and more than material. He retains the Aristotelian conviction that in the blood a *vis vitalis* (principle of life) is operational. H. Butterfield, *The Origins of Modern Science: 1300–1800* (New York: The Free Press, 1965), ch. 3.

There are two types of methodological naturalism. In a broader sense, methodological naturalism posits that all empirical phenomena, including those at a higher level, have a basis in nature and thus lend themselves to the methodological research of the natural sciences. This naturalism can therefore be defined as the claim of the natural sciences in general to explanatory competence in regards to living reality. The claim implies that the natural sciences do not offer room for metaphysical arguments or God-talk to give an account of the so-called "irreducible complexities" that would reveal themselves in living organisms.

Methodological naturalism in a narrower sense focusses on physics. It can be understood as the claim of physics to explanatory competence with regards to the living world. This naturalism is thus more specific. It stipulates that all forms and processes of life, no matter how complex, have a physical basis, which makes physical explanations possible. Meanwhile, neither the broader nor the narrower variants establish claims that are exclusive. Neither pretend that the natural sciences are capable of *completely* explaining all phenomena.

Methodological naturalism, in the broader as well as in the narrower sense, has a strong position. The methodological importance of the natural sciences, particularly physics, is based on wide research practices. Take the research of thought processes, as it is carried out today within cognitive neurology. Thinking takes place on different levels; it can be characterized as an emergent phenomenon on a natural basis. On the one hand, it is emergent, for the qualifying function of thought, i.e. the activity of logical analysis, is determined by logical laws, that cannot be found in nature. On the other hand, thought does have a natural basis, for the logical thought activities correlate with neurophysiological processes; in fact they are ultimately based on molecular processes that take place in the brain. Cognitive neurology and biophysics have a variety of instruments at their disposal to chart these processes. What occurs in the brain cells of humans escapes the theory of modern logic but is a continuation of what has been happening in the brain cells of animals for millions of years. This infrastructural continuity justifies methodological naturalism, i.e. the idea that logical thought processes can be elucidated on the basis of cerebral and molecular processes. It does not legitimate ontological naturalism, for methodological naturalism, taken in itself, does not pretend that cerebral and molecular processes are the real and only causes of logical thought processes.

It is clear that our concept of cause and causal explanation needs to be adjusted. Cerebral processes correlate with thought processes; they do support but they do not cause the latter. Causality is level-bound, determined by the idionomy of a domain, i.e. through physical, biotic, logical, or other laws. Causality can never form an explanatory link between the domains. Explanations of thought processes based on natural causes are therefore possible but circumstantial and indirect, for they ignore the peculiar causality that is inherent in logical thought. Logical causality is determined by causes that are referred to as reasons, and that are polished, in logic, to the premises of a logical argument. Reasons are causes in their own right. They are of importance for beings that can distinguish valid from invalid reasons. Reasons are normative, that's to say, reasons are not causes that compel us, but causes that urge us to draw correct conclusions in conformity with logical laws of identity, excluded contradiction, *modus ponens*, etc. Animals have no idea of causes induced by laws of thought. Their behavior can only be explained on the basis of physical and biological causes. Explanation of human behavior demands additional considerations.

The wisdom of methodological naturalism is this: the natural sciences can explain every thing; they cannot explain everything completely.

6 THE PROBLEM OF DAVID CHALMERS

Now it becomes clear why I have so many reservations about the naturalistic explanations of the human mind that are propounded by the philosophy of mind and that I brought up for discussion earlier. Representatives of the philosophy of mind in the twentieth century have constantly stressed the embodiment of the mind, and with good reason. Neuroscientists and cognitive psychologists have shown the untenable position of Cartesian mentalism or cognitivism: the attempt to see the mind as the autonomous center of thought and the will, separate from the body and the material world. They have made it very clear that mental consciousness is sustained by neurophysiological functions of the brain and rooted in the material reality of space and time.

No matter how true it may be that mental and bodily functions go hand in hand, the human mind cannot be reduced to the body. One cannot do justice to the intrinsic coherence between mind and body in a reductionistic or materialistic philosophy. Thought is not a bodily function that has fallen upward. Mental activities cannot be reduced to bodily processes. Neither the early American behaviorism of J. B. Watson, B. F. Skinner, and others, who regarded the mind as a the sum of conditioned reflexes of the body, nor the later identity theory of the Australian philosophers U. T. Place and J. J. C. Smart, who simply identified the mind with the brain, have been able to make this acceptable. In the final analysis these schools of thought were not able to account for the colorful diversity that the mind displays in the arts, culture, and science and that differs so fundamentally from the physiological uniformity that prevails in the human brain.

By evolutionary processes the mind has developed a multimodal variety of competencies. The human person possesses a coherent but articulated variety of mental functions. This is the reason that Hilary Putnam, Jerry Fodor, and others introduced so-called functionalism (after 1960) as a subsequent stage of the philosophy of mind. In the theory of functionalism a sharp distinction is made between a thing and the diverse functions for which it can be used, in this case a distinction between the human brain and its mental functions. This distinction is often justified by making a comparison with the computer. For the computer, too, is a material thing, a piece of hardware. Yet it also represents, from the user's point of view, a multitude of functional possibilities because it can run a great diversity of software programs (music, word processing, data management, illustration, games, etc.).[28]

Still, the difference between the software and hardware of a computer is not comparable with the difference between minds and brains. To be sure, there is also a marked difference between software and hardware. The processor activates software instructions of a very

[28] H. Putnam, "Minds and Machines," in S. Hook (ed.), *Dimensions of Mind* (New York: New York University Press, 1960), pp. 138–64; J. A. Fodor, *The Language of Thought* (New York: Thomas Y. Crowell, 1975).

particular nature. Nevertheless, hardware and software have been designed by engineers outside the system, carefully attuned to each other in a total technological concept. This cannot be said of the system of internal relationships that have developed in the synergy of the human mind and body. That system developed from within.

Furthermore, the computer with its many programs of application is a closed mechanical regulatory system without any awareness of a transcending order. The human mind, on the contrary, is oriented toward transcendent normative principles, i.e., toward logical laws, moral standards, etc., that it follows (and frustrates at times) by a free will. The mind is not forced to follow these principles but feels obliged to follow them; a computer does not feel at all. Norm principles are not part of a closed regulatory circuit; they affect an open mind, a responsive consciousness. In short, mental functions are not technological applications but idionomic competencies that display a fundamental receptiveness for norm principles that transcend and constitute the human mind.

At this point the paradox of every materialistic view of consciousness becomes immediately obvious. Even if, in the future, the program of artificial intelligence – as conceived by Paul and Patricia Churchland, Daniel Dennett, and others – could completely explain human consciousness in terms of motor-sensorial and neuro-endocrine processes; yes, even if it could simulate all mental activities and copy them on silicone chips, then the content of conscience and computer software would still compare like apples and oranges. For with the comparison questions arise immediately. Why are digital computer processes not accompanied by individual experiences, and mental consciousness processes are? Why do people, unlike computers, in their conversations and in folk psychology, time and again, give personal account of their actions in terms of beliefs, longings, and expectations? Why are we, people, so aware of what happens in our brain? In fact, why is the human person human, and not a calculator or a zombie?[29]

---

[29] For Paul M. Churchland see *Scientific Realism and the Plasticity of Mind* (Cambridge, MA: MIT Press, 1979) and *A Neurocomputational Perspective: The Nature of Mind and the Structure of Science* (Cambridge, MA: MIT Press, 1989), where he wants to replace psychology with a hard neuroscience. For Patricia Churchland see P. S. Churchland and T. J. Sejnowski, *The Computational Brain* (Cambridge, MA: MIT Press, 1992). For

It is especially David Chalmers, the *enfant terrible* of the philosophy of mind, who in a pioneering article, "The Puzzle of Conscious Experience," has brought to the fore the fundamental shortcomings of functionalistic physicalism. Chalmers formulates his view as follows. Even if we could solve the "easy problems" of consciousness and could demonstrate in humans a strict correlation, or isomorphology, between consciousness and brain activities, and could explain physically how the brain integrates sensory stimuli into information and translates information into verbal expressions, then we are still left with a final problem: how do we account for first-person experiences? We are left with the "hard problem": "why is all this [brain] processing accompanied by an experienced inner life?"[30] Chalmers states:

> The hard problem ... is the question of how physical processes in the brain give rise to subjective experience. This puzzle involves the inner aspect of thought and perception: the way things feel for the subject ... There are facts about conscious experience that cannot be deduced from physical facts about the functioning of the brain. Indeed, nobody knows why physical processes are accompanied by conscious experience at all. Why is it that when our brains process light of a certain wavelength, we have an experience of deep purple? Why do we have any experience at all? Could not an unconscious automaton have performed the same tasks just as well? These are questions that we would like a theory of consciousness to answer.[31]

All too easily the philosophy of mind has capitulated to the third-person perspective, the objectivizing analysis of the natural sciences. As a result it doesn't know what to do with the human I, with the

---

Dennett see *Darwin's Dangerous Idea*. The elimination of first-person awareness, the phenomenological I-experience, occurs, according to Dennett, through the third-person perspective, the objectification through the natural sciences. He sells the latter as "hetero-phenomenology."

[30] D. J. Chalmers, *The Conscious Mind: In Search of a Fundamental Theory* (New York and Oxford: Oxford University Press, 1996), p. xii.

[31] D. J. Chalmers, "The Puzzle of Conscious Experience," *Scientific American* 273 (December 1995), 80–86. Chalmers searches for a non-Cartesian form of body–mind dualism. See also his book, *The Conscious Mind*. No matter how correct the questions that Chalmers asks are, his theory of consciousness cannot totally separate itself from scientism; it describes the I-consciousness as epiphenomenal, i.e. incidental or superfluous: "Something can be superfluous and still be relevant." Epiphenomenalism is precisely the charge that Searle levels at Chalmers.

first-person perspective of subjective experiences. It is clear, nevertheless, why the philosophy of consciousness, cognitive psychology, and the neurosciences have become so fascinated by ontological naturalism. This naturalism contains a hard kernel of truth. No matter how exclusive the human mind is, it displays embodiment and situatedness. It has incarnated itself in a corporeal being. It has situated itself in levels of reality that it shares with plant and animal organisms. Its exclusivity is paired with an inclusivity that even reaches into the material mode of being. Thus, as far as I am concerned, George Gaylord Simpson may assert: "Man is the result of a purposeless and natural process that did not have him in mind."[32] It is indeed a truth, but this truth is meager fare!

Emergence thought is an invitation to open ourselves up to a richer truth. It is this truth that escapes the sciences, or to put it more correctly, that precedes the sciences. In this pre-scientific truth, residence of our daily life experience, we realize that the third-person perspective of science is rooted in the first-person perspective of our I-experience. The "I" (our ego) is the point of departure of all our modal functions and competencies, including our logical function. I know that the logical function of thought has for centuries claimed a central place for itself as "scientific reason" and is cherished by many scientists as the root of our human existence. But reason is not primordial. Reason does not think. I think. This I-experience is given with our humanity and came to realization, long ago, in the process of emergent evolution and humanization.

But this I, too, does not have the first word. For the I is not a thing in itself. In the way a mirror image is nothing without its original. In the way a person on stage is nothing without the alter ego that is being personified at the spot. The human I is relational, dependent, and has no basis in itself. The I refers. It can only be constituted and thrive in encounters. I recall here the tragic experiences of a number of young children who grew up in extreme isolation or in the company of animals. Time and again it was shown to be impossible to rehabilitate those feral children; their becoming human was broken in the bud.

---

[32] Simpson, *The Meaning of Evolution*, p. 345.

In other words, the objectivizing third-person perspective of scientific reason is not an original position. It is a derivative form of knowledge. It is rooted in an I, in the subjectivity of first-person experiences. That is what Chalmers has seen correctly. But I add: the I, too, is not original. It is in turn rooted in a thou, in the inter-subjectivity of second-person experiences. The human person is addressed. He or she is a you before becoming an I.

With this the mystery of our being human grows. For the I of other people is as relational and non-original as my own I. Although to be human in a community of people offers cohesion, it does not afford a final basis. Where does science, in fact where does humanness, find its deepest basis? Perhaps I may draw the reader's attention to a fact to which all great mystics have pointed through the ages: humans can descend in their soul. Once they travel this road, then the human I proves to be rooted in a divine Thou as its ultimate ground. For this reason John Calvin begins his famous *Institutes* with a thesis that has become almost incomprehensible in an age of secularism: "Man never attains to a true self-knowledge until he has previously contemplated the face of God, and comes down after such contemplation to look into himself."[33]

My final conclusion is that the third-person perspective of science is based on the pre-scientific intimacy of first- and second-person experiences. Yes, the deepest stirrings of the human heart and the deepest motivations which also guide scientists are more than internal deliberations. They have a spiritual birthplace. They touch the divine. Thus we have to reflect not only on the fruits of science but also on the matrix or womb of science. That's to say, science and, in particular, evolutionary science, does not reside in an ivory tower; we need to explore the spiritual context in which it has developed.

[33] J. Calvin, *Institutes of the Christian Religion*, trans. Henry Beveridge (Grand Rapids, MI: Eerdmans, 1964), 1.1.2.

CHAPTER 10

Augustinian faith and evolutionary science

The central question of this chapter is: how does scientific knowledge, in particular the insights of evolutionary science, relate to religious faith? Still influential in Christian circles, especially in Roman Catholicism, is the scholastic model that was developed by Thomas Aquinas. It is a model that sees reason and faith as two complementary sources of knowledge and, for this reason, strives for a synthesis between both (section 1). In this chapter I wish to plead for an alternative approach, a non-synthetic or hermeneutical model in the spirit of Augustine's adage, *fides quaerit intellectum*, faith seeks understanding. In this model faith functions not as an extension and completion of reason but as a source of inspiration and as a hermeneutic frame of reference for rational knowledge, also for the theory of evolution (section 2). Crisis symptoms surrounding this theory lead to the formulation of four hermeneutical ground rules (section 3). At the end of this chapter I shall attempt to bring some of my personal experiences into the discussion (section 4).

1 THE CREATION ACCOUNT AND THE STORY OF BECOMING

Is the theory of emergent evolution and irreducible novelties not a presentation of issues derived from Scripture, and then presented in the guise of science? I must deny this. The Bible is a document of faith: the story of God's dealing with humankind and the world. In this story one does not encounter the concept of evolution, let alone the abstract, scientific notion of emergent evolution. I would not even exclude the possibility that some Bible readers would have great difficulty with the concept of emergent evolution as I have presented it in this book. They may ask themselves doubtfully

191

whether we, human beings, have indeed descended from the family of apes, even if that be via innovative intermediate stages. In any case, the question will arise whether humankind can arise directly from the hands of a good God, as the Bible indicates, and at the same time have originated laboriously through complicated processes of becoming and emergent evolution.

Creation and becoming are not identical. The biblical creation story (Gen. 1–2:4a) proclaims God to be the ultimate origin of all things, including human beings. But the story of becoming which follows (Gen. 2:4b–7), a text unjustly referred to by Old Testament theologians for more than a century as the second creation story, does not deal with the event of creation but with the process of becoming of the world *after* it was created. Earth and water were on hand, and the text recounts how God, in the becoming of human beings, worked as a potter. He molded the clay, thus choosing mediated processes. In colorful, imaginative language the Bible reports, "The Lord God formed the man from the dust of the ground and breathed into his nostrils the breath of life, and the man became a living being" (Gen. 2:7). Creation and evolution are thus not equivalent. There can only be becoming, also becoming in terms of evolution, on the basis of creation.

To create out of nothing is one thing. To cause something to originate out of existing material is another. The first, God's creating act, brought about the second, a world developing in time and space. Creation became the starting-point of time as an endless process of mediated action: of becoming from, and becoming toward. Thus creation and becoming have to be distinguished carefully. God's creative acting is emphatically described in Scripture as "finished" (Gen. 2:1–2). But the processes of genesis, of cosmic expansion and evolution on earth, which have come forth from the creative act, are not finished at all. To the contrary, the becoming process began after the creation. Reality became temporal realization of the potential of creation.

This view of the origin of the world is far removed from the theory of origins that is usually referred to as deism. In deism, God is the creator of the world as well, but only as a clockmaker who, in the beginning, fabricated the timepiece with such precision that it continues to tick along without anyone having to look at it. The

Bible writers speak a different language. They live with the prayer that God will "not abandon the work of his hands" (Ps. 138:8). God guides the process of origination and disclosure, certainly where it concerns humankind, created in his image. Especially in Christ he has made a brand-new start by preparing for the world, broken by sin and ensnared in guilt, a way to its final destination. Creation, brought to self-awareness in human creatures and to wholeness in the kingdom of God, isn't that the ultimate meaning of the history of the world?

The topics of creation, the history of salvation, and the kingdom of God are expressions of faith, grounded in biblical revelation. The opinions about evolution and emergence presented in this book are theoretical concepts, based on rational considerations. Do keep these two separate! Faith is not a primitive attempt to theorize about origins, nor is the God of faith a God-of-the-gaps, an additional explanatory factor to fill lacunae in scholarship. Similarly, the concept of emergence is not a faith vision but a scholarly proposal to deal with the logical, methodological, and material deficiencies of evolutionary naturalism with the help of the idea of idionomic novelty.

To be sure, faith and theory do influence each other; now the question is, how? In an earlier chapter the Intelligent Design theory gave us reason to reconsider the traditional, scholastic view of reality. In the tradition of scholasticism faith and science are displayed as two independent but complementary sources of knowledge, aimed at mutual accommodation and synthesis (see ch. 2, section 3). In his attempt to do justice not only to the idea of separate sources of knowledge but also to the ideal of a synthesis, Thomas Aquinas, in the Middle Ages, called nature (and natural reason) "the preamble to grace."[1] He also formulated the well-known adage *gratia naturam non tollit sed perficit.*[2] That is, divine

[1] Thomas Aquinas, *In librum Boethii De trinitate expositio* (1261; English: *Commentary on Boethius's Book On the Trinity*), 1q. 2a. 3. See J. A. Aertsen, "Thomas Aquinas (1224/5–1274)," in Klapwijk *et al.* (eds.), *Bringing into Captivity Every Thought*, pp. 95–121.

[2] Thomas Aquinas, *Super Sententiis*, 2d. 9q. 1a. 8. The First Vatican Council (1869–70) confirmed Thomas Aquinas' distinction between the natural knowledge of the sciences and philosophy and the supernatural knowledge of the Christian faith and theology. This supernaturalism is also the point of departure of John Paul II in his encyclical *Fides et ratio* of 1998. In it the Pope refers to Augustine as well as Aquinas. He ignores the fact that the

grace does not support nature but perfects it. That's the reason why, according to Aquinas, Christian theology crowns the profane and preparatory work of the secular sciences. From their side, these sciences have to open themselves to their supernatural perfection. Science works by reason; faith has an additional and complementary value. Science can show on rational grounds, for instance, that God exists; Christian theology can then show, on biblical grounds, that this God can be found in Christ and his church.

Aquinas' synthesis ideal was based on pious intentions. Science is autonomous but it should prepare the way toward faith and sacred theology. But this alleged autonomy of reason, although in Aquinas' view relativized and related to the truth of the Christian faith, had disastrous results in the long run. Once it was defined as a profane and more or less secular activity, science began to profile itself *etsi Deus non daretur*, as though God does not exist. In modern times the split between secular and sacred became complete. Science began to regard itself not as relatively autonomous but as a completely autonomous affair. It manifested itself in fact as methodological atheism. And seeing the advances of modern sciences and their impact on culture and society, this methodological atheism became, in a few centuries, a practical atheism. From the nineteenth century on, science without God evoked a world without God.

And what became of the Christian synthesis ideal that Thomas Aquinas cherished? It was totally lost from sight. Even theology, put on a pedestal by Aquinas as the sacred counterpart of secular knowledge, was caught in the bewitching influence of worldly science. It began to judge itself by science's standard and to compete with it. Eventually theology could only make its complementarity come about by using religious explanations and sophisticated God-talk to take advantage of remaining lacunae in the theories of secular science. These gaps in science, it now suggests, must be *loci Dei*, places where God's presence can be detected and where his intervention can be demonstrated. The all-encompassing synthesis ideal of the Scholastic era has shrunk remarkably here! It is fragmented and reduced to incidental referrals to a divine intervention into the

typically scholastic distinction between a natural and a supernatural order of knowledge is lacking in Augustine.

innerwordly order of things; it looks like a *deus ex machina* doctrine. This complementary theology, which we encountered earlier in Dembski's filter theory, is a vulnerable view. For the idea of God as filler of the gaps in scientific knowledge is in constant need of corrections, given the progress of science.

2 *FIDES QUAERIT INTELLECTUM:* A HERMENEUTIC HORIZON

What, then, is the relationship between faith and science? Let us start with the acknowledgment of the idionomic character of the various levels of human consciousness: of religious consciousness (which gives rise to faith) as much as of analytical consciousness (which gives rise to science). We may be able to determine the mutual relationship of faith and scientific reason with the help of the Church Father Augustine. Augustine was deeply convinced that God does not only grant a person faith, but that He is the source of all knowledge and wisdom. Thus faith, according to him, is not irrational but inquisitive. This inquisitiveness is expressed in the famous motto: *fides quaerit intellectum*, faith seeks understanding.[3]

Augustine makes a different connection between faith and reason than Thomas Aquinas. Aquinas asserted that reason is an autonomous faculty of human nature with the proviso that the natural knowledge of reason finds its fulfillment in and thus has to be attuned to the supernatural knowledge of faith. In this way Aquinas posited and relativized the autonomy of reason. Augustine, on the contrary, does not want to posit or to relativize the autonomy of reason. He totally rejects the autonomous position of reason.

Augustine has good reasons for that. He keeps himself distant from the GNP paradigm *(gratia naturam perficit)* of medieval scholasticism and its dualistic basis: the fundamental distinction between natural reason and supernatural faith. Augustine's starting-point is the unity of the human being, created in God's image for

---

[3] The expression *fides quaerens intellectum*, also employed by Anselm, originates in Augustine's saying, *crede ut intelligas* (believe in order that you may understand). Augustine refers here to Is. 7:9 in the Vetus Latina (Old Latin Bible): *nisi credideritis non intelligetis* (unless you will have believed, you will not understand).

fellowship with Him, whose heart is restless until it finds rest in God. The spiritual center of the human being is the heart (in the biblical sense of the word). For this reason, humans by nature have a religious inclination. They have in faith a spiritual impulse, not only to discover God but also to discover the majesty of God's acting in all of His creation. Even the intellectual exertions of science, though they have an idionomic character, are not a strictly independent faculty in human consciousness. They are motivated, in the final analysis, by deeper aspirations, by the natural inquisitiveness of faith. Here we have the purport of the FQI (*fides quaerit intellectum*) paradigm.

How Augustine put his FQI formula into practice could give rise to critical questions, but we deal here with the major topics.[4] The formula states that faith is aimed at rational insight. Not thought but faith has the primacy. Faith is properly basic. But the primacy of this faith is not a token of obscurantism, not a blind trust in authority. Faith can mature into rational understanding. Augustine's view begins with the faithful acceptance of God's Word; this is followed by the attempt to find recognition and confirmation for this faith in God's world. The cognitive interest of science is not a separate and secular human ability. The unfolding of rational knowledge is motivated and stimulated by the context of meaning within which it operates. Knowledge has a need for the inspiration of faith and the light of Scripture, for Scripture sheds light on the problems of everyday life. For Augustine faith is, one could say, the religious framework in which humans try to understand things.

How can we translate this Augustinian vision for our times? This vision implies that neither science nor individual scientists ever begin with a clean slate. In every investigator a religious (or pseudo-religious) belief about the world precedes the theoretical analyses of science. In Christians this religious expectation coheres with biblical revelation. But faith, and the worldview that derives from faith, can also have a non-Christian, a humanistic or even an atheistic

---

[4] In his conflict with Pelagius, Augustine criticizes the rational abilities of the "natural human being" and he stresses the primacy of faith. Nevertheless, in conformity with the intellectualism of Greek philosophy, he tends to present reason as a more exalted level of knowing than simple faith in the authority of Scripture. See A. P. Bos, "Augustine, 354–430," in Klapwijk *et al.* (eds.), *Bringing into Captivity Every Thought*, pp. 49–66.

orientation. Faith and the attendant worldview form the ultimate framework of reference within which we order our theoretical insights; they are the final hermeneutical horizon of our knowledge and understanding of reality.[5] Faith is the determinative interpretative framework of our factual knowledge, for it places all that is temporal and temporary in the light of what has, for us, eternal worth. For example, by seeing the world as a divine creation or, in case of an alternative commitment, as a purely material process, faith sheds light on the problems with which science is confronted, it colors the solutions that are brought forward, and it determines the direction in which scientific interest develops.

Thus the practice of science in a Christian way does not imply the establishment of an alternative paradigm of science, as Dembski and other adherents of Intelligent Design suggest. Christian science is normal science, a methodological standard procedure for acquiring empirical knowledge on distinct modal levels of reality. However, it is practiced in such a way that the tendency to reductionism and absolutization of what is relative is opposed and perspectives of liberation and *shalom* are disclosed.

The great extent to which faith inspires science became clear at the beginning of the modern period. Many think here of the well-known conflict between Galileo and the church, in which the church unjustly intervened in scientific research. I call this conflict a regrettable misstep of a passing nature. More important was that the sources of Christianity were rediscovered, in particular the biblical belief in creation. This belief in creation freed theoretical science from the 2,000-year regime of Greek-Aristotelian metaphysics. First, it knew of an almighty Creator and thus reacted against the notions of form and matter as the ultimate principles of being. Further, it knew of an all-encompassing creation order and thus rejected the idea of a teleological order that would be inherent to nature. Finally, it knew of universal creation laws and thus opposed the dualistic view that laws of circular motion would determine the heavenly spheres and laws of rectilinear motion the sublunar or earthly reality. Because of this hylemorphism, finalism, and dualism

---

[5] Hermeneutics is the theory of interpretation. Hermes was in classical Greek mythology the messenger of the gods and the interpreter of their will.

the investigation of nature at the end of the Middle Ages had become completely stuck. But belief in the unity of the world as a reality created by God liberated theoretical thought from the speculative ballast of these Aristotelian doctrines and from the ancient depreciation of nature. Creation belief stimulated empirical-scientific research. It renewed the most basic questions in science and raised new, hypothetical expectations about the universal coherences of the world, the mechanics of the cosmos, the mysteries of life, and the well-being of humankind.[6]

Why couldn't such a faith also shed light on the scientific questions of our times? Why would it not, in particular, be able to contribute to a breakthrough in the often petrified opinions in regard to evolution? Why would it not be able to help us in identifying the tendencies to absolutize that cleave to evolutionary naturalism? In the evolution debate, too, regrettable incidents can be reported between religion and science. But here, too, the biblical faith in creation, even if it is, in itself, not of a scientific nature, may have liberating effects in science, provided the churches do not, as in the time of Galileo, read in the Bible what it does not say, and provided faith does not push itself forward as a substitute for science by introducing God as a complementary explanatory factor.

Therefore, in the spirit of Augustine, I plead for a non-synthetic or hermeneutic model of the relation between religion and science. In the hermeneutic model, philosophy and the special sciences operate consciously or tacitly (to use a word from Michael Polanyi) within a preconceived context: the interpretative framework of faith. In this formulation "faith" cannot simply be equated with Christian faith! Also the expectational horizon of a non-Christian religion, also the metaphysical worldview of Aristotelian hyle-morphism, yes, even the modern ideologies of ontological natur-alism and evolutionary materialism are hidden expressions of a religious belief; they can be considered as interpretative frameworks in which scientists give meaning to the dynamic of the material and living world. The evolution debate often appears to be a strictly

---

[6] P. Harrison, *The Bible, Protestantism, and the Rise of Natural Science* (Cambridge: Cambridge University Press, 1998); R. Hooykaas, *Religion and the Rise of Modern Science* (Grand Rapids, MI: Eerdmans, 1972).

rational discussion but in my view these rational discussions are ripples on the surface of our knowledge. The actual debate does not take place on rational grounds but, as the philosopher of science Michael Ruse often emphasizes, on a deeper level of insight; religious core convictions are at issue.[7] Religious beliefs play a hidden role in all theories, says Roy Clouser.[8] As long as we do not recognize this religious involvement, the theoretical discussion will remain play fighting. As soon as we acknowledge this religious interest, a really critical dialogue can take place, a reasoned discussion in which we no longer hide but articulate our deepest concerns and motivations with respect to the origin of life.

How do philosophy and the special sciences relate in this hermeneutic context? The answer that follows is given in brief form. Of old, philosophy has profiled itself as a universal science, a discipline that deals with the most general topics. The other sciences separated themselves; they have particularized into specialized disciplines. We can therefore distinguish between philosophy as a totality science and the natural sciences, social sciences, ethics, theology, etc., as specialized sciences. As totality science, philosophy analyzes the mutual relations between the special sciences; it also analyzes the relationship between scientific theory and pre-scientific or practical life experience. Christian faith is part of the latter. Thus philosophy can mediate between faith and science with cognitive tools. Philosophy has to raise the question in what way and to what extent the results of the special sciences are influenced by faith.

In short, not only faith but also philosophy interprets those facts that are brought forward by the special sciences. They are both of hermeneutical significance. Yet there is a basic difference. Faith presents an ultimate or religious interpretative framework, e.g. by speaking of the world as a divine creation. Philosophy is and remains an idionomic science. It offers a conceptual and publicly testable interpretative framework, e.g. by analyzing evolutionary processes in terms of emergent evolution.

---

[7] M. Ruse, *The Evolution–Creation Struggle* (Cambridge, MA: Harvard University Press, 2005).
[8] R. A. Clouser, *The Myth of Religious Neutrality* (Notre Dame, IN: University of Notre Dame Press, 2005).

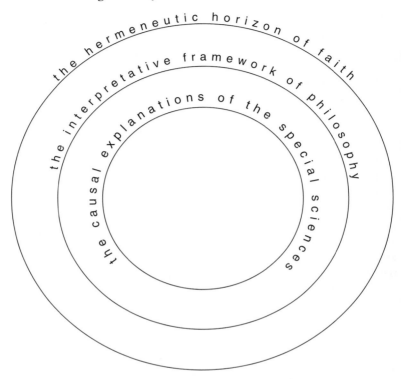

the hermeneutic horizon of faith

the interpretative framework of philosophy

the causal explanations of the special sciences

Figure 10.1 Faith, philosophy, and the special sciences

This description of tasks, of which Figure 10.1 gives a schematic representation, is of direct importance to our topic. The theory of emergent evolution is a philosophical theory. The theory does not explain evolutionary phenomena as biology does, but it attempts to interpret these phenomena in the framework of an ascending series of idionomic organizational levels. Faith in creation or in creaturely orderings probably could support this interpretative viewpoint, but the theory itself is founded on a scientific basis. In short, the theory of emergent evolution is a philosophical view that, being sensitive to the ultimate and all-encompassing hermeneutic horizon of faith, penetrates into discussions of the special sciences by providing an interpretative framework of emergent levels of being, a framework that makes clear how in the genealogy of living organisms continuity and novelty can go together.[9]

The theory of emergent evolution represents an ontological pluralism in the sense that it wants to do justice to the irreducible differences in levels in this world. In the first instance, it connects directly with the objective facts of living nature and with the causal explanations that the evolutionary sciences bring forward. In the second instance, confronted with the new phenomena and general principles of biological organization in this area, it attempts to deepen these causal explanations by interpreting them in the context of an ontological stratification model. However, the more we explore the contours of this interpretative scheme, the more often we encounter the boundaries of what we can explain and understand. What is the coherence, the unity, and the deepest origin of this plural reality? In the final instance, i.e. at the boundaries of the explanatory building of the sciences, we encounter ourselves. We become aware of the human condition. We encounter the subjective choices and the deeply held expectations that lie at the basis of our understanding of the world. Yes, we come face to face with the basic trust that stretches out to the inscrutable mystery of reality, that comes to symbolic expression in religion. Albert Einstein described it in these words: "The most beautiful thing we can experience is the mysterious. It is the source of all true art and science. He to whom this emotion is a stranger, who can no longer pause to wonder and stand rapt in awe, is as good as dead: his eyes are closed."[10]

The mystery of reality demands an attitude of modesty and receptivity, an attitude that we, working in the sciences, can give shape to by means of what I like to call an "open philosophy."[11] Emergence thought attempts to be a specimen of such an open philosophy. On the one hand it attempts, to the bitter end, to

[9] Our conceptual scheme of philosophy (see ch. 9, section 1) is not comparable to the synthesis model held by scholasticism. It does not pretend to be able to correct or complete scientific research from out of faith understood as a supernatural source of knowledge.

[10] Einstein's quotation is from his book *What I Believe* (1930), cited from S. M. Ulam, *Adventures of a Mathematician* (New York: Charles Scribner's Sons, 1976), p. 289.

[11] J. Klapwijk, "A la recherche d'une philosophie ouverte," a series of articles in French, *Hokma. Revue de réflexion théologique* 70–76 (Lausanne, 1999–2001). See specifically: "Prologue. Entre étonnement et perplexité," *Hokma* 70 (1999), 1–5, and "Epilogue. L'ouverture de la philosophie," *Hokma* 76 (2001), 16–23.

explain what can be explained and wants to do justice to the irrefutable indications of evolutionary continuity. On the other hand, it wants to be receptive to what in experience forces itself upon us as possible indications of a newness that is so original that it transcends this chain of continuity.

Faith is indeed related to science and scholarship. It points to something beyond causal explanation and interpretative understanding. Especially the creational perspective of the Bible shows what humankind with all its scientific methods transcends: the presence of a God who is the spiritual source and the ultimate lawgiver of all being. God is presented to us not only as the creator of the world but also the lawgiver. He is the deepest origin of all the creation orderings that have come to light in the disclosure process of time. On every level of reality things can only exist as an answer to divine laws. Whether they concern physical processes, biological phenomena, or moral behaviors, according to Scripture, God's laws constitute the very condition for the existence of created reality. Ultimately it is in the light of these divine laws that even the sciences try to explain the world. All in all, there is good reason to distinguish the causal perspective of the special sciences, the emergence perspective of philosophy, and the creation perspective of faith, and yet, to keep them together. They clarify each other, as text and context.

There is faith that broadens insight. There is also faith that restricts insight. Within the latter I include the creed of evolutionary naturalism. The naturalist, too, encounters the idionomic nature of emergent phenomena and the basic difference between physical things and things with supra-physical characteristics. In practice that person, too, allows for the basic differences between dead material and living reality when he or she works in the garden, takes the dog for a walk, or takes the kids to school. As soon as the naturalist has to determine his or her theoretical position, however, that person can do nothing but flip a switch and, in the spirit of Thomas Hobbes, reduce all expressions of life to matter in motion.

It is often suggested that evolutionary naturalism is based on the objectivity of rational arguments while the Christian faith rests on the subjectivity of religious feelings. This representation of affairs is disputable. The question needs to be posed whether it is, in fact, naturalism that undermines the objectivity of reason and the validity of science. Suppose naturalism is right, and our cognitive abilities are no more than a cerebral tool of bipedal primates, derived by genetic variation and natural selection from the struggle of existence; that would be the ultimate parody! For then human knowledge in its deepest impulse is not focussed on truth but on fitness and pugnacity. Then scientific discussions become boxing matches in the academic arena. Yes, as an extreme consequence of this position we would have to nominate a new kind of scientist for the Nobel Prize, scientists who – like Trofim Lysenko under Stalin and Alfred Rosenberg under national socialism – are willing to use science as an instrument of power in the fight for self-interest. Fortunately we are far removed from such an apocalyptic scenario. Nevertheless, the danger of scientific derailment always lurks in the background of a worldview that, when it comes to critical situations, knows no higher standards than the ruthless laws of nature.

3 PAKICETUS, THE SWIMMING UNGULATE

It has been suggested that evolutionary naturalism, in view of its inherent contradictions, is in a paradigmatic crisis.[12] There may be something to that. Some Christians seek to deduce the correctness of the Bible from this alleged crisis, and to bring creation belief forward as an unavoidable alternative. As if creation and evolution are two equivalent options in solving the origin problem. I'm not going to fall into this trap. The Bible is not a scientific reference book but "God-speaking literature."[13] And the creation story of Genesis 1 is not a theory about the genealogy of nature but an

---

[12] The book by the Australian biochemist Michael Denton, *Evolution: A Theory in Crisis* (Bethesda/Maryland: Adler and Adler, 1985), is well known. See also the skeptical attitude of the DNA chemist Robert Shapiro in regard to current evolutionary theories, in *Origins: A Skeptic's Guide to the Creation of Life on Earth* (New York: Bantam, 1987; London: Penguin Books, 1988). In subsequent work Shapiro appeals to a "life principle," the idea that under strict circumstances primitive organisms shall inevitably emerge: *Planetary Dreams* (New York: John Wiley and Sons, 1999). Proponents of Intelligent Design have also suggested that the Darwinian paradigm is at the point of collapse.

[13] C. Seerveld, "Reformational Christian Philosophy and Christian College Education," *Pro Rege* (Dordt College, Sioux Center, Iowa) 30:3 (March 2002), 1–16; 4.

unmasking of idolized forces of nature, contained in a hymn to the true Origin of the world.

Still, the biblical message, precisely because it desacralizes nature and restores it to its creaturely worth, can be a source of inspiration for science. In fact, it has functioned this way in the western world for many centuries, as a wellspring where modern scholarship could flourish without myth or mystification. Especially at the onset of modern times the biblical message was an inspiring basic experience. The creation account, rediscovered in the original Hebrew language by Reformers and Christian humanists, became an indispensable frame of reference for the theoretical innovations of Kepler, Newton, Boyle, and other great scientists who overthrew the mega-structure of Aristotelian-medieval cosmology.

This story has another side as well. Secularization also increased with the rise of modern science. Agnostics and atheists seized their opportunity. Blind to the meaning of the biblical perspective on creation they succeeded in transforming the desacralization of nature and the revaluation of earthly life as a life before God's face into a purely innerwordly matter, often even into a purely material affair. According to them, there is only matter, and knowledge of matter explains everything. Hobbes, Büchner, Moleschott, and others worked out these beliefs in a colorful assortment of materialistic philosophies which in the nineteenth century converged in the credo of Ludwig Büchner: force and matter produce mind. Finally they grasped at the Darwinian notions of variation and selection to chart the road from matter to spirit in the sense of evolutionary naturalism. And once again Augustine's dictum became true: *fides quaerit intellectum*. In the evolution debate not only the Christian faith in the divine origin of the cosmos but also the naturalistic faith in a material origin of the world can serve as a source of inspiration. Materialism, too, proves to be of hermeneutic significance for evolutionary science.

Every belief can become of heuristic and hermeneutic significance for the sciences, even the most one-sided ideological view. For not only the religious longing for the absolute Origin of the world, but also the pseudo-religious striving of ideologies to absolutize something in the world into its origin has the need of scientific confirmation. Philosophical materialism is a good example. Whoever absolutizes the physical or material mode of being as the deepest ground of reality would want to back up this position with solid arguments and commit him- or herself to a fundamental investigation of matter. This commitment causes something paradoxical to occur. Materialism does not only bias the research of matter; it also fosters this research, in its own way.

We are now in the position to generalize Augustine's adage. We can formulate the following four hermeneutic rules:

(1) Every religious or ideological (pseudo-religious) position develops and entertains certain expectations about the world.
(2) Every pattern of religious expectations condenses itself into a coherent worldview, often elaborated into a philosophy.
(3) Every worldview or philosophy elicits scientific investigations aimed at the confirmation of the position that is taken.
(4) The significance of scientific research is idionomic and thus reaches farther than the expectations and motivations induced by the worldview of its originators.

These hermeneutic rules are also applicable to our topic, evolutionary naturalism. Gripped by the idea that the world has evolved directly from physical matter, and that the biological kingdoms formed according to strictly mechanical laws, this type of materialism has produced all kinds of research programs that probably would never have been developed without that ideological expectation. I do not say that the results obtained have confirmed the ideological starting-point, yet they have made it plausible that life has a material basis, that biological kingdoms show phylogenetic relations and that the mind is rooted in force and matter.

For Darwin too, naturalism – or at least a moderate form of naturalism – was a source of inspiration.[14] I give a simple example. It brought him to the hypothesis that whales were originally land animals that have returned to the ocean. At the time this thesis shocked people, but Darwin's expectation worked its way into scientific research programs. And sure enough, not long ago, paleontologists in

---

[14] Naturalism had a reductive character but no materialistic roots in the thought of Darwin. In a well-known passage at the end of *On the Origin of Species* (sixth edition) he refers to God as the creator of the most elementary life forms or life form.

Pakistan were able to confirm Darwin's thesis with the excavation of *Pakicetus*, a swimming ungulate. A surprising find! The fossil remains show *Pakicetus* to be a hairy, hoofed animal, the size of a wolf, with a smooth snout and a long, sweeping tail. Approximately 50 million years ago the animal moved on land with ease, but it also dived into the sea when this proved to be advantageous. These were adequate reasons for paleontologists, particularly Hans Thewissen, to audaciously present the animal as an "archaic cetacean."[15]

In the history of science, religious and ideological positions often play a double role, sometimes positive, sometimes negative. They can block or inspire the project of science. In the latter case they give motivation and inventiveness to its development. Karl Popper judges that this has been the case with Darwinian naturalism. On the one hand he regards Darwinism, because of its overall claims, to be a metaphysical type of research. On the other hand he acknowledges that this program has given rise to fruitful discoveries.[16] Nevertheless, I would add that success is no guarantee for the future. A spirit of renewal can change into rigid views. The rise and set of Aristotelian natural philosophy in premodern times shows that even a privileged research program can succumb to a paradigmatic crisis.[17]

Is the theory of evolution, as the Australian molecular geneticist Michael Denton once suggested, "a theory in crisis?" Certainly, there are arguments that can be brought forward to support this thesis. For those who support an evolutionary naturalism, and conclude that all phenomena of life – not only the phenomenon of

---

[15] In 2001 Hans Thewissen and co-workers presented a species of *Pakicetus*, and a related species, as "archaic cetaceans" (cetacea is the order of whales and dolphins), the missing link between even-hoofed ungulates and cetaceans. J. G. M. Thewissen *et al.*, "Skeletons of Terrestrial Cetaceans and the Relationship of Whales to Artiodactyls," *Nature* 413 (2001), 277–81. Since this article other fossil animals have been excavated and suggested for this function.

[16] Popper, *Objective Knowledge*.

[17] The prevalent perspective of an ideology can run out of energy. Thus, after Plato's metaphysics, the more empirical approach of Aristotle had a favorable effect on the research of nature. But in the late Middle Ages even the Aristotelian philosophy of nature had rigidified into a totalitarian teleological system. At that time, the mechanization of the world picture was experienced as a liberating, anti-metaphysical position. Methodological naturalism is a fruitful elaboration of this in the areas of material and living nature. At present, this anti-metaphysical approach has changed into ontological naturalism, again a monolithic metaphysics.

the whale but also the phenomenon of science – are fully explainable as end-products of the mechanisms of random variation and differential survival, saw through the branch on which they are sitting. They suggest that science is nothing more than a sophisticated organ that the human species has developed to survive in the struggle for life, in the same way that other organisms have developed jaws or claws. This suggestion is treacherous because it undermines the trust in the independence and emergent surplus value of reason. It destroys the universal nature of science: its orientation toward a standard of truth that – and this has been a deeply rooted Christian conviction through the ages – binds all people together, precisely because it transcends all people.

I come to a paradoxical result. The Christian faith is often regarded as a threat to the theory of evolution, and, yes, it has given reason for this thought on more than one occasion. I am of the opinion, however, that this faith can form a sound basis for a theory of evolution. Neo-Darwinian naturalism, on the contrary, that presents itself as an armored defender of all evolutionary science, appears, in its ideological consequences, to undermine the truth of evolutionary theory; in fact it even speaks against the validity of its own opinions. For this reason I agree with the words of the American philosopher of religion Alvin Plantinga:

Modern science was conceived, and born, and flourished in the matrix of Christian theism. Only liberal doses of self-deception and double-think, I believe, will permit it to flourish in the context of Darwinian naturalism.[18]

The biblical creation motif can be considered to be of fundamental significance for our subject. This is not to say that the Bible, unacquainted as it is with the topic of biological evolution, would sanction or suggest the theory of emergent evolution. But the Bible does offer room to think in this direction, if we may – in keeping with previous analyses – understand Augustine's view of time in

---

[18] A. Plantinga, "Darwin, Mind and Meaning," *Books and Culture* (May/June 1996), 16–18, 35. That modern science came to flourish within the matrix of the Christian faith is partly correct. In the beginning of modern times Christianity still set the tone in the western world but among the philosophical avant-garde, particularly Francis Bacon and Descartes, a secular rationalism already prevailed. In the centuries to follow this would become the standard hermeneutical horizon for western science.

such a way that what God created in the beginning appeared as novel millions of centuries later.

4 PERSONAL EXPERIENCES

Do not forget, esteemed reader, I speak from personal experiences. For years I have asked myself whether there are enough reasons to place the evolutionary process in the framework of a theory of emergence based on the idionomic sovereignty of distinct organizational levels. My reservations were not sparked by creationist sympathies, for I have long felt that in creationism the reverence for the biblical creation account is not free from literalism. Neither did my reservations flow from an affinity with Christianized essentialism (see ch. 12, section 5), for in the essentialist identification of constant species with supra-temporal essential forms based on the creation order, I detected the after-effects of a Platonic doctrine of ideas. Nor was I in the sway of design theories in the spirit of William Paley or Intelligent Design, for there I discovered traces of a scholastic synthesis. Neither did I see a passable route in evolutionary naturalism, for this is a way of reasoning infused with logical and philosophical inconsistencies. The neo-positivist ideal of a unified science was entirely foreign to me because the recent development of science gives evidence of a fundamental diversity of sciences and scientific domains. And, last but not least, it was clear in my mind that the truth of methodological naturalism did not contradict the novelty of emergent phenomena. The way to a theory of emergent evolution and ontological stratification thus seemed to be paved with promising vistas.

Why did I hesitate, then? I wavered because I did not understand which powers could cause new domains with above-physical laws to emerge from lower domains, yes, from physical nature. How could novelties spring forth from physical nature if they were not caused by the laws of physical nature? If they were caused by above-physical laws, where did the validity of these laws come from? If, on the other hand, they were caused by physical laws, then isn't the supposed idionomy of above-physical laws and domains in the final analysis still a mental illusion?

One counter-argument kept me going: that in the final analysis the validity of physical laws, too, cannot be explained. For every physical explanation occurs in the light of physical laws and thus presupposes such laws. Every attempt to explain physical laws would thus amount to a *petitio principii* (i.e. the attempt to prove what is the starting-point in the proof; in logic one usually speaks of begging the question). I found this conclusion to be convincing. The validity of physical laws is unexplainable and yet indisputable. Nevertheless, this conclusion appeared to be too meager for me to subsequently claim the validity of above-physical laws using an argument by analogy.

In this murky situation, faith in God as the creator of the world became for me increasingly significant. I read and reread the writings of the Church Father Augustine, and I considered his concept of time as a creature of God. I felt I could understand him to say that time is a process of disclosure of all the potential that God has enclosed in His creation, thus also the disclosure of creaturely orderings.

The understanding of time as a universal process of disclosure of all that is enclosed in created reality made clear to me that nothing forces us to conclude that the origin of emergent domains with their idionomic regimes was brought about by bottom-up causation on the basis of physical laws. In the revealing light of time, why do we not reject aprioristic reductionist claims, I asked myself. Are we not entitled to accept as original data, beside the physical order, the biological, logical, economic, moral order, etc., in which scholars as well as practical people profile themselves? Why don't we consider these orderings to be realized by time, yes, as successive expressions of what have been the holy intentions of the creator from the very beginning? The deepest mystery of evolution is not the emergence of new realities; it is time. It is the all-embracing process of time that, from the origin of the cosmos, again and again has brought new realities to light.

For good reason, evolutionary naturalists emphasize moments of chance and randomness in the evolutionary process. But do they prove in this way the omnipotence of physical laws and the contingency of life? The facts speak a different language. Random events have unchained orderings that are anything but random. Contingency catalyzes functionality and purpose; it has elicited, again and again, higher and more complex levels of meaning. Thus believing people have good reasons to say that God called the physical nature into being and that He, at the same time, incorporated all higher levels of ordering into His creation as potentials from the beginning. Thus they are also justified in saying that humans are, at the same time, a product of evolution and created according to God's image. Darwin's theory does not undermine the picture of creation but clarifies it.

In the light of this conclusion I present the fundamental diversity of emergent domains and idionomic laws as a scientifically justified hypothesis, even as a not-unimportant ontological paradigm that is attuned to the empirical facts. Moreover, I place this diversity, for myself, in a religious-hermeneutic context. I do not, however, lose the difference between the scientific perspective and the religious framework from sight. The theory of emergent evolution and ontological stratification is in itself a hypothetical proposal that needs to be tested scientifically. The religious framework in which I situate it is for me a spiritual incentive to explore the pluralistic image that I have formed of the world with a greater scientific openness than would ever be possible in the reductive climate of Darwinian naturalism.

CHAPTER II

The organism is a whole.
The world is a habitat

Emergent evolution is a theory that is of importance for the life sciences for various reasons. First, it dispenses with the Aristotelian idea that life originated by *generatio spontanea* (spontaneous generation of life from inanimate matter), a view that was disproved by the bacteriologist Louis Pasteur in 1862 but, under the term "abiogenesis," is still secretly cherished by evolutionists. The theory also liberates us from the twist of thought that reason is the sheer product of an evolutionary process that was discovered by that very same reason. Furthermore, it causes us to reflect on the question of whether the standard picture of evolution pushes us into a physicalist straightjacket. It also draws our attention to the many sides of the evolutionary process: its idionomic development on physical, biotic, vegetative, sensitive, and mental levels. It also focusses us on the question of how, in a living organism, higher and lower functions correlate and how basal functions contribute to the unfolding of higher life forms. Finally, it confronts us with another kind of correlation: the question of how the evolution of life forms is accompanied by changes in the surrounding world.

The correlation problem brings us into contact with the direction in philosophy that is known as holism. Thus, in this chapter I first give a brief introduction to the concept of holism (section 1). I then ponder the last two points: the correlation between higher and lower functions in the totality structure of a living organism (section 2), and the correlation between an organism and its environment (section 3). Subsequently I ask for attention to the globalizing implications of the holistic view (section 4). I round off this chapter with some comments about alternative forms of holism (section 5).

I J.C. SMUTS, HOLISM, AND EVOLUTION

"Holism" is a term derived from the work of the South African general, statesman, and scholar Jan Christiaan Smuts: *Holism and Evolution*. Holism is, literally, thinking in wholes, in accord with Aristotle's aphorism: "The whole is more than the sum of the parts." Indeed, wholes often display new and different characteristics that are not present in the constituent parts. That's the reason why there is a certain affinity between holistic thought in its interest in wholeness and emergence thought in its interest in newness.[1]

Two kinds of holism can be distinguished: a primary form that has little to do with emergence, and a pregnant form that has much to do with it. Primary holism deals with the part–whole relation that one might encounter on a single level of being, e.g. the physical (in the relation of atoms to the molecules made up from these atoms), the vegetative (in the relation of cells to the tissues these cells make up), or the logical-analytical (in the relation of concepts to the proof that is built up from them). The novelty of these level-bound wholes is relative. Take the liquid character of water. Under certain conditions liquidity is a characteristic of water as a whole, not of the parts, i.e. of the individual H_2O molecules. Nevertheless, this liquidity of the whole can be explained from the structural characteristics of the atoms and molecules that make up water. No wonder, for whole and part are subject to the same physico-chemical laws; the behavior of the whole can be explained from the structural characteristics of the atomic and molecular parts. The liquid character of the water is a novelty but not in the sense of emergent newness.

An entirely different matter is the pregnant form of holism that Smuts had in mind. This kind of holism brings us into contact with wholes that cannot simply be reduced to a junction of already existing components. It draws our attention to configurations of being with properties that are original and that cannot be fully explained by the characteristics of the constituent parts. These

---

[1] Holism can be seen, in general, as a reaction to the separation philosophy that, from the time of Descartes, has characterized modernity by making a fundamental opposition between subject and object, soul and body, reason and world.

irreducible wholes exhibit entirely new qualities. Here Smuts had in mind the properties one encounters in the "organized complexity" of living organisms. The properties of such wholes can be designated as emergent. When I discuss holism in this chapter, I specifically deal with this pregnant form of holism.

I return to my starting-point. We have encountered two forms of correlation. First, we concluded that in an organism the higher and lower functions correlate, i.e. they form a whole in the sense of one totality structure. We then concluded that the organism and the milieu in which it lives correlate, that is, they form a whole in the sense of one habitat of life. I see the totality structure, discussed in the next section, as well as the habitat of life, discussed in section 3, as two instances of pregnant holism. It is worthwhile to consider their implications.

2 ENZYMES, NEURONS, AND EMOTIONS

In the process of emergent evolution living things manifest themselves as a totality structure with a qualifying mode of being that is irreducibly new. How can one logically bring together a phenomenon that is in itself well known with such a new mode of being? We should note that the latter is not a surplus added to an otherwise unaltered substrate. Emergence implies innovation of the total structure of the phenomenon in question. Morgan and Alexander have already pointed out that, in emergence, innovation also occurs in the substrate of the structure in which emergence arises. Take sensitive observation. It is a novelty that is typical of animals, and foreign to plant and unicellular organisms. Nevertheless, the sensitive capacity was only capable of being realized in the animal system through a general adaptation of the physical, biotic, and vegetative substrate, among other things by the development of hormonal substances, nerve cells, and sensory organs.

Every form of life, including the biosystem of bacteria and plants, can be seen as a whole, an integration of modes of being, or, in the terminology of François Jacob, as a *holon* or *integron* (see ch. 6, section 3). In every living organism a totality structure presents itself that transcends the physical domain. This state of affairs cannot be undone by a one-dimensional, materialistic appeal to "the closed system of Nature." Of course, I do not detract from one of the most fundamental principles of physics, the law of conservation of energy, which is of decisive significance for closed systems in the physical domain. But this law does not take away from the fact that in living organisms subjacent functions, including the physical, have opened themselves up to higher functions and are attuned to the highest or qualifying function of that organism.

Each phenomenon of emerging evolution can be seen as an incisive step in the process of disclosure of the world. In view of this fact, one may perhaps speak of interdependence between emergence and evolution. In any case it is certain that emergence takes advantage of evolution. In an organism the disclosure of a super-structure is dependent on the evolution of the infrastructure. Thus in the origin of life on earth the specific biotic function of bacteria could only shape itself after a whole series of material conditions was met. Some of these necessary conditions were the cooling of the earth's surface, the separation of land and oceans, the polymeriza-tion of molecules, and the crystallization of amino acids, nucleot-ides, and protein aggregates. Similar pre-adaptations occurred with respect to the vegetative function of plants, the sensitive function of animals, and the mental functions of humans. These, also, could only realize themselves when in certain organisms the evolutionary process had prepared the necessary sub-structures.

Could the converse also be true? Can we say: evolution takes advantage of emergence? No matter how incomprehensible this may be, it appears at times – I express myself carefully – that the process of becoming on earth, despite its capricious and unpredictable course, did indeed anticipate the biological forms that were forth-coming. Is it possible that chance and anticipation go hand in hand?

In a previous chapter I recounted the thesis of Monod, that new forms of life were a successful gamble as much as the lucky numbers in the casinos of Monte Carlo. Perhaps he is right! Perhaps the development of life is a gamble . . . and, at the same time, more than that. To understand the latter one shouldn't talk to the gamblers in Monte Carlo, but rather to the bookmakers and bankers. For it is the people with big money who have discovered that games like roulette and backgammon can be arranged in such a way that, in spite of all risks and uncertainties, the organizers acquire winnings in the long run. These people have overcome the gamble of the game with their design of strategic rules based on the laws of chance. My question is this: can't the processes of evolutionary change on earth have been something like that, an unpredictable gamble and at the same time an occurrence governed by strategic rules? If so, then they would be contingent and, at the same time, scripted. They would anticipate novelties, structural changes, and long-term gains for life. I give three examples of anticipation for consideration, one on the physico-chemical, one on the biotic, and one on the sensitive level.

My first example deals with enzymes. At some point in time unicellular organisms emerged from the aggregation and polymerization of molecules. The emergence of these unicellular systems could only succeed through the timely availability of biochemical substances, including enzymes.

In chemistry one encounters catalysts, often metals or metal-containing compounds, that serve as accelerators of chemical reactions. Biological systems also possess catalysts: enzymes that can speed up metabolic reactions in all forms of life, from sulfur bacteria to human beings. Enzymes have evolved from inanimate matter. Given their modal basic function, they are not more than complex physico-chemical structures, proteinaceous substances that one encounters in the living cell. Also the catalytic action of enzymes, taken in itself, is not biotic but chemical in nature. For this reason, this action can, in certain circumstances, also take place outside the living cell. Think of enzymes in detergents used in the home.[2]

Nevertheless, enzymes have their primary and principal significance in living organisms. Speaking in ontological terms, they have besides a physical function a biotic function that is not to be ignored. Enzymes have a key position in processes of homeostasis. They are an indispensable condition for life, yes, an integral component of the biological cell in the service of the maintenance of life. Evolutionary theoreticians assume that in the history of the world enzymes evolved right alongside other parts of the cell. Indeed, but the problem is that even in the very earliest prokaryotes

---

[2] These detergents are mixtures of inorganic substances with an enzyme component produced by bacteria.

enzymatic substances must already have been available in a pre-liminary form at the moment of their origin. It is as though these prospective enzymes, despite their accidental physical origin, con-stituted themselves at just the right moment to make the coming of life on earth possible. In that sense I can hardly avoid speaking of anticipation: an anticipation of novelties that took place on the physico-chemical level. In short, enzymes are chemical substances, yet they have presented themselves just in time to be indispensable basic ingredients for the origin of living organisms.

My second example is more complex; it deals with neurons. Living organisms react very differently to external stimuli. Unicel-lular organisms react directly to stimuli from their environment, even if amoebae and ciliates do this differently from simple bacteria. The reactive pattern of plants is more complicated. Stimulus and response are not directly related but the relation is mediated by organs that plants have developed (roots, leaves, flowers, etc.) to enable them to deal with the possibilities and limitations of the environment. The relationship between animals and their environ-ment is even more intricate.[3] The bodies of animals are also equipped with organs and attuned to the *Umwelt*, i.e., to the world in which the animal lives, but external stimuli are processed internally. The response is steered by observation and inner experience. The sus-ceptibility to stimuli that is common to all living organisms is here sublimated to a sentient response. Susceptibility to stimuli is not just a sensitive surplus. It implies a renewal of the total reaction possibilities of the animal system, and in this neurons or nerve cells play a central role.

I want to elucidate this. The cells in the body of all living organisms have a reactive structure. In animals, however, right down to the most primitive cnidarians and flatworms, nerve cells have developed, in addition to skin, connective tissue, and muscle cells. In animals the sensitive function correlates with the vegetative function of the body. Thus feelings of hunger, fear, and sexual excitement in higher animals go together with a neural stimulation of sensory organs. In lower animals sensibility, in the absence of sense organs, is coupled to synaptic stimuli and the transmission of

---

[3] I do not consider sponges in this discussion.

impulses between connected nerve cells. With invertebrates, which lack brains and where the nervous system consists of a few nerve ganglia, sensitivity is located in these knots of nerve cells. Even in minute multicellular animals sensibility is present, related to elementary nerve pathways in the body surface.[4] In all these animals the nerve cells transmit stimuli from outside the body to other nerve cells, to muscles, and to other organs.

Neurons do not display feelings. They do not, themselves, belong to the sensitive level. They do seem to anticipate it. Being a part of the organic (vegetative) infrastructure, neurons have, in the evolutionary process, laid the groundwork so that animal feelings could unfold. In short, the nervous and endocrine systems of the body, already present in simple form in invertebrates, are in themselves insensitive, yet they have developed into an integral part of the sensitive totality structure of animals.

My third and most complex example concerns emotions. The emergent development of consciousness in humans is based on underlying feelings but has also changed these feelings drastically. Originally there were animal feelings, but in the totality structure of the human person they were transformed into typical human feelings, known as emotions.

Contrary to William James, who described an emotion simply as "a feeling of bodily changes,"[5] I make a distinction between feelings and emotions. Animals have feelings such as hunger, pain, sexual urges; they share these feelings with human beings. People also have feelings of a different sort: emotional feelings such as rage, shame, humor, and compassion. Emotions, too, are bodily feelings; they are often paired with accelerated heart rate, tension, etc. But remarkable about emotions is that they have content, they are feelings *about* something. They do not only say something about the emoting subject but indirectly also about the concern in which

---

[4] In protozoa and sponges primary nerve cells are lacking. Here fibrils present in the protoplasm can transmit stimuli. It is very questionable whether one can speak in unicellular organisms of sensitivity, or *petites perceptions*, as Leibniz uses the word. In plants the situation is different again. Devoid of any perceptive abilities they only show irritability, i.e. receptivity to their environment, for example to the light used in photosynthesis and photoperiodic regulation.

[5] William James, "What is an Emotion?," *Mind* 9 (1884), 188–205: "Our feeling of the [bodily] changes as they occur *is* the emotion" (pp. 189–90).

this knowing subject is emotionally involved. Emotions take place on the sensitive level, as do other feelings, but they are concerned with – that is, they anticipate – a higher level affair, i.e. the intentional content of human consciousness.

This point, too, I wish to clarify. For good reasons cognitive psychology during the 1970s disassociated emotion from the corporeal explanatory model of William James and the mechanistic stimulus/response model of behaviorism. Emotion is, indeed, more than a bodily reaction. However, today there is too much of an opposite tendency, insofar as emotion is now defined as a cognitive attitude. The opinions of the American philosopher Robert Solomon are well known. In his book, *The Passions*, he describes emotion as a cognitive judgment. Emotions would thus not be causal mechanisms but intentional orientations, not irrational or bodily impulses but propositional attitudes.[6] With this cognitive interpretation Solomon runs the danger of losing sight of the bodily and sensitive aspects that are an essential characteristic of the emotions. The cognitive interpretation provides no answer to the question of why emotions so often appear to us as irrational, as not open to reasonable arguments. Others are more careful. They suggest correctly that cognitions are antecedents of emotions but not constituents. They precede emotions but they are not part of them.[7]

An e-motion is, literally, an out-movement: a feeling that is not primarily steered by inner needs but by external factors, that is to say, by a mental representation. I can be emotionally moved by what strikes me mentally: the image of war casualties, a deed of self-sacrifice, a heroic act, a beautiful goal. Mental images call forth

---

6   Solomon designates emotions as "an evaluative (or normative) judgement, a judgement about my situation and myself and/or about all other people." Describing them further, he says: "They are extremely subtle, cunning, sophisticated, cultured, learned, logical, and intelligent." R. C. Solomon, *The Passions* (New York: Anchor Press/Doubleday, 1977), pp. 187, 430. Martha Nussbaum tends toward a similar viewpoint when she defines emotions as intelligent value judgments, appraisals that provide us with insight into what and who we value, and that are, for that reason, indispensable for self-development and as pillars for morals. M. Nussbaum, *Upheavals of Thought: The Intelligence of Emotions* (New York: Cambridge University Press, 2001).

7   W. Lyons, *Emotion* (New York: Cambridge University Press, 1980); R. B. Zajonc, "Feeling and Thinking. Preferences Need No Inferences," in *The Selected Works of R. B. Zajonc* (New York: John Wiley & Sons, 2003), ch. 14.

emotions in the form of social engagement, religious ecstasy, moral sensibility, esthetic wonder.

Sometimes people say: only a person can be truly happy or sad. Why only a person? Because it is only of a person that one can say he or she has good reasons for it, reasons that are supplied by the mind. Reading Kafka or Kierkegaard, one realizes how much emotions of shame, remorse, anguish, or doubt offer a bodily basis for the struggles of the mind. Thus, a human being is more than the sum of body and mind. The emotions build a bridge. They well up in the body but they anticipate the mind. They arise spontaneously without complicated reasoning and attach themselves as feelings of sympathy or antipathy, approval or aversion, etc., to all those concerns over which the mind forms judgments. Emotions are just that, feelings, but feelings with antennae. Thus my thesis is: emotions are oriented feelings, feelings that reflect concerns with which we are cognitively and intentionally engaged. The emotion itself is not intentional; it is a "feeling towards" (Peter Goldie): a sentient urge toward a more-than-sentient concern.[8] Why can only people, overcome by emotions, blush, laugh, or cry bitter tears? Because they have good reasons for it!

In summary, no matter how one puts into words the coherence of higher and lower modes of being – in terms of anticipation or interdependence – enzymes, neurons, and emotions appear to function as intermediaries in a totality structure that needs to be holistically understood. In the process of evolution the appearance of an emergent mode of being is not an event that leaves the basis unaffected. To the contrary, basis and superstructure correlate. Emergence is inclusive. It is dependent on a preceding or simultaneous rearrangement of the subjacent modes of being. To put it another way, what is considered to be, from a functionalistic viewpoint, a process of emergent development, can be considered to be, from a holistic viewpoint, a process of internal disclosure.

Nowhere does the integral renewal of structure so prominently come to light as in human beings. Phylogenetically and ethologically,

---

[8] P. Goldie, *The Emotions: A Philosophical Exploration* (Oxford/New York: Clarendon Press, 2000). Goldie correctly emphasizes that emotions are feelings. However, to distinguish them from moods, he continues to describe them in terms of intentionality, as Sartre and Solomons do.

humans are closely related to animals. Instinctive and animal traits are therefore not foreign to them. As spiritual beings, persons have these traits under control; they are integrated into the humanity and dignity of the person. Persons take responsibility for feelings and behaviors, right down to the hidden wink and the smallest gesture. These are integrated in a process of free actualization of the self. Human beings – I assume normal circumstances – have become accountable for the entirety of their actions. Their affinity with animals is biologically undeniable, but it is transformed and integrated into a new, typically human, totality structure. This human totality structure transcends the totality structure that is unique to animals. Just as the totality structure of animals transcends that of all the organisms that precede it. And just as the totality structure of all living things is a grand triumph over the regulated order of inanimate matter. In other words, the hierarchy of modal forms and functions that we described earlier reveals itself as a hierarchy of transcending totality structures. The theory of emergent evolution is a perfect paradigm of holism!

3 THE LIFE-WORLD

Living organisms not only profile themselves as totality structures with correlative relations between the higher and lower modal functions, they also manifest themselves as structures that have close correlative relations with their environment. This relationship to the environment can be designated as the life-world.

I would note that philosophers usually understand the concept of life-world in a rather exclusive way, namely as the world in its specific significance for human individuals. The ideas of the German philosopher Martin Heidegger are illustrative. Heidegger came to the overwhelming conclusion that humans cannot be defined as animals endowed with reason and confronted with a material world. To the point, he describes the human being as *Da-sein*, i.e. as "being-there" or "being-in-the-world." With this he suggests that the human being and its life-world are inseparable. They are so inseparable that we cannot say a sensible thing about human individuals without including the world in which they live, or a sensible thing about the world without realizing that this world is as humans experience it.

The life-world is a thoroughly human world, full of meanings that we as people attach to things, whether it concerns natural things, cultural products, or social phenomena. The person who thinks that one can only view a thing correctly with the detached view of a scientist or technocrat is alienated from him- or herself and the world. With the objectifying view of science we precisely lose the real world from view, the world in which we relate to each other and care for each other. Human existence and the life-world, subject and object, belong together from the very beginning. In the understanding of ourselves we implicitly include the world and our fellow humans. And in our dealings with the world and fellow creatures we implicitly meet ourselves, for in every word and gesture to the other, we realize ourselves.

The tragedy of our times, according to Heidegger, is that we have sold our souls to science and technology, i.e. to a sterile, rational approach *to* and control *over* the world. In doing so, we have broken the bond that connects us *with* the world. We have adopted the scientistic model that Descartes introduced in modernity. In this model, the human being is a rational subject. All other things are objects of rational knowledge and technological control. All things, including living organisms, thus change into inanimate mechanical objects. In the Cartesian thought model a radical split has been effectuated between humans and world, as subjects and objects. We, moderns that we try to be, have appropriated this subject/object split in our everyday practice.

And what a price this has cost us! We have objectivized the world into a conglomerate of things at our disposal, over which we decide and can exert control. We have cut the ties that bind us to the world. Scientism has resulted into separation thought, and this separation philosophy has resulted in a destruction of the life-world. We no longer feel at home in the world. We suffer from self-alienation, dehumanization, disorientation, loneliness, anguish, and meaninglessness. That we are overcome by such negative feelings is for Heidegger proof positive that human beings and the world, in the deepest sense, belong together. A livable world demands engaged people. And engaged people demand a world with a human face, a world in which we feel at home and recognize ourselves.

Separation thought demonstrates the need for holism thought. In the spirit of Heidegger one could say that we must learn to see the world again in holistic terms and in an ecological perspective. Our world is an integral unity. It is an ecosystem, a world in which people have found their home (*oikos*). In this home human subjects are concerned with fellow subjects and objects in their surroundings with an attitude of care.

Heidegger applied the concept of the life-world to the coherence of the human subject with its fellow humans and with surrounding things. I have to correct this human-centered vision, a tough remnant of Cartesian philosophy. I propose, in this section, to generalize the concept of life-world, and to apply it to the coherence of all living beings and their habitat. In all of nature we find animate and even inanimate things that are equipped with subjective abilities and with relationships with their surroundings or, as biologists are wont to say, their *Umwelt* or *niche*. These non-human subjects we can indicate as "natural subjects." Noting their qualifying function, we can typify these natural subjects as physical, biotic, vegetative, and sensitive subjects.

In modern philosophy humans have elevated themselves to the status of exclusive subjects of the world. All other things, including living organisms, are reduced to objects of rational knowledge and technological control. However, if we place human beings in the great perspective of emergent evolution and ontological stratification, a perspective in which all things and all organisms manifest themselves as entities in their own right, then the exclusive position of the human as subject evaporates. Thus we have to bid farewell to Descartes, and indirectly to Heidegger too, in order to do justice to the subjective character of nature. My proposal requires a drastic change, not only of our thought but also of our language with respect to subjects and objects. GTEE, the general theory of emergent evolution, implies the notions of ontological hierarchy and stratification. In such a theory of modal levels we have to define anew (1) what is a subject, (2) what is an object, and (3) what is their mutual relationship.

(1) The notion of a thing as a natural subject must be central. Things in nature are, in themselves, not objects, i.e. things seen from the analytical perspective or value-judgment of the human

subject. Things have an intrinsic worth. We have come to know them as entities equipped with an idionomic diversity of modal functions and properties. Thus they can be called subjects in the authentic sense of the word: they are subjected to modal laws. Examples abound. A quartz crystal is a physical subject. A sulfur bacterium, too, can be seen as a physical subject but at the same time it qualifies itself as a biotic subject. A pine tree is a physical and biotic subject but it qualifies itself as a vegetative subject, etc. The basis of thought is that natural entities such as minerals, bacteria, plants, and animals present themselves as idionomic subjects because they have different modal functions and heed different modal laws. Thus these modal functions can be described as "subject functions."

(2) On levels where a natural entity is not a subject, it can nevertheless be present as an object. A thing in nature that presents itself as a subject on a lower level can, at the same time, be an object at a higher level. Then it is an object in the sense that it is an essential component of the habitat of organisms that manifest themselves on this emergent level. It obtains an objective meaning for the subjects that are present here. I will again give some examples. Hydrogen sulfide is in itself a physical subject, but in the evolution process that took place, eons ago in ancient oceans, it emerged into a biotic object for the sulfur bacteria that, since then, as biotic subjects, take up the hydrogen sulfide and metabolize it into sulfate. A pine tree is a vegetative subject, but with the advent of the animal kingdom it emerged as a sensitive object; since that time the pine tree has had an objective significance as a refuge for birds, squirrels, and other animals. Thus, emergent evolution is to be seen as an ascending development with ecological implications, for not only organisms but also the surrounding entities gained an ontological surplus value. They brought new qualities to light, which correlated with the subjective characteristics of the organisms involved. These additional qualities of things can be called "object functions." For the sake of completeness I add that, with the coming of *Homo sapiens*, things in nature also gained significance as objects on a mental level. They became logical objects, artistic works, economic wares, juridical goods, etc. In that specific sense one can, in the spirit of Descartes, designate nature as an object for

	Minerals	Bacteria	Plants	Animals	Humans	
mental object					↑ → mental subject	noosphere
sensitive object				↑ → sensitive subject		zoosphere
vegetative object			↑ → vegetative subject			phytosphere
biotic object		↑ → biotic subject				biosphere
↑ → physical subject						cosmosphere
	Minerals	**Bacteria**	**Plants**	**Animals**	**Humans**	*idionomic spheres* / *entities*

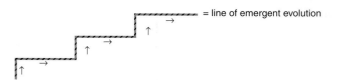

= line of emergent evolution

Figure 11.1 Holistic representation of emergent evolution

human reason. But from an ontological point of view the subjective status of nature remains the undeniable basis for all the objective meanings that, in the course of the evolutionary process, human beings have given to it.

(3) I come to the following conclusion. Even if a thing is to be characterized as a subject, this subjectivity does not exhaust its ontological status. For two reasons. In the first place, each living subject is oriented toward an intersubjective network of co-subjects and an *Umwelt* of objects. Furthermore, entities themselves can have, beside their subject functions, object functions at a higher level: as environmental factors they have come to participate in the upward direction of life by developing object functions that are attuned to higher subjects. On each level of being, subjects assume correlative connections with the surrounding world, on the one hand with

co-subjects in life communities and, on the other hand, with objects in environments for life. In short, we have reason to honor living nature as a complex, ontological network of subject/subject relations and subject/object relations on diverse levels. I have attempted to depict the network of subject/object relations in Figure 11.1.

4 FROM BIOSPHERE TO NOOSPHERE

Emergence is an inclusive process with globalizing effects. Lower modes of being are involved in the origin of higher levels of being in two ways: via supervenient subject functions and via emerging object functions. In section 2 we saw how subjects disclose themselves in the totality structure of an organism in favor of a supervenient subject function. In the previous section we noted how subjects participate within an emergent mode of being via object functions. In other words, life elevates itself in an emerging genealogy of living organisms. And life broadens itself in a globalizing expansion of new life-worlds or life-spheres. Thus there is reason to not only examine the modal diversity of the biological species, as we did earlier, but also the typological diversity of the life-worlds.

I begin with the origin of one of the earliest life-worlds, that of the unicellular, prokaryotic microbe. This genesis was not some miniscule incident, the change of a molecular clump into a cellular mini-system in an otherwise unaltered domain in space and time. On the contrary! As soon as life came on the scene, a threshold was crossed and the world changed. New significances loomed, not only in the organisms but also in their surroundings. Matter transcended itself, not only in the microbe but also in the microbiological milieu. Three and a half or four billion years ago the earth became, for the first time, biologically significant. Matter and energy became nutritional substrate, nursery ground, and expansion room for countless populations of micro-organisms. The world obtained a new appearance, a new qualification as life-world. The new biotic mode of being realized itself as a new realm of being: an idionomic cosmos of biotically qualified subjects and objects. Subjective necessities of life began to interact with objective conditions for life, with all the means and provisions for life that the swirling ancient ocean offered. In this way the sterile planet Earth, in an equally sterile universe, called a *cosmosphere*, obtained a different status. It became a *biosphere*: a habitat supplied with oxygen, for bacteria, bacteriophages, blue-green algae, unicellular green algae, and protozoa. Endless eons later the world of plants began to delineate itself, also in a correlative unison of subjects and objects. The event of emergence not only brought a new class of subjects into being, it also caused a new type of objects to appear. The vegetable kingdom is not just a set of botanical systems in a purely material space. It is, rather, a *regnum*, a sovereign kingdom of plants, a full-fledged universe, a finely tuned biosystem of organisms and their habitat. Plants are populations of vegetatively qualified subjects rooted in a vegetatively renewed environment, turned toward the source of light necessary for photosynthesis, sheltered against extreme temperature fluctuations, and attuned to the rhythm of days, seasons, and tides. The *Umwelt* has immensely wide bounds. Properly seen, even the orbits of sun, moon, and stars received a vegetative qualification; they became a protective guard around the newly established kingdom. The world expanded into *phytosphere*, a space characterized by plant life.

With the arrival of animals the world again exploded into a surplus of meanings, attuned to the sensitive and perceptive possibilities that are peculiar to animals. Things, by their perceptibility, began to participate in the sensitivity of animals: they became visible, audible, and touchable. They suddenly appeared to be adorned with colors, sounds, and smells that previously had not been perceived by any living creature, and were, until then, meaningless. With the sensitive competencies of the animal, and the attendant activities of hunting, eating, mating, and nesting, the world acquired an observable presence. It became a field of perception, a hiding place, a spawning ground, a nesting area, and so much more. The world as *sensorium animale*, perception space for animals, is also a category all its own, infinitely richer than the habitat of plants or the biotope of microbes. The emergence of the sensitive mode of experience marked the emergence of a new way of being, a sovereign universe, the *zoosphere*. As a new network of sensitive relationships, the zoosphere is partly determined by subject/subject relations, such as predator and prey, parents and brood, herd and individual, and partly determined by subject/object relations such as trout and stream, nuthatch and nest, and mole and meadow.

With the coming of humankind the world opened up once again, now as a world of culture and human care; this needs no further explanation after my description of Heidegger's views. Culture is the world in human perspective, the world as a spiritual home, a habitat for humanity, yet supported by the physical and above-physical constants of nature. Culture is based on a free choice. In it the humanity of the human species takes shape but also, alas, its inhuman possibilities. Culture has to be fought for, along an avenue marked by blood, sweat, and tears. Culture is culture-history, an odyssey on which little progress has been recorded through the ages, except in the area of technology. There is suffering in nature but that cannot be compared to the excruciating violence that people can inflict on each other. Culture, being free from the yoke of nature and living in circumstances fit for human beings, is in other words an ideal that is only realized in fits and starts. Culture is a world of its own, a world designated by Teilhard de Chardin as the *noosphere*, the sphere of the "nous," i.e. the human mind.

As soon as we have relinquished our modern, anthropocentric view of the world as nothing but an object that is at the disposal of human subjects, an overwhelming panorama of five strongly divergent worlds in their own right unfolds before our eyes: the cosmosphere, the biosphere, the phytosphere, the zoosphere, and the noosphere. These spheres have developed into relatively inde-pendent domains and, apart from the cosmosphere, they all have a subjective and an objective side. They are governed by idionomic laws that are determinative for living subjects in close interaction with their environment. Therefore, one could say, these laws have sovereignty in their own sphere.

But do not forget the other side of the picture. The spheres have diverged, yet they continue to relate to each other. They are in a tight mutual coherence. For in the process of emergent evolution the later domains did not only emanate from the earlier ones but also continue to build on them. In other words, the world in which we live is not only a pluralism of spheres but simultaneously one holistic reality. This has incisive consequences for the delicate position of human culture.

Often, culture is played off against nature. This fails to recognize the holistic coherence between nature and culture. Culture is built on nature and incorporates nature in an objective sense. Wherever humans are present, the appearance of the world is humanized and nature becomes a component of culture. The human presence alters nature and uses it for human purposes. Humans are busy changing nature into agriculture, aquaculture, silviculture, viniculture, technoculture, and the like. Even the so-called objective view with which science surveys the physical universe is, upon closer examination, a typically human view: an abstract-logical representation and appropriation. For example, that the universe originated through a Big Bang is an opinion that can only retrospectively be designated in this way by intelligences equipped with auditory nerves. The Big Bang could not be "heard" since sound does not travel in a vacuum.

The human world is not only more complex than the worlds formed earlier, in which protista, plants or animals were the highest subjects, it is also more differentiated. With the emergence of human levels of being, human activity systems also originated, such as science, economics, art, politics, family life, and religion. All these activity systems in fact began to form a world of their own. In so-called primitive cultures this diversity is not immediately apparent, for there these systems are often intertwined under the auspices of a tribal chief or shaman.[9] In modernity these systems have been more clearly differentiated. Formal divisions often have occurred between church, state, science, the economy, etc. In each system a particular mode of being pushes itself forward as the leading function, such as the religious, political, scientific, or economic. In essence the noosphere is thus a container concept asking for noetic specification. The human life-world is a network of habitats in which people participate in various role patterns as churchgoer, citizen of the state, academic, or business entrepreneur.

The human habitats represent, despite mutual intertwinings, spheres that are relatively autonomous or, as I prefer to say, relatively

---

[9] In *Les Formes élémentaires de la vie religieuse: Le système totémique en Australie* (Paris: Presses Universitaires de France, 1912), Emile Durkheim shows on the basis of research on the Aroenta tribes in central Australia that also in tribes considered to be primitive, religion and culture are extremely complex systems that determine tribal consciousness and penetrate all social relationships.

idionomic. Every sphere has its own group dynamic and its own laws that are, contrary to the laws of nature, normative in character: they can be followed or disobeyed. In every sphere a universal normative principle forces itself upon us, a principle that is constitutive for that particular sphere. Take the economic sphere. Ecomic actions are determined by the general principle of mutual benefit. This implies that a transaction is economic when it renders a benefit to demander and supplier. This demand for mutual benefit is a typical humane standard. It is with the help of this trade principle that the human species – as "naked ape" confronted with dire shortages of food, clothing, and shelter – transformed the competitive violence of the animal kingdom into a humane solution, namely peaceful advantages for both parties.

The above does not imply that economic or other normative laws developed in the same way for all times and all places. The human life-worlds are idionomic but also dynamic. On the late-Roman *latifundia* (estates), with their households served by slaves, other economic rules prevailed than on the virtually self-sustaining medieval serfdoms with their feudal lords and villains. Yet other rules crystallized in the open-market relationships of western capitalism and in the planned economies of communism. When I speak about the universality of the economic, I exclusively intend to designate the universality of the economic principle, i.e., the demand for mutual benefit based on exchange. Concrete economic laws are, like all concrete standards, not universal but particularized. They fit into a historical tradition and are adapted to natural and societal circumstances.

People must always elaborate – or "positivize," as experts in law and philosophy say – the universal principles of the noosphere into concrete laws or rules. The rules have to be adapted to and actualized in the natural and societal circumstances that prevail. The principle that economic relations are bound to a demand for mutual benefit may be universal, but this does not say anything about the concrete form in which trade and market relations actually occur. Sometimes a serfdom, sometimes a patriarchal system, sometimes a free-market convention, sometimes a state economy appears to be decisive for exchange relations. In short, norm principles are general and transcend cultural boundaries; concretized standards and rules are time-bound, confirming cultural boundaries. This is how matters stand in economy. This is also how they stand in juris-prudence, morality, and religion.[10]

In the history of human culture the dynamic of emergent evo-lution becomes fully apparent only when this history is seen in an ecological perspective. In civilization, human beings do not only change themselves, they also transform the surrounding nature and bring it to a higher level. Thus, as market merchants they transform natural things into economic goods under the demand of mutual benefit. Thus, as artists they transform natural materials into artistic works under the norm of esthetic creativity. And thus, as priests they also transform material, plant, and animal ingredients into sacred grounds, mysterious rituals, and consecrated offerings under the standard of the sanctification of life. In culture nature obtains a human face without denying its natural origin.

I conclude with a critical note. Modern humans use nature but they also misuse it. The human presence on the globe is at present so dominant that pristine nature is disappearing rapidly, even in the polar areas. Yes, it seems that modern humans are capable of des-troying, and in the hunt for profits are even likely to destroy, nature, i.e., to destroy the preceding non-human life-worlds for their own benefit. However, there are limits to the exploitation of nature. Those who have an eye for the holistic and ecological coherences of culture and nature, as I sketched it above, realize that the unbridled destruction of nature must result in the revenge of nature and in human self-destruction. The catastrophic consequences that the uncontrolled harvest of timber and unlimited warming of our globe have in numerous countries demonstrate that humankind is indeed engaged in the destruction of the house in which it lives. GTEE unleashes a compelling criticism of modern society.

5   NEW AGE AND BRAHMAN

The evolutionary process presents itself to us as a holistic event in the pregnant sense of the word. In the various spheres of animate

---

[10] For a discussion on positivization of norm principles see Klapwijk, "Pluralism of Norms and Values," 158–92.

nature and culture, life has evolved into a hierarchy of totality structures, each one transcending the one below it. It is a hierarchy in the sense that more and more complex structures have originated, and that in each structure the highest organizational level has gained control over, and received feedback from, the lower levels. In a critical reflection on Darwinism, Karl Popper has contributed to this hierarchical view of evolution. He describes the process of multimodal evolutionary development as a "growing hierarchical system of plastic controls." I quote some sentences from his book *Objective Knowledge:*

Darwinism, with all its great virtues, is by no means a perfect theory. It is in need of a restatement which makes it less vague. The evolutionary theory which I am going to sketch here is an attempt at such a restatement. My theory may be described as an attempt to apply to the whole of evolution what we learned when we analysed the evolution from animal language to human language. And it consists of a certain *view of evolution* as a growing hierarchical system of plastic controls, and of a certain *view of organisms* as incorporating – or in the case of man, evolving exosomatically – this growing hierarchical system of plastic controls.[11]

Indeed, the hierarchical system of subjects endowed with increasingly higher and more inclusive life forms has exosomatically externalized itself on earth: it is as if it has stepped out of its own body. It has objectivized itself in a hierarchy of habitats. Nowhere is this externalization so clear as in the noetic spheres in which human beings dwell. Science cannot exist without libraries. Technology cannot fabricate without machinery. The economy cannot run without markets. And religion cannot adore without temples. I am of the opinion that neo-Darwinism has not clearly chosen a position in this regard. It is particularly the evolutionary naturalists, preoccupied as they are with a one-sided continuity axiom, who have not succeeded in doing justice to the idionomic variety of life forms, and the life-worlds they occupy.

No wonder that in the past few decades holistic counter-movements have developed. A striking example of this is the New Age movement. In this movement, an anti-reductionistic and spiritual view of reality has come to the fore, a view that likes to orient itself

[11] Popper, *Objective Knowledge*, p. 242, italics by Popper.

on eastern religions and mysticism, and particularly on Brahman, the ancient divinity of the Hindus, the spiritual source of all that exists. Brahman is not only the animating power that flows through all living beings. Brahman is also the deeper unity of material nature and of the cosmic universe. In their spiritualistic worldview, the adherents of New Age also want to do justice to evolutionary developments and emerging moments. They see the world as caught in an expansive process in which life has opportunities to internalize itself and in which cosmological renewals, indeed a New Age era, is immanent.

Anthroposophical and astrological influences play a role in these views. New Age orients itself to the equinox, the position on the starry sky to which the axis of the earth points on the first day of spring. This spring equinox moves and transcribes a circle, as is well known, once every 26,000 years along the twelve constellations of the zodiac. According to the adherents of New Age, this creates twelve time periods or ages, of over 2,000 years, in which humanity lives, every time under a different star. Until 2,000 years ago we had the Age of Aries, the Ram, symbol of the Arab-Jewish period. At present we are in the Age of Pisces, the Fishes, symbol of Christian culture. Soon we will enter the Age of Aquarius, the Water Carrier. Aquarius represents the New Age in world history, an age in which new spiritual relationships will be revealed.

It is not without reason that I signal these things. I want to make it clear that holism is no panacea against one-dimensional and reductive ways of thinking. In the holism of the New Age speculative thinking has soared. It has alienated itself from the empirical sciences. Correctly Fritjof Capra and others have denounced the reductive tendencies in modern science and criticized the purely mechanistic explanation of biological phenomena.[12] But, incorrectly I feel, these thinkers have lost sight of the basic given of material continuity in inanimate and animate nature and have taken flight into uncontrolled, pseudo-scientific, and semi-religious fantasies.

In the evolution debate reductionistic and holistic ideas are often in sharp opposition. At least they should be able to find each other in the acknowledgment of the foundational significance of the

---

[12] F. Capra, *The Tao of Physics* (Boulder, CO: Shambhala, 1975).

physical mode of being for all the higher domains, not only for the biological kingdoms but also for the position of the human species. This is in large measure also the view of G. Ledyard Stebbins, botanist and one of the architects of the modern evolutionary synthesis. In his book *Darwin to DNA* Stebbins emphasizes that reductionism and holism are to be seen as being of equal and complementary significance. I would put it another way: the debate on evolution invites us to unite the mechanistic ideas of material continuity and the holistic idea of emergent innovation into a concept of evolutionary development that does equal justice to the material and the spiritual dimensions of the world.

CHAPTER 12

The slumbering temptation of essentialism

In preceding chapters I criticized the philosophical presuppositions of Darwinian naturalism. In this chapter I want to lay my own philosophical starting-points on the table. I will do this in a critical discussion with Herman Dooyeweerd, who was a philosopher at the Free University of Amsterdam and gained international attention with his magnum opus, *A New Critique of Theoretical Thought.*[1] Dooyeweerd had serious scientific objections to the standard theory of evolution. In his "philosophy of the cosmonomic idea" he emphasized the meaning of the creation order, as I have also done. However, in his understanding of this creation order, he succumbed to the slumbering temptation of essentialism.

In this chapter I try to demonstrate that, beside creationism, essentialism can be regarded as one of the toughest strongholds of a conservative Christianity in its view of the living world. And I see Dooyeweerd as one of the most talented representatives of this essentialism.

I begin with a brief introduction to Dooyeweerd's philosophy; with him I argue for the necessity that philosophy bases itself on the standpoint of experience (section 1). In this connection I explain the difference between metaphysical and empirical philosophy (section 2). The modus operandi of a philosophy that is based on the standpoint of experience I present as the reflective-empirical method (section 3). I will show how the reflective-empirical method also applies to living nature, and how Dooyeweerd employs it to typify biological species (section 4). Subsequently I attempt to clarify how Dooyeweerd's identification of species with typological laws founded in the creation

---

[1] H. Dooyeweerd, *A New Critique of Theoretical Thought.* I quote from the first edition: Amsterdam: H. J. Paris, 1953–58.

order inevitably leads to essentialist metaphysics (section 5). Finally I demonstrate how a renewed reflection upon experience can lead to an overcoming of essentialism (section 6).

I IS THERE A CREATION ORDER? HERMAN DOOYEWEERD

I know of no other thinker who has studied more thoroughly Augustine's distinction between the creation order and the process of its realization in time than Dooyeweerd. This makes his philosophy of great importance for us. We are dealing here with an exceedingly dynamic theory, a theory that sees the fullness of creation gradually come to light in the grand disclosure process of time. Time discloses itself in the birth of the cosmos, in the expansion of intergalactic space, in the consolidation of our solar system, in the genesis of bacterial, plant, and animal forms on earth, and, yes, in the origin of human beings, and in the realization of cultures and civilizations.

Dooyeweerd's philosophy has the double-faced head of Janus. Alternatingly, it sees time as a process of time and as an order of time. At times it presents itself as a dynamic process philosophy *à la* Whitehead, a view that interprets reality as the realization of the ongoing process of time. At other times Dooyeweerd's philosophy presents itself as a static systems theory, a view that analyzes the temporal world as a network of cosmic structures founded in the creation order. In this structural setting Dooyeweerd also speaks of time, even of universal or "cosmic" time. However, then his concern is not about time as an all-inclusive process of time but rather as an all-inclusive order of time, an order that determines the temporal coherence of the creational ordinances. Now, the basic thought is that the world has opened itself up in conformity with this order of time. The time order is seen as a sort of matrix, a measure for all that develops in the process of time, also for living organisms.[2]

---

[2] Dooyeweerd has elaborated the idea of the disclosure of temporal reality primarily in the direction of culture; see *ibid.*, vol. II, pp. 181–92, 331–65. He has a larger concern, however, namely the apotheosis of time in all of reality. Time discloses itself in the basic structures of nature and culture. All these partly modal, partly typical structures (section 4 in this chapter) are described as "grounded in the order of cosmic time," *ibid.*, vol. I, p. 29.

Dooyeweerd's idea of cosmic time is thus twofold. In the first instance it is an idea that brings to light the dynamic and successive character of time as a temporal process. In the second place, it reveals itself as an idea that seeks to illumine the structural and expressive character of time as a temporal order. And when it comes right down to it, in Dooyeweerd's thought the expressivity of the temporal order supersedes the successivity of the temporal process.

In view of this expressivity of time there is, in the first place, no room for the idea of an evolutionary development in the sense of Darwin's "descent with modification." Dooyeweerd designates lower modal structures as "earlier," but this is especially in the sense that they are more elementary and are thus earlier in respect to the higher ones in a structural sense. In the same way higher modal structures are designated as "later," but this is especially in the sense that they presuppose the earlier structures and surpass them in the so-called transcendental direction of time.

Hence there is, in the second place, no room for the idea of emergence. That the temporal disclosure of events in the world could be accompanied by idionomic novelty, with new law structures becoming functional, seems unfitting to Dooyeweerd. The reason he gives to support this is that what time has disclosed must have been enclosed in time from its very beginning. All structures that time has brought to expression – the biological species included – must have been, in one way or another, enclosed in the cosmic time order. The cosmic time order brings to expression the a priori and universal validity of all those structures that are grounded in the creation order. In regard to structures grounded in the creation order, Harry Cook, historian of biology and editor of this book, speaks strikingly of an "archetypal manner of thinking." He asks: "Is it possible that archetype thinking, prevalent among romantic and later nineteenth century biologists, influenced Dooyeweerd?"[3]

Dooyeweerd does not deny the innovative significance of time. For him it is present in the "anticipations" that delineate themselves

---

[3] Georges Cuvier in France, Richard Owen in Britain, and Louis Agassiz in Switzerland and the United States, three famous biologists of the time, all spoke of basic animal types or, as some authors called them, archetypes. See Ernst Mayr, *The Growth of Biological Thought: Diversity, Evolution, and Inheritance* (Cambridge, MA: The Belknap Press of Harvard University Press, 1982).

in the process of time, or, to be more exact, in the fact that in the development of living organisms the lower modal functions open themselves up in favor of the higher functions (see ch. 11, section 2). But that the innovative nature of time displays itself also, and even primarily, in the emergence of new idionomic orderings, concretely speaking in the origin of living beings with higher modal functions, falls outside the purview of his thought. He does recognize that there is a correlation between structural laws and the subjects that obey these laws, between the "law side" and the "subject side" of reality, as he puts it. But this insight does not lead to the recognition that biological or moral laws, for example, only became valid at the moment that biotic organisms or moral subjects appeared on the world stage.

One question may have occurred to the reader already: is there such a thing as a divine creation order? This question can, in my view, not be answered in science. But whoever doubts this as a believing person simply *has* to read Psalm 119, an endless song of praise to the glory of God's laws and creational ordinances. In correspondence with this, the Christian church has confessed, through the ages, its faith in God as the almighty creator of heaven and earth, who upholds His creation, and who also makes life livable by subjecting it to His ordinances, in spite of the protestations of a series of modern theologians.

Still, these theologians are correct on two cardinal points. It is not self-evident that *every* structure that manifests itself in the world is a pure and full reflection of God's creation order. Furthermore, the order of creation should be understood in the light of the expectation of the kingdom of God, as depicted in the messianic visions of Israel's prophets.[4] Thus the self-evident appeal some people make to the established structures as ordained by God – those in power are

---

[4] J. Klapwijk, "Reformational Philosophy on the Boundary Between the Past and the Future," *Philosophia Reformata* 52 (1987), 101–34; 110–15. The Bible includes the created world in the messianic contours of a pilgrimage to the kingdom of God. The creation order has a conserving and a prophetic content. It speaks of God's purpose from of old, and of his intentions for the present and the future. The heaven and earth of Gen. 1 point to the new (=renewed) heaven and earth of Rev. 21, and vice versa. For this reason a theology of creation has to be eschatological at the same time, i.e. has to think from out of the coming kingdom of God. By translating creational structures into kingdom structures, it can lay the groundwork for a theology of hope.

especially liable to promote this fallacy – is often badly misplaced. For societal structures are in many respects contingent, a result of conflicts of interest and power plays. Natural structures are similar; they are usually a result of the clash of interests. Biological species are perhaps the clearest example of the latter, engaged as they are in a ruthless competition. The biological species represent creaturely ordinances, but under the pressure of time. They are reproductive communities with patterns of stability that have consolidated themselves historically but that are not unchangeable.

One could say of Dooyeweerd that he too readily exchanges species in the form of structures with variable patterns of durability for species in the form of structures with invariable and essential characteristics that are based on the creation order. I would designate this definition of biological species as "essentialism." It is this essentialism that limits the dynamic of Dooyeweerd's thought considerably. For suppose that biological species are not variable patterns of organization but archetypical expressions of a divine master plan; this would make evolution all but impossible. Then the conclusion forces itself upon us that the thesis of the genealogical change of species, no matter how strongly it is supported by the facts, is scientifically untenable. And that is, in short, Dooyeweerd's position. For him, no Darwinian evolution, not to mention emergent evolution!

The intriguing part of Dooyeweerd's position is that he does not want to derive his rejection of the idea of an evolution of species from metaphysical principles or from isolated Bible texts.[5] He relates his rejection to the view that every respectable, scientific theory, philosophy included, has to start from daily life experience. This is a challenging starting-point that I share. The general tenor of this chapter shall therefore be: philosophy should be based on the standpoint of experience. Just as all other theoretical disciplines, philosophy has to give an account of experience and of all that presents itself to us in experience. How we shall implement this starting-point in our philosophy of living nature, and whether Dooyeweerd has held himself to this central thesis in his essentialist

---

[5] Creationists derive the dogma of the constancy of species primarily from the statement that God created all living creatures "according to their kinds" (Gen. 1:11–12, 21, 24–25).

approach of species, we shall have to examine in the sections that follow.

With this I have given a first impression of the incisive philosophical questions that will be the topic in this chapter, and of Dooyeweerd's position. In the sections that follow I want to elucidate these questions further. For this reason the discussion will become – I say it as a warning – somewhat abstract and academic. Those who so wish may choose to skip this part. But then they would also miss the account I give of my own philosophical position.

2 THE STANDPOINT OF EXPERIENCE AND METAPHYSICS

The standpoint of experience implies a rejection of every form of philosophy that can be designated as metaphysics. In the modern sense of the word, philosophy is to be described as anti-metaphysical. Philosophy is anti-metaphysical because and in so far as it distantiates itself from the super-empirical world as it was presented in classical, medieval, and early-modern philosophy. Today's philosophy does not lend itself to theoretical speculations about the first principles, the divine foundation or the highest purpose of being, or about the hidden essence of things. Philosophers have discovered that the scientific search for a world that transcends the possibilities of human experience is meaningless and that all attempts in that direction overestimate the ability of human reason.

I share these objections to the overestimation of reason that is part and parcel of the concept of metaphysics. In an earlier chapter my objections led to a critique of the thought of Alexander and Morgan. Their philosophy made a promising start but ended in a fog of confusion when it made theoretical predictions about God as the final apotheosis of the whole process of emergent evolution. Such an eschatological fantasy is not rooted in religious faith or in living experiences of God but arises from the metaphysical considerations of an intellectual elite.

Metaphysical propositions are theses that go beyond the realm of experience in the sense that they cannot be tested on the basis of empirical data. When a metaphysician takes the floor there soon prevails, depending on the ambience, a painful or respectful silence, because the argument, in all its loftiness, strikes one part of the audience as unprovable, another part as irrefutable. Metaphysics is by definition a theory that is neither provable nor refutable and is, therefore, pseudoscientific. Its pseudoscientific character results from the fact that metaphysical arguments do not meet the demand for empirical verification or falsification to which modern science has committed itself.

I do not suggest that metaphysics rests entirely on a misconception of what science is. It has a legitimate aspect that is often lacking in other philosophies. It lies in the valuable opinion that science – I use the word "science" here again in the broad sense of scholarship or *Wissenschaft*, i.e., the general pursuit of theoretical knowledge, thus including philosophy – does not have to limit itself to empirical phenomena, i.e., entities that appear in human experience as its content. Science is interested not only in what appears in experience as its content but also in what we do *not* experience as its content, something that remains hidden in experience and still deserves our attention. Metaphysics reminds us of this specific preoccupation with what is hidden in experience, in spite of itself (see below).

Regrettably, the rejection of metaphysics in modern philosophy is often coupled with naturalistic and atheistic claims. That would seem to me to be a mistake. No matter how anti-metaphysical science may be, this does not imply that one cannot speak about God in academic discourse. One can bring God into a scientific discussion to the extent that He has revealed Himself within empirical reality in the experiences and testimonies of faith and in the historical traditions of religion, as Christian theology is doing. One could even call theology an empirical science because and insofar as it is based on the authentic experiences of people with God.[6]

---

[6] Christian theology can be seen as an empirical discipline, which reflects on the correlation of religious experience and divine revelation. It bases itself on faith experiences that are grounded in revelation. For this reason it is a theology of experience and of revelation at the same time. Its counterpart is the so-called natural or metaphysical theology which has, from the Middle Ages on, with the help of proofs of the existence of God, pushed itself to the fore as a theology that bases itself on logical arguments as a rational support of Christian theology.

The method of philosophy is, negatively defined, anti-metaphysical. In a positive sense we can define it as empirical. I would like to elucidate this point further. Right-minded philosophy bases itself – as all other empirical disciplines, including theology, do – on the standpoint of experience. Please note, I am writing about experience here in the broad sense of the word! Experience is more than the protocol observations of laboratory and field researchers. It is also more than the simple "sense experiences," i.e. the observations of colors, forms, and the like, to which British empiricists have appealed since the time of Locke and Hume. It is, rather, the full range of sensations that are common to the human being in the daily practice of life, the "everyday life experience" in the broadest sense of the word. These may include, as far as I am concerned, experiences of God, as I already mentioned above. I add that everyday life experiences – whether they are sensory, moral, or religious experiences – need to always be critically screened before the sciences can appeal to them. There is, after all, always chaff among the wheat and no appeal to experience, no matter in what discipline, has the hallmark of infallibility.

The daily life experience is a "con-crete" experience. This means, literally, it is a "grown-together" experience, an experience that is comprised of a variety of cognitive interests on different modal levels. In daily life, non-sensory forms of interest always accompany sensory observation: among others, economic, esthetic, symbolic, and moral in nature. When someone sees a piece of jewelry, for example, that person does not only have an experience of form and color, but also encounters its economic worth, its artistic design, its symbolic significance, etc. Whether one watches ripening grain, a painting, a playing child, or roaring traffic, one always sees more than what is at hand. Beside the sensitive content, one also notices characteristics that are esthetically, economically, and morally, etc., relevant.

Well then, philosophy and the other sciences – taken in the broad sense defined above as the general pursuit of theoretical knowledge – base themselves on the standpoint of experience. They attempt to think through, analytically and systematically, the impressions that we encounter in daily life experience. But given the fact that this experience of the world is con-crete and includes diverse cognitive interests, science would be overcome by all those data if it did not go about its task in a selective manner. Therefore science has differentiated into a variety of special disciplines, each of them focussing on a special cognitive interest that, as a rule, represents a single modal domain. Scientists select, for example, exclusively physical evidence, biotic observations, economic data, or esthetic impressions, in order to come to a physical, biological, economic, or esthetic theory, respectively. Of course, there are also interdisciplinary sciences, but we call these "inter-disciplinary" precisely because they presuppose the diversity of cognitive interests and modal areas of expertise.

In short, the experience to which the logical analysis of a single science is oriented is no longer the comprehensive experience of concrete and multimodal entities in daily life. It is an abstracted type of experience related to a single modal facet of things in the world. And yet, no matter how abstract this mode of experience may be, it retains a link with the pre-theoretical world of experience as a whole, from which it is abstracted. It does not lose itself in a senseless search for metaphysical ideas that, as a deeper source of explanation, would lie behind or beyond the world of empirical phenomena.[7]

3 THE REFLECTIVE-EMPIRICAL METHOD

Although philosophy is based on the standpoint of experience and although in that sense one can designate it an empirical science, it is nevertheless different from all other sciences. Most of the sciences have developed into specialized disciplines with particular modal domains of experience as their focus. Philosophy has profiled itself in a different manner. From of old, it has encompassed all parts of the project of theoretical knowledge.[8] It was the "mother" of all

---

[7] In the last two centuries, Wilhelm Dilthey, Edmund Husserl, Martin Heidegger, and Dooyeweerd rediscovered the daily life experience. The "critical" philosophers in the tradition of Kant had written it off in an earlier stage as "naïve" experience: a form of experience that the modern person would have outgrown thanks to the light of scientific reason. With the rise of positivism this scientistic way of seeing things has become exceedingly popular. But it is not realized that the special sciences too, in their appeal to empirical data, give account of elements that are abstracted from pre-theoretical experience.

[8] Harry Cook reminded me that this general status is still symbolized by the academic degree of Ph.D.

sciences, of physics, logic, and ethics, and it had a scope of interest that was as wide as the world. Now that the "children" have left the parental home, with their specific cognitive interests, philosophy still represents the general interest in knowing, in a manner that does not hinder or repeat the work that the special sciences do.

To put it another way, a new division of labor has come into existence. On one side there are the special sciences, focussed on the content of experience, that is, the *facts of experience*. Their angle of approach and input is strongly determined by the levels of reality. They analyze the empirical data that are collected on one or more modal levels of reality. On the other side we see philosophy. Philosophy is a totality science, focussed on something that the investigators in the special sciences pass by unnoticed, namely the general presuppositions that are contained in our experience of reality, that is, the *conditions of experience*. In this somewhat unusual attention, not for specific contents of experience but for the general conditions of experience, the angle of approach of philosophy manifests itself.

I mention two examples. The ethologist who investigates the mating behavior of animals is focussed on empirical facts, but employs, wittingly or unwittingly, a general notion of what an animal is. The judge who in his verdict concludes that the defense of the accused is in conflict with the truth seeks to establish the empirical facts, but assumes a general notion of truth. The empirical facts are the field of research of the special sciences – of ethology, jurisprudence, etc. – but the general notions that play a role in our experience are the investigative field of philosophy. Philosophy, being a totality science, does not concentrate on particular facts but on the general presuppositions that shape our experience of the world. Philosophy wants to know: what makes an animal an animal? And what, precisely, is truth? Of course, the philosopher can also be interested in particular facts of experience. But be careful, for he or she always does so with a deeper interest in the structural conditions that are at issue: the general presuppositions that give form to the experience of facts.

In this way the mutual division of tasks between the specialized sciences and philosophy becomes clearer. The one is a special discipline, aimed at the "hard" facts of experience. The other is a totality discipline, fascinated by the often difficult-to-grasp and thus easily ignored "soft" presuppositions of experience. The method of special science is empirical in an objective sense of the word; we can designate it *objective-empirical*. Its power lies in the systematic analysis of what presents itself in experience as objective, factual material. The method of philosophy is also empirical, but in a reflective sense of the word. It relates the content of experience to the subject of experience. It reflects on the way we, humans, experience facts and on the universal conditions to which this experiencing of the facts is bound. For this reason I designate the method of philosophy *reflective-empirical*.

I return here, once more, to the nature of metaphysical philosophy. Metaphysics, too, has been preoccupied since the time of Parmenides and Plato with the universal conditions that lie hidden in experience. That is the element of truth in all metaphysics. But metaphysics attempts to inflate these universal conditions in the experience of temporal reality into a world of its own above time and space, yes, into "absolute ideas" or "supra-temporal essences" that would be the foundation of the empirical world. The incisive implications that this essentialism has had for biology I shall discuss before long.

Contrary to metaphysics, empirical philosophy knows itself to be bound to the world of experience. For this reason, it enters into discussion with the special sciences. Its task is threefold: (1) It analyzes the structural conditions that are basic for the way in which we, human beings, experience the world. (2) It compares the empirical positions and claims of the various special sciences. (3) It develops to be the critical conscience of the special sciences.

The difference I have indicated between the special sciences, fixed as they are on objects of experience, and philosophy, focussed on the conditions of experience, may sound rather abstract. Let me therefore illustrate the difference between them with the example of visual observation. When one pays attention, one is always struck in the first instance by things immediately before our eyes: the objects of observation. But with some thought one has to conclude that in observation other factors also play a role, factors that are perhaps not an objective given but that are, nevertheless, a necessary condition for observation. As an example, take the necessity of a light source. Suppose it was cloudy all day. Then in the evening I can say: "I did not see the sun, but it tried its level best or else I wouldn't have seen a thing!" With such a comment I say, in fact, that in visual observation the sun is not an object of observation but a condition for observation; it makes visual observation possible.

This is just an example. But just as we can distinguish between objects and conditions for observation, so we can also make a general distinction between the objects and conditions of experience. The special sciences and philosophy make a different use of this distinction. The special sciences investigate the objects or contents of experience, say the empirical facts, while philosophy analyzes the basic conditions to which experience is bound, say the "light-source" of our knowledge. Philosophy has discovered that experience and knowledge are bound to basic conditions in terms of universal laws and standards. It attempts to recover what the character is of these standards of knowledge and how they steer our experience.

Philosophy is interested, for example, in the logical-analytical mode of experience. Philosophy wants to know what makes the process of logical analysis possible. Thus it ignores the objects of logical analysis, zooming in, instead, on truth as a universal standard of analytical knowledge. Truth is not an object of knowledge; nevertheless, no one who seeks insight can disregard the principle of truth. Truth is a universal standard and thus an indispensable condition for making correct analytical distinctions. It is a source of light, a law that is, ultimately, determinative of the validity of all our analyses of objects.

Logical analysis is a modally determined form of experience and knowledge acquisition. There are also other modally determined forms of experience. Philosophers also search for the basic conditions of these non-logical forms of knowledge, for the general standards to which we appeal in the case of technical, moral, esthetic, or religious knowledge. For even in our technical, moral, esthetic, and religious practices we appeal to universal standards, in this case to the normative principles of efficacy, solidarity, beauty, and trust in God. These, too, are laws or ordering principles that we cannot objectivize because they form the basis for our knowledge of objects.

I return to the opening thesis of this chapter. Right-minded philosophy bases itself on the standpoint of experience. In that respect it closely resembles the other empirical disciplines. It does, however, have its own contribution to make. While the other disciplines attend to particular objects of experience that delineate themselves on one or more modal levels, philosophy has a more general intent. It is a totality science. It remains faithful to the world of experience as a whole. And one of its most serious tasks will always be to reflect on the universal laws that constitute and regulate experience on the various modal levels.

4 THE REFLECTIVE-EMPIRICAL METHOD AND LIVING NATURE

The question that now forces itself upon us is this: do laws also play a constitutive role in our experience of living nature? I can only answer the question in a positive way. The experience of phenomena in living nature, too, is an oriented experience, determined by ordering principles. We experience nature as an ordered whole, in which regularities assert themselves. Living nature does not constitute an exception; it shows an impressive regularity. People bring forth people, Aristotle noted more than two thousand years ago. That would seem to be a platitude. It is an ultimate wisdom.

Living nature does not present itself to us as chaos. We recognize what takes place in nature; we observe it with preconceived expectations. We know in advance that organisms unfold according to principles of self-regulation, homeostasis, reproduction, etc. We categorize natural phenomena according to preconceived intuitions. Suppose that we see two trees, the branches of which have grown together. We interpret this conjoined growth as entirely different from the embrace of a mother and baby baboon that, in threatening circumstances, hold tightly on to each other. Why do we interpret them differently? Because we recognize the behavior of animals and the growth habit of plants in advance as incommensurate phenomena. Different modal viewpoints are in question. We know that the patterns of life at a sensitive level answer to different modal principles from the patterns of life at a vegetative level.

In our experience of nature, modal laws play an important role. These laws can be seen as conditions for experience that articulate, a priori, our knowledge of the natural world.[9] In fact, these modal a priori's are so tightly linked to our daily life experience that we immediately sense differences among a wave that is breaking, a branch that is bending, and a head that is bowing. The modes of being ensure that we make a distinction between inanimate and animate things. They ensure that we in the living world make distinctions among microbes, plants, animals, and what is human. They ensure that we operate with discrimination even in human society and intuitively experience differences in levels among institutes such as science, economics, art, politics, and religion.

It is here that I point to the work of Dooyeweerd once again. For Dooyeweerd too, the pre-theoretical life experience is more than the sum of sensory impressions. It is an oriented experience of reality, determined by ordering principles in the sense of modal laws that hold for the various levels of reality, also in nature. However, a crucial point in Dooyeweerd's philosophy is that human experience is not only determined by modal laws but also by type laws. He even dedicated the third and largest volume of *A New Critique of Theoretical Thought* to a discussion of these type laws.

What are type laws? We deal here with an incisive difference. Modal laws, as I said earlier, are laws that are level-bound, determinative of the functions and characteristics of entities on any organizational level of reality. Type laws, in Dooyeweerd's views, are not level-bound. They are laws that are typical for entities as a whole. He calls them typical because they put their stamp to a

---

[9] We are concerned here with ontic a priori's, not with epistemic a priori's in the sense of Kant. Kant's epistemic a priori's were a result of the Cartesian split between the knowing subject versus the objective world, so that the laws of nature changed into a priori's of reason. In my view a priori conditions for knowledge are simultaneously a priori conditions for being, given the intrinsic coherence of subject and object. Not only the a priori's of nature but also the a priori's of culture (truth, justice, etc.) are, at the same time, constitutive principles of experience and of the world that is experienced. This spontaneous and inclusive experience of reality is pre-theoretical. It precedes the "methodical split between subject and object" (the investigative area) that characterizes the structure of scientific thought. In scientific thought, a modal domain as a (non-logical) object has been said to "stand over against" the scientist as a logical subject (in German this object is therefore designated as "Gegen-stand"). But this so-called "opposition of subject and object" can be misleading, for the topic under investigation is more than an object; the Gegenstand encompasses not only objects but also subjects. Biology – to take an example – not only investigates the food or habitat of animals but also animals themselves. An animal is not a biological (sensitive) object but a biological (sensitive) subject.

collection of entities, thus typifying the group. In short, type laws are laws that determine the specific identity of a class of entities. They do not touch on modal nature, i.e. the question about the "how" of something: is it physical or psychic, etc.? They touch on the typical peculiarity, i.e. the question about the "what" of something: is it gold or silver, a lion or a tiger, etc.?

With this latest example we encounter, all of a sudden, the topic of biological species. From the time of Darwin's *Origin of Species*, the species problem has been of primary importance in evolution theory. Evolutionary research concentrates on the mutual relationship and possible evolutionary succession of species, even though the phylogenetic tree – given its many dead end branches – will probably never be reconstructed in its entirety. Dooyeweerd's preoccupation with type laws has radical consequences for his view of species and their genealogical development, however. For him the taxonomic distinction of phyla, classes, orders, families, genera, and species is an expression of (more or less comprehensive) biological types. And the identity of these types is determined by type laws, understood as a priori ordering principles that are anchored in the divine creation order.

Here things become exciting. Suppose that the species reflect type laws, and these type laws are a derivative of immutable creational laws, can there then still be any mention at all of a change in species? Earlier I took the role of pleading for the reflective-empirical method as a method suitable for philosophy. But what is the consequence of this method? Doesn't reflection on the basic conditions for human experience lead us, with Dooyeweerd, to the acceptance of the traditional doctrine of the constancy of species, whether we want to do so or not?

5 TYPE LAWS: AN ESSENTIALIST ERROR

Starting with the difference between the "how" and the "what" of things, Dooyeweerd states that the empirical world is not only regulated by modal laws, determinative of the "how-ness" of a thing, but also by type laws, determinative of the "what-ness" of a thing.[10]

---

[10] Dooyeweerd, *A New Critique*, vol. III, p. 39.

In doing so, he allies himself with a long philosophical tradition. Already in ancient and medieval times, philosophers searched for the what-ness (*quidditas*) or essence of things. *A New Critique*, vol. III, is in fact a continuation of classical essence philosophy. Dooyeweerd too aims at the essence of a thing when he speaks about the identity structure of a thing.[11] For the identity structure is the entirety of determinations that defines the type, i.e. the essential characteristics or identity of a collection of things.

There is a difference from the ancient definition of essence. Ancient thinkers saw the essence of things as modeled after a realm of eternal ideas (Plato) or of supra-temporal forms of being (Aristotle) that would transcend empirical reality. Dooyeweerd correctly dismisses these views as a product of metaphysical speculation. He does not present identity structure as a metaphysical archetype or as a supra-temporal form of being beyond the world of experience. In his view identity structure is a type law, i.e. a law that is typical of a collection of things and that is presupposed in experience.[12] Is this type law indeed presupposed in experience?

Dooyeweerd applies his essentialist view to biological species. In an earlier context I described the biological species as a reproductive community with a variable but historically balanced pattern of durability (see ch.5, section 1). The species represent a structural design, the components of which came together, in a long evolutionary process, to form a building plan or body plan that is typical of such a group. For Dooyeweerd too, the species represent a building plan. Not, however, in the sense of an evolutionarily developed building pattern but as a blueprint that determines the essential characteristics of a group in advance. In his view the species represent, just as the higher taxa of systematic biology do, identity structures in the sense of type laws. And those type laws are, in the

---

[11] Dooyeweerd uses individuality structure as a standard term. The title of volume III is "The Structures of Individuality of Temporal Reality." The term "individuality structure" is misleading for it is not individuality that is up for discussion. I have therefore consistently substituted the term with "identity structure." Dooyeweerd's concern is the structure that typifies the identity of a *collection* of individual things.

[12] "We have observed that a *type*, as a *structure* of individuality, has the character of a law," Dooyeweerd, *A New Critique*, vol. III, p. 97.

final analysis, creation laws that make it possible that our experience of living nature is an ordered and oriented experience.[13]

Views of a similar nature are found in Dooyeweerd's discussion of the book by the zoologist Jan Lever, *Creation and Evolution*, at that time widely read. Lever's starting-point here is the God-given creation order. He also defends modal differences as creaturely differences that are determinative of the plant and animal kingdoms. The "dogma of the constancy of species" he rejects, however, with a selection of arguments.[14] Dooyeweerd reacts to this with the thesis that the species "are founded in the divine creation order and determine, in final instance, the nature of plants and animals" and that they "as 'ordering types' make possible our specific experience of plants and animals, and thus cannot be variable."[15] In short, according to Dooyeweerd, the species have to be understood as a law-like type. For this reason a later species can never have originated from the genotypic alteration of an earlier species.

Dooyeweerd distinguishes more and less general structural types. Therefore, among all the biological taxa, the species have a crucial function for him. He calls them "the most individualized structural types" or "the lowest communal types of the plant and animal kingdoms."[16] Not that he automatically identifies the species concept with the species concept as developed by John Ray and Carl Linneaus in the seventeeth and eighteenth centuries. There is, in his view, a fundamental difference between the structures of creation

---

[13] "The structural types of plants and animals are . . . ordering types that belong to the law side, and not to the factual side of our empirical world . . . As *ordering types* they have a constant and foundational character in the order of time because they make *possible* our experience of the plant and animal worlds." Translation by H. Cook from Dooyeweerd, "Schepping en evolutie," *Philosophia Reformata* 24 (1959), 113–59; 132.

[14] Later, in his book *Geïntegreerde Biologie* (Utrecht: Oosthoek, 1973), Lever suggests that the taxonomic distinction between the kingdoms should be dropped. His arguments are that all organisms share a common genetic language, packaged in the structure of DNA, and that they have a common metabolic system, based on adenosine triphosphate. These arguments I do not consider to be decisive. The presence of DNA information and ATP metabolism in all living organisms can better be explained by a theory of emergence. Lever only wants to distinguish between organisms with a vegetative trend, directed at nutrition, and organisms with an animal trend, directed at behavior. Unlike the directedness toward behavior, the directedness toward nutrition, whether this occurs autotrophically through photosynthesis or heterotrophically through absorption or digestion, is not a trend but a basic characteristic of all living systems.

[15] Dooyeweerd, "Schepping en evolutie," 146.   [16] *Ibid.*, 143, 146.

and our fallible formulations about these structures. He also recognizes that in the carriers of genetic factors structural changes can occur, but then only in polytypical species.[17] He admits, furthermore, that the species – or at least the populations that correspond with a typological species – must have been realized, in history, into what they are now. But the manner in which this occurred is unknown. In short, the species are a type structure, the type structure is a law, and the law is immutable.

This hidden essentialism causes great tensions in Dooyeweerd's thinking. On the one hand he presents the species and the above-species categories as a pre-ordered framework of typological options. On the other hand he recognizes the possibility that certain populations which correspond to a species, as generations come and go, have changed within the typological field into what they are now. The manner in which this has occurred completely exceeds our ability to think, however.[18] He calls this inability *docta ignorantia*, learned ignorance.[19] Perhaps nowhere is the tension between the dynamic of his thinking and the dominance of the essentialist tradition so poignantly expressed as in the quotation that follows, a passage in which he designates the problem of descent more or less indifferent in the light of typology!

Naturally one cannot exclude, a priori, the *possibility* that many of the species as we know them today realized themselves as ordering types via a process of gradual or more saltatory structural alteration of groups of individuals in whose ancestors another species type was revealed, even if this possibility is not scientifically verifiable . . . The realized type must be measured according to the ordering type of the species, which is constant according to its law-ordered nature. In view of this, the problem of the actual descent of the individuals belonging to one species is, at least to a certain extent, indifferent.[20]

[17] New types can only arise within the species; ibid., 133, 143.
[18] In a letter to the South African biologist J. J. Duyvené de Wit (February 12, 1964) Dooyeweerd writes: "Whether a genetic line runs from a unicellular organism via multicellular organisms to the first human being we *cannot* say. The answer to the question 'How did God create' lies beyond our human-creaturely and scientific abilities." (We are indebted to Dr. J. Glenn Friesen for sending us a copy of this letter; H. Cook.)
[19] Dooyeweerd, "Schepping en evolutie," 156.
[20] *Ibid.*, 146. I note a comparable tension in the work of Dick Stafleu, who elaborated Dooyeweerd's philosophy of nature in a modern manner. Stafleu describes the species in an essentialist sense as an immutable character, a timeless cluster of structural laws.

Dooyeweerd's argument here falls fundamentally short. Of course, one can make a distinction between the "how" and the "what," between the modal structure and the typological characteristics of a thing or organism. Besides, modal structures have the character of laws, even of idionomic laws. In that sense one can indeed call them general conditions for experience. But Dooyeweerd does not make it plausible that one can also give the predicate of law to the type structures of systematic biology, i.e. to the typological categories of phylum, order, and class, or to the smaller categories of family, genus, and species. He also does not make it plausible that these type structures are a priori determinants of the world of experience, from which one could infer the immutability of species as creational laws. To the contrary, scientific research has convincingly demonstrated that the species are patterns of relative durability but without a fixed identity. The knowledge of all these patterns – modern taxonomists have identified at least two million species – we shall have to gain laboriously by experience, education, and research. The species are – to come back to an earlier distinction – not a priori conditions for experience but factual contents of experience. My conclusion is: the supposed constancy of species is *not* implicit in the reflective-empirical method but is deduced from the metaphysical distinction that essentialists make between a temporal reality with populations that can modify, and a supra-temporal reality of species that represent imperishable forms.

Perhaps someone will object in favor of essentialism that the content of our experience is always individual and variable, but that a species and the characteristics of a species are, to the contrary, general in character. On the basis of this assumption one could conclude that, in the final analysis, a species and the characteristics of a species are not an empirical content of experience but an a priori condition for experience.

Nevertheless, this constancy of species in a structural sense does not exclude that the corresponding populations in a subjective sense are subject to change. On this basis he states: "Evolution signifies the subjective realization of species." M. D. Stafleu, *Een wereld vol relaties: Karakter en zin van natuurlijke dingen en processen* (Amsterdam: Buijten & Schipperheijn, 2002), pp. 198–210, in particular p. 208. A further comment is clarifying: "In a strict sense I do not say that the species change subjectively, but the populations that correspond with a species" (personal communication, June 30, 2003, tran. H. Cook).

That argument does not hold water. Although the act of experiencing is an individual process, the content of what an individual person experiences can nevertheless be a general characteristic. If I see a cow I establish not only individual but also general traits, such as an animal that grazes, chews the cud, and has hollow horns. Thus the content of an experience can be general. It can also be variable. Thus the well-known black and white markings of Holstein-Friesian cattle are not a general standard of nature; they have been derived from an ancient parental stock and were selected as the breed became established. These characteristics of the breed are not general on the basis of an a priori in nature, but on the basis of social conventions and human interventions. Dooyeweerd would no doubt allow this in regard to the characteristics of bovine breeds but not in regard to the characteristics of the species. But in my view it is difficult to understand why the distinction between breeds, say between Holstein and Jersey or Aberdeen Angus cattle, is just a factual content of experience while the distinction between species would suddenly be a general condition for experience. Furthermore, since the advent of biotechnology, not only the artificial modification of breeds but also the genetic manipulation of species lies within human reach.

I shall not contradict essentialism's claim that the living world is characterized by type laws. There are countless laws determinative of a particular type of micro-organism, plant, or animal. Think of microbes such as *Vibrio cholera*, the cholera bacterium, that moves by means of a flagellum. Think of plants such as *Kalanchoë daigremontiana*, that multiplies by small plants on the leaves of the maternity plant. Or think of the many spiders which, like *Latrodectus mactans*, the black widow, catch their prey in a web spun of very fine protein threads. Indeed, the cellular structure, the pattern of growth, and the behavior of all species is type-bound. These types are determined by law.

Thus type laws are not to be ignored. They are a spontaneous and obvious presupposition in our daily life experience. They are also an obvious and unconscious starting-point in our biological research. However, type laws do not have a separate status. They are not to be identified with irreducible essences that originated from an original creating Word. Even less are they to be associated with an intelligent design that would have been inserted, in-between times, so to speak, in the phylogeny of a population.

If the analyses of this book are correct, then biological laws are not typically but only modally determined. They present themselves as a limited set of universal, level-bound principles but with germinative power and an inconceivable adaptive ability. That is to say, these universal principles have particularized themselves into a great diversity of standard applications. Type laws can be considered to be standard applications of elementary biological principles. They are ingenious key formulas that have been repeatedly tried out in the evolutionary process, and that have been codified, letter by letter, in the genome of every living organism in order to survive in the struggle for existence. Also, the cholera bacillus, the maternity plant, and the black widow are carriers of such a standard solution. These standard solutions are not immutable types but typified elaborations of universal modal principles with a high degree of durability.

6 ESCAPING ESSENTIALISM

Throughout the centuries, essentialism has been, next to creationism, one of the toughest strongholds of conservative Christianity with respect to the doctrine of the constancy of species. That's the reason we have paid so much attention to it and focussed on Dooyeweerd's essentialist view of identity structures and type laws.

Dooyeweerd's essentialism has not been without opposition. Earlier I referred to the critical views of Jan Lever. In conclusion I want to bring forward some reservations expressed by Dirk Vollenhoven, a colleague of Dooyeweerd at the Free University in Amsterdam and one of his closest allies in the struggle for a religiously inspired scholarship and an integrally Christian philosophy. The position of Vollenhoven is instructive. Just like Dooyeweerd, he is not a creationist; he does not build his philosophy on literalistic interpretations of the creation message in Genesis. And just like Dooyeweerd his starting-point is a theory of modal spheres and laws that in faith can be seen as expressions of a divine creation order.

What is not present in Vollenhoven's philosophy is a theory of type laws that would hold for the essence or immutable identity of a group of entities. Thus, his philosophy also lacks the application of these type laws to living nature and, similarly, the identification of species and higher taxa in biological systematics with these type laws. In my view this is the main reason why Vollenhoven in the later part of his career could be much more open to modern evolutionary research than Dooyeweerd.

In the severely summarized text of a speech that appeared after his death, Vollenhoven offers a dynamic view of living nature under the central theme: "The genesis *within* the kingdoms." In this framework he brings not only procreation but also transformation forward as the two key concepts for a theory of biotic nature. From this starting-point he comes to a positive recognition of the evolutionary process.[21]

Vollenhoven takes explicit distance from Dooyeweerd's position. He notes: "Dooyeweerd assumes the constancy of species . . . That is, in my view, a late-Aristotelian thought: the becoming *only* of the individual thing." Vollenhoven intends to say: the idea that only individual things and organisms are developmental, but general things (species, etc.) are constant, was unjustly taken over by Dooyeweerd from the later thought of Aristotle. However, besides the becoming of individual things and organisms there is also procreation, i.e. the reproduction of biological groups and populations. The process of procreation can be described as a general process of becoming as far as living nature is concerned. In this general process, Vollenhoven finally concludes, transformations occur, partly in a negative sense in the form of a degeneration of the species, partly in a positive sense in the form of an evolution of species.

In all of this Vollenhoven has one strict reservation. For him, evolution occurs within the fundamental diversity of the biological kingdoms, not across the boundaries of plant life and animal life. The idea that the kingdoms themselves could have evolved from each other and even from inanimate matter completely falls outside

---

[21] D. H. T. Vollenhoven, "Problemen rondom de tijd," in A. Tol and K. A. Bril (eds.), *Vollenhoven als wijsgeer: Inleidingen en teksten* (Amsterdam: Buijten & Schipperheijn, 1992), pp. 170–98. For the quotations that follow see pp. 180–82. They have been adapted by Jaap Klapwijk and translated by Harry Cook.

the horizon of Vollenhoven's views. What may have been the reason for this is not clear to me. Probably he assumed that an evolution of the kingdoms out of each other and out of material reality would be a failure to acknowledge the ontological hierarchy of modal levels and ultimately would lead to a naturalistic monism. Thus, over against Dooyeweerd he makes a plea for a restrictive or kingdom-bound form of evolution:

In plants and animals, procreation occurs. And with this there can be transformation, in the negative sense (degeneration) as well as in the positive sense (evolution). Neither can be denied . . . But it is then a matter within the kingdoms, within a certain kingdom. How far this goes one has to leave to the investigators of the kingdoms concerned; do not say, therefore "the species are immutable" . . . But one can only speak of [an objectionable] *evolutionism* . . . in the case of a genesis that crosses the boundaries between the kingdoms . . . The species concept is too vague over against evolutionism. Species is, as a concept, a collection of characteristics; this is too vague because we are dealing with concrete things . . . In addition, species is too often considered in too static a way (perhaps due to an Aristotelian confusion between *eidos* and *morphè*) . . . "Species" as a concept can be used to kill anything labeled as transformation. To summarize: species is, as a concept, too vague, too fixed, not concrete enough . . . The concept of kingdom is clearer: kingdom with a number of [modal] functions that are determinative.

It is clear that Vollenhoven did not yet consider the concept of saltatory or emergent evolution, no matter how much this concept supports and dynamizes the ontology of modal structures. But it has been one of his major contributions to the Christian philosophical tradition of which in the last century Dooyeweerd and he were important spokespersons that he – unhindered by the notion of type laws – has indicated a way to escape from essentialism. Vollenhoven's position demonstrates that neither a careful analysis of the biblical creation account nor the Judeo-Christian belief in a divine creation order necessarily leads to the doctrine of immutable species.

   I conclude, connecting with ideas presented at the beginning of this chapter. Philosophy is a methodical reflection on experience and, in particular, on the basic conditions under which we experience the world. It can bring us to the recognition of an ontological hierarchy of modes of being as the a priori framework within which we experience life on earth with its variety of kingdoms and wealth of species. The evolution of these species can, to a large extent, be seen as a linear process within the biological kingdoms corresponding to the idionomic laws of these kingdoms. At crucial times, however, it has manifested itself as emergent evolution, an evolution that crossed the modal boundaries of the kingdoms and disclosed higher domains with supervenient modal functions and properties.

However, as soon as philosophy ends in the essentialist view of invariant species as law-like structures to which living organisms and populations would, in advance, have to conform in the evolutionary process, it loses contact with empirical reality. It then becomes an Aristotelian or pseudo-Christian metaphysics, even if one should make an appeal to the order of creation. Whatever the creation order may include, it can never be in conflict with the facts of experience and the robust results of the evolutionary sciences.

In this book I have raised this question: can we find traces of purpose in the living world and its development? Or is evolution, in the final analysis, a blind and capricious natural process that has nothing to do with a purpose or meaning, not to mention the lofty intentions of a divine creator?

Most scientists agree that science falls short in answering this question. I share this viewpoint. To be sure, the phylogeny of life confronts us with remarkable novelties; it even places before us the puzzling hierarchy of ontological arrangements. On this basis we may perhaps speak of a purposeful process and a pathway of meaning. But science does not disclose to us an entrance to God and His purposes. It does not bring us to the creator of the world. Nor does it bring us to the doctrine of species constancy as being a reflection of the creation order, as essentialism suggests. If, nevertheless, science wants to speak of a purpose or meaning perspective, then it should not connect this to the unchangeable *status* of species, but, rather, to the *direction* in which the species have developed over hundreds of millions of years. For the phylogeny of life is directional in the sense of an emergent development in which, ultimately, creatures appeared that, despite their rootedness in matter, prove to be carriers of a spiritual mystery.

Which secret? There is a rumor that humans are pilgrims en route to a city of shalom. But here too the limits of science are clear. For this rumor is carried by faith; science cannot confirm it. I hope to return to this topic in the final chapter. In the penultimate chapter I dwell on a number of questions that have not yet been answered.

CHAPTER 13

Questions surrounding the emergence process

Evolutionary history progresses along an obstacle course. Who shall say how often nature, from the beginning of its cosmic origin, had to cross a hurdle to reach a new level of being? For the sake of clarity I have discussed, until now, no more than five ontological levels: the physical, the biotic, the vegetative, the sensitive, and the mental. With this I have pointed to the distinctive or leading functions of material things, bacteria, plants, animals, and human beings.

This fivefold division is in all probability far too simple a representation of the topic. It is likely that the process of emergent evolution proceeded in a more nuanced manner and requires much more philosophical analysis than can be offered here. In this chapter I want to call attention to a number of lacunae in this research. To begin, we have to take into account that there are more modal levels and thus also more ontological transitions in the evolutionary process than is indicated above (section 1). There is also a need for an additional analysis of what constitutes the irreplaceable value of the human person, and what is the relationship of spirit, soul, and body (section 2). Further discussion is also needed about the question of how the ontological profile of humans developed in the evolutionary process (section 3). Because naturalistic axioms often stand in our way, I conclude this chapter with a summons to more openness of spirit (section 4).

I HIDDEN CONFIGURATIONS IN NATURE: PRIONS

There have probably been more critical transitions in evolutionary history than the fivefold classification above would indicate. It is not impossible that already in the physical universe crucial transitions took place after – some might even like to say "before" – the moment of the Big Bang.

The initial events can hardly be imagined. At the origin of the universe, now usually dated to be 13.7 billion years ago, nuclear particles that developed probably combined soon after to form hydrogen and helium atoms. Heavier atoms such as oxygen, nitrogen, and metals could not form spontaneously. Cosmologists such as Fred Hoyle and William Fowler suggest that they were assembled in the nuclear furnace inside early stars that may have been formed 300 million years after the birth of the universe. Molecules would be of an even later date, possibly formed after stellar explosions in interstellar dust clouds.

Simple experiments in quantum mechanics have given researchers reason to speak of parallel universes. Suppose that the universe is indeed, in a qualitative sense of the word, manifold. Then the "Theory of Everything" proposed by physicist Steven Weinberg in his remarkable book *Dreams of a Final Theory* becomes problematic.[1] Then structural changes may already have occurred in the genesis of the astrophysical universe, emergent innovations that may give good reason for theoretical physicists to develop a "metabletics of matter" in the future.

It is entirely possible that in the living world also, more idio-nomic arrangements of being than we analyzed above have come to the fore in the passage of time. Biologists such as T. Dobzhansky and G. L. Stebbins emphasize that, in the development of life on earth, emergence occurred numerous times.[2] Do we need to go further back and take into account a preparatory phase of life? Did life on earth in the almost impenetrable Cryptozoic (Pre-Cambrian) period cross an early hurdle with the introduction of an elementary life form that preceded the biotic mode of being as we now know it? It could be that eons ago in the ancient ocean, amino acids and nucleotides clumped together into a pre-biotic aggregate with the ability for replication, comparable to those that Manfred Eigen

---

[1] S. Weinberg, *Dreams of a Final Theory: The Scientist's Search for the Ultimate Laws of Nature* (New York: Pantheon Books, 1992).

[2] Stebbins, *Darwin to DNA*, considers the origin of eukaryotes, multicellular organisms, invertebrate and vertebrate animals, warm-blooded birds, mammals, and human beings as instances of emergence.

brought to light in his laboratory, and that only from the "RNA world" of nucleic acid life, on a following level of complexity, unicellular micro-organisms evolved.[3]

When considering pre-biotic evolutionary stages we perhaps need also to think in an entirely new direction. In the early 1980s Stanley Prusiner discovered minuscule particles that can infect the brains of cows with BSE ("mad cow disease") and of sheep with scrapies. These particles consist of a protein without a nucleic acid genome, i.e. without the hereditary material that is characteristic of life on earth. Prusiner called this pathogenic protein a prion. Other prions proved to be capable of causing comparable diseases in deer and in humans. In the latter case, the illness is known as Creutzfeldt-Jacob disease. Prusiner is currently of the opinion that mammals have a gene that codes for normal prions and that these prions can be converted, spontaneously or by contact with abnormal prions, into disease-causing prions.[4]

I do *not* suggest that prions represent, in themselves, a pre-biotic phase of life. On the contrary, it is clear that not only disease-causing prions but also normal prions presuppose biotic forms of life, or that they are in a symbiotic relationship with them. Nevertheless, the remarkable mode of existence of prions may give us a hint how there could be a protein-like pre-form of life that incarnates the principles of self-regulation and proliferation, but without the coding ability that is inherent to the principle of DNA transmission.

What is the status of the biotic mode of being, dominant in unicellular organisms and subjacently present in all multicellular systems? Even if one would entirely ignore the possibility of a prebiotic form of being and simply state that the principles of self-regulation, homeostasis, metabolism, reproduction, and DNA

[3] W. Gilbert, "The RNA World," *Nature* 319 (1986), 618. C. R. Woese, "A New Biology for a New Century," 173–86.

[4] For his research on prions, Prusiner was awarded the Nobel Prize in Physiology and Medicine in 1997. For the distinction between normal and pathogenic prions, see S. B. Prusiner, "Detecting Mad Cow Disease," *Scientific American* 291 (July 2004), 86–93. Recently Prusiner and co-workers announced the laboratory synthesis of prions: G. Legname, S. B. Prusiner *et al.*, "Synthetic Mammalian Prions," *Science* 305 (2004), 673–76.

transmission determine the biotic level of being, then other differences in levels are not excluded. Perhaps a critical boundary was crossed, as Stebbins suggests, when within the realm of unicellular organisms eukaryotes appeared and took their place beside the prokaryotes.[5] In fact, quite a number of biologists consider the difference between prokaryotes and eukaryotes – remember that the latter and all their descendants only occur in the last quarter of the history of life on earth – to be greater than that between plants and animals.[6]

The topic is even more complicated when photosynthesis and the receptivity for light that occurs in some of the prokaryotes, particularly the blue-green algae, have also to be seen as a new competency, a crossing of a boundary toward a higher level of being. It is worth mentioning that taxonomists from the 1990s on have divided the kingdom of the Prokaryota into two domains, the Bacteria and the considerably smaller Archaea (see ch. 5, section 4). The structural implications of these new divisions in domains and kingdoms are, as yet, difficult to ascertain. Not every taxonomic distinction based on criteria for the kingdoms necessarily corresponds with what we have in mind: an ontological ordering based on modal levels and idionomic competencies.[7]

How plants and animals evolved is not entirely clear either. There are good indications that these branches of the tree of life have both developed from out of the unicellular eukaryotes. Both developed via emergent self-transcendence but along separate paths. It happened in such a way that the vegetative mode of being that came to the fore in the plant kingdom was also realized in the vegetative body structure of animals. Yet there is a remarkable difference. In the animal body with its flexible organs and all its possibilities for interactivity this vegetative structure has become subservient to the higher, sensitive body structure.

---

[5] Eukaryotes, as we saw earlier, are distinguished from prokaryotes by membranes that surround the nucleus and that are part of such cellular organelles as mitochondria and chloroplasts.

[6] E. O. Dodson, "The Kingdom of Organisms," *Systematic Zoology* 20 (1971), 265–81.

[7] The taxonomic distinctions discussed in this paragraph are also described in an overview: W. F. Doolittle, "Uprooting the Tree of Life," *Scientific American* 282 (February 2000), 90–95.

The position of the Fungi (molds and their relatives) and their relationship to the plant and animal kingdom is also debatable. These organisms lack chlorophyll and the ability to carry out photosynthesis and, for this reason, cannot synthesize their own nutrients. They distinguish themselves in many cases by having a predominant haploid phase and being heterotrophic, i.e. obtaining nutrients by external digestion of dead or living organisms. Phylogenetic analysis, using DNA and protein sequence determinations, has led some investigators to postulate that fungi are more closely related to animals than to plants; others assume that fungi are the ancestors of plants. Whatever is the case, all the investigations into modes of nutrition, life cycles, cell types, phylogeny, and the like are only peripheral to the question that concerns us here: do the fungi represent a separate kingdom of organisms, and if so, on the basis of which idionomic competence?[8]

The status of animals also needs to be clarified more fully. Whoever just refers to the sensitive feeling of animals as an idionomic competence is not saying very much. The sensitivity of animals is difficult to gauge. We can only assess it from the outside, by neurophysiological measurements and observations of behavior. Sensitivity is probably an ambivalent concept. It can indicate outer and inner experience, sensory perception and psychic feeling. Have the sense experiences of elementary animal organisms and the inner feelings of advanced chordates developed from each other in a continuous, one-dimensional line? Or must we assume that in the development from lower to higher animals emergence gave rise to a higher sphere of competence and a new type of sensitivity?

An even thornier question is how the sensitivity of animals correlates with their instinct. For instinct, too, is an ambiguous concept with a multitude of meanings, a storehouse where zoologists and philosophers stow all the animal inclinations and behaviors that they do not know what to do with. Nevertheless, instinctive acts are

[8] R. H. Whittaker proposed the idea of a separate kingdom of the fungi (see ch. 5, section 4). American scientists suggest that the differences between the genes of fungi and of plants could be utilized to reconstruct a time scale of development of plants and fungi. Since fungi appear to have developed 1.3 million years ago, they are evidently the pioneers of plant life. Plants would have developed much later, 700 million years ago. E. Pennisi, "Molecular Approach to Mushroom Hunting," *Science* 293 (2001), 1027–28.

of great importance; they include the social instincts and all kinds of communicative abilities that, at times, make animals strongly resemble human beings. In what follows I want to make some further comments about the relationship between animal instinct and human consciousness. In any case the ambiguity of the concepts of sensitivity and instinct could indicate that in the diversification of animal functions, emergence in the sense of self-transcendence has taken place.

2 JOHN PAUL II ON THE EVOLUTION PROBLEM

The topic of emergence and self-transcendence becomes even more urgent in the case of human beings. More than any other creature on earth, the human person is a puzzling and enigmatic being. Even though human beings are a product of emergent evolution, from a taxonomic point of view they do not represent a kingdom as plants and animals do. *Homo sapiens* is only a single species. But it is a species with a distinctive feature: the mind or mental consciousness. And because humans are capable of reflecting upon themselves and upon the deeper, spiritual root of their existence as "per-son" (see ch. 9, section 2), this mental consciousness can also be designated as self-consciousness and even spirit, i.e. a consciousness that is breathed through with a higher or divine reality.

Considering the human species, I want to make some comments about five topics in this section: the so-called self-consciousness of monkeys (for comparison), religious consciousness, the relationship of mind and body, the concept of the soul as formulated by Pope John Paul II, and the multiformity of the mind. We shall see that from these topics shall flow a new series of evolutionary questions.

The supposed self-consciousness of monkeys   In the 1970s, the animal psychologist Gordon Gallup disputed the thesis that consciousness of self is an exclusive characteristic of human beings. He did this on the basis of the "mirror test." Under anesthesia, Gallup applied a dab of paint to the forehead of several species of monkeys. Whenever the animals, once they awoke, scratched their forehead after a look in the mirror, Gallup ascribed self-consciousness to them. Older chimpanzees and a single orangutan appeared to be aware of themselves, but apes and monkeys lower on the evolutionary scale seemed to be staring at a stranger. In 2001 and 2006 the mirror test was repeated with dolphins and elephants and, here too, a form of self-awareness was detected. Or not?

Consciousness of self is not the same thing as the recognition of one's own head as a part of one's body with the help of a mirror. For with self-consciousness or self-awareness we normally think of something else entirely: the inner concern of a human being with his or her own existence. We think here of the ability of the human person to engage in conversation with him- or herself and, in a normative sense, to give account of what he or she is or does. This definitely involves more than the Gallup experiment would indicate. Only humans are capable of carrying out a dialogue with themselves in terms of knowledge of, and accountability to, themselves. Thus, human consciousness is self-consciousness, and self-consciousness is more than higher-level consciousness. It is an awareness of personal integrity, probably even a vague sense of divine presence.

Religious consciousness Human consciousness – I noted this earlier – plays itself out on several levels, also on the level of faith and religion. Beside logical, technical, and moral consciousness, human beings also display religious awareness. This last point is controversial. Many people do not feel themselves to be religious in the least. They deny religious consciousness as well as spiritual connection with God. Do self-consciousness and knowledge of God belong together?

In my view the thesis is indeed defensible that the consciousness of non-believers and dissenters, too, has a spiritual basis and a religious expression. For secular people also have the innate impulse to see their temporal existence in the light of ultimate reference points, even if they give an innerworldly expression to this spiritual motivation. Examples of innerworldly religion are the absolutization of reason, the exultation of artistic creativity, the adoration of sports or pop idols, or also – as I tried to demonstrate in this book – the reduction of all life forms to random expressions of matter. In this urge to absolutize what is relative, secular people mirror themselves in what transcends their individual existences and in an introverted way give evidence of an unconscious contact with the divine.

Mind and body In its confounding multiplicity, the mind or mental consciousness is not an addition to the body. The human being is a unity, just as each living organisms is, in its own way, a unity. The human person represents a totality structure in its own right. Thus, the human mind is *not* an independent entity. The mind is not an immortal soul descended into a perishable body, as Plato postulated, not a timeless intelligent form realized in a material organism, as Aristotle assumed, and not a rational substance at the helm of a mechanical vehicle, a ghost in a machine, as Descartes suggested. What is it then?

Human consciousness is entirely entwined with its modal substrate functions. Every rational argument and every moral act gives evidence of sensitive, vegetative, biotic, and even of molecular processes. "Without phosphorus, no thought" is the well-known pronouncement of the Dutch materialist Jacob Moleschott.[9] That pronouncement is very one-sided but not incorrect. The mind is matter, but matter that has been brought to a successively higher level of existence in the process of emergence.

The concept of the soul formulated by Pope John Paul II The world came to life and the human being flowered into a person with unending and incomparable worth, called to enter into fellowship with God. This is one of the central truths of the Christian faith, and I subscribe to it. Thus I feel a close affinity with the following statement of the late John Paul II in a papal message of 1996 to the Pontifical Academy of Sciences:

The Church's Magisterium is directly concerned with the question of evolution, for it involves the conception of man: Revelation teaches us that he was created in the image and likeness of God . . . In other terms, the human individual cannot be subordinated as a pure means or a pure instrument, either to the species or to society; he has value *per se*. He is a person . . . But even more, man is called to enter into a relationship of knowledge and love with God himself, a relationship which will find its complete fulfillment beyond time, in eternity. All the depth and grandeur of this vocation are revealed to us in the mystery of the risen Christ.

---

[9] J. Moleschott, *Der Kreislauf des Lebens* (Mainz: Von Zabern, 1852): "Ohne Phosphor keine Gedanke!"

As he continues, I take distance from his position. Here the Pope inserts, with an appeal to the encyclical *Humani Generis*,[10] a dichotomy between the body and soul of the human person:

[I]f the human body takes its origin from pre-existent living matter, the spiritual soul is immediately created by God . . . Consequently, theories of evolution which, in accordance with the philosophies inspiring them, consider the mind as emerging from the forces of living matter, or as a mere epiphenomenon of this matter, are incompatible with the truth about man. Nor are they able to ground the dignity of the person.[11]

The Pope is, not unjustifiably, apprehensive about evolutionary naturalism as a philosophical source of inspiration. But with the dualistic view of a body that has evolved from matter, and a soul that has arisen by a special creation, the Pope takes away from us the biblical view of the unity of the human person as a creature that, in all its mental and bodily activities, lives *coram Dei* (Luther), i.e. before the face of God. In fact, he confirms here, albeit within a Christian frame of reference, the classical Greek dualism of body and soul, enabling him to express his agreement with a Darwinian evolution theory in a restricted form. As if the body came into existence via the mediated process of evolution, while the soul would be introduced into every human embryo, at the time of conception, as an immediate result of God's creative intervention, bypassing all genetic and evolutionary developments.

The multiformity of the mind   A remarkable characteristic of the human mind is multiformity and variability. The mind is first of all multiform in the sense of multi-modal. Rooted in the physical body, it has unfolded in a multiplicity of idionomic functions, some of which are analytical, technical, economical, moral, and religious awareness. With these modal competencies corresponds, we discovered (see ch. 8, section 2), a multitude of idionomic activity systems in modern society, such as science, technology, economy, etc.

---

[10] John Paul II here appeals to the pronouncement: "animas enim a Deo immediate creari catholica fides nos retinere iubet" (for the Catholic faith exhorts us to maintain that the spirit is created directly by God) in the encyclical *Humani Generis* of Pope Pius XII, *Acta Apostolicae Sedis* 42 (1950), p. 575.

[11] John Paul II, "Message to the Pontifical Academy of Sciences," *The Quarterly Review of Biology* 72 (1997), 381–83.

Moreover, the mind is extremely variable. Human beings are not instinctively bound to stereotypical patterns of behavior as are the drones, the workers, and the queen in a hive of honeybees. They have to take free decisions. They act in systems of activity that they have themselves created and in which they fulfill a diversity of roles. Thanks to the flexible use of their mental abilities, i.e. their freedom of choice, they devote themselves, now to professional obligations or to studies, then to care tasks, sport, music, and so on.

3 ONTOLOGICAL PROFILE AND EVOLUTIONARY PROCESS: NEANDERTHALS

We have encountered the exceptional position of the human being. As I said before, neither the capabilities of the body nor the competencies of the mind make the human being unique. The human being is unique because all its bodily and mental functions are rooted in the I–Thou relation, the spiritual bond of love of the human I with God and fellow people. It is this pre-functional, intimate relationship to others that marks every human being as a person with a unique and indispensable value in itself (see ch. 9, section 2).

And yet, this unique creature is not an isolated and independent being. On the contrary, with all its mental and bodily functions, and even as a spiritual being, it is closely interwoven with the material world, also in the evolutionary respect. Emerged from nature with all other living creatures, only humans have shown themselves to be capable of transforming nature into culture, into the field of endeavor where the mind can work. Seen from a functionalistic perspective, the mind is the distinctive characteristic of the human person. It has manifested itself in a great diversity of mental functions and societal systems. From this multifunctional position of human beings, new evolutionary questions come to the fore. I want to highlight two of these.

My first question: did the variety of mental functions of *Homo sapiens* emerge at one time or did it come to light step by step? Did analytical insight, technical skill, artistic creativity, moral sensitivity, and the like appear simultaneously? Or did human individuals in prehistoric times fall back to the instinctive behavior of preceding hominids for the greater part only to successively gain a greater and greater participation in what we would now recognize to be the human identity? Paleo-anthropological data are annoyingly ambivalent on this point.

Let us consider esthetic awareness. Archeologists have determined that *Homo sapiens*, more than 100,000 years ago, made specific markings with red ochre on the walls of caves near the mouth of the Klasies River in the Republic of South Africa. Were these markings an early symptom of artistic sensitivity or did they only have a practical signaling function? Questions of this sort arise about other locations as well. Not long ago, researchers found a collection of perforated snail shells, about 75,000 years old, in the Blombos Cave near Cape Town. All the holes in the shells proved to have been made in the same place in the shell.[12] What must we think of all this? Did early human beings decorate themselves as early as that with chains of beads? Or were the perforations purely fortuitous, and must we maintain the current opinion that artistic human talent did not develop until a much later period, say 40,000 years ago? It is known that prehistoric humans searched for precious stones at that time, and made cave paintings, not only in Spain and France but also on the African and Australian continents.

Comparable questions arise in regards to the moral awareness. Let's consider *Homo neanderthalensis*.[13] At the time of the first discovery of fossil remains of Neanderthals in 1856 and 1908, they were depicted as primitive brutes with club or stick. This image became more human when traces of temporary settlements were discovered. In recent years another change of opinion has occurred. Carvings on the remains of chewed-off human bones found by old locations of fires have created the impression that the Neanderthals were thoroughgoing cannibals. Is this opinion correct? These

---

[12] C. Henshilwood, "Middle Stone Age Shell Beads from South Africa," *Science* 304 (2004), 404.

[13] Neanderthals were indirectly related to *Homo sapiens*. It is assumed that the last representatives became extinct approximately 25,000 years ago near Gibraltar. I. Tattersall gives an account of these Neanderthals in *The Monkey in the Mirror: Essays on the Science of What Makes Us Human* (New York: Harcourt, 2002), ch. 5.

ancient people possessed a good-sized brain, refined artifacts, and sophisticated hunting techniques. It was determined that they also took care of their wounded, and that they even developed burial rituals. Must our conclusion be that their morality was present from the beginning but was suppressed in times when the interest of the group demanded it? Or should we conclude that moral, and perhaps also religious, sensibility emerged in a later stage, after logical and technical awareness had developed?

My second question: what was the impetus for the origination of the human mind? What developments in the life of pre-human primates formed the necessary conditions for the origin of those specific abilities that are characteristic of the ontological profile of human beings? To put it another way, how were human mental functions able to rise above the pre-mental functions that one encounters in living nature? Did emergence of the mind imply that at a given moment human awareness as a unit superseded the instinctive drives of animals in favor of technology, culture, and worship? Or was it a case of innovations one by one, that is to say, self-transcendences, now here, then there?

If we assume the first hypothesis – I name this the accumulation hypothesis – the pre-human beings followed the bed of animal instinct as long as possible, until the emergence of, shall we say, logical insight elicited a sudden chain reaction of cognitions of a different sort. One could imagine its course in a few words as follows. Logical analysis became the substrate for technical ability, that is to say, analytical distinctions were put to use for distinguishing means/end relationships. Technical insight, in turn, became a substrate for lingual consciousness, i.e. signals were employed as efficient means to the end of transmitting meanings. Lingual consciousness became a substrate for moral awareness, or also, words and gestures were used to express good intentions. Moral awareness became, finally, a substrate for experiences of faith; to put it another way, love and good care were experienced as a budding awareness of divine presence. And in this entire process of functional changes, human beings began to recognize themselves as spiritual creatures, equipped with personal attention and responsibility over against God, themselves, and fellow creatures.

In short, in this perspective, the ontological stratification of organizational levels and modal functions that we have encountered in the order of nature continues itself in the order of culture, in an anthropological hierarchy of mental arrangements. From this perspective, the initial emerging movement from the animal kingdom in the direction of the human species became, at the same time, a giant step, for it released, even though it was on the basis of a natural continuum, a many-sided cultural change. The process of hominization came to expression in an accumulation of functions and in a series of mental innovations. Time will tell if sufficient empirical support from the past will be found for this accumulation-model of human genesis.

If we start from the second hypothesis – one could call this the integration hypothesis – then the assumption is less massive. In this case typical human competencies developed from time to time and occasionally, even if they later integrated into the totality structure of the human person. Those functions came into being at different times and on diverse continents, elicited by catastrophes and other specific circumstances. While in the accumulation model the higher mental functions built upon the lower ones in a regular order, in the integration model they connected, from case to case, to the instinctive abilities that animal ancestors had developed beforehand. One could imagine that hundreds of thousands of years were necessary for the completion of this process. This leads to the delicate and almost embarrassing question whether there were ever on earth beings that we might have to consider, on the basis of their one-sided abilities, as partly human.

The integration model of human genesis too is a model that awaits testing by empirical sciences, including paleontology, ethology, and comparative psychology. According to this model, logical insight is probably an extension and innovation of the mimetic learning behavior of higher animal species. Technical ability developed from the fabricating abilities of apes. Lingual facility was an idionomic rearrangement of the sign language as we encounter it among chimpanzees and bonobos. Solidarity and care for the neighbor arose out of the spontaneous acts of reciprocity among pre-human primates. In short, all kinds of solutions that animals had, until that time, employed instinctively in their struggle for survival, gave rise to mental functions because human beings brought them to a higher level by conscientization. Hominids became human because they became, at crucial moments, critically and normatively aware of actions that had, until that time, been carried out instinctively, if they occurred in the animal kingdom at all. They coordinated these actions into an ontological profile that corresponds to the unique worth that we nowadays grant to the human person.

According to which model, accumulation or integration, the genesis of human beings took place cannot be determined by philosophical reflection. That is a lesson that can be learned from a comparison with animal and plant life. With regard to animals and plants we can make a distinction between their ontological profile and the evolutionary process by which they originated; yet the ontological profile does not legitimize conclusions with reference to the evolutionary process. The ontological profile of the animal demonstrates that the sensitive structure is based on a vegetative substructure, for observation and feeling in animals are dependent on morphogenetic and physiological processes, that we also find, *mutatis mutandis*, in plants. Evolutionary research has nevertheless indicated that animals did not originate from plants.

Well, also in regard to human beings it is important to separate the ontological profile and the evolutionary process. Even if it is possible to bring a systematic order in the ontological profile of human beings, the question of how, in the becoming of *Homo sapiens*, human characteristics evolved from subhuman characteristics cannot be answered by philosophical reflection but only by continued empirical research.

4 THE LAST GREAT NARRATIVE

I don't know how the questions I have raised in this chapter with regard to emergent evolution will be answered in the future. In any case, I see no reason why we should have to consider a theory that is based on emergent evolution to be in conflict with the biblical message of creation. With two caveats. First, do not read the Bible as a journalistic account; it is, rather, a collection of faith-inspired writings that witness to God as origin, sustainer, and finisher of all existence. And, secondly, do not consider evolutionary science to be a theory of the development of the species only in the sense of gradual adaptations but also in the sense of boundary-crossing innovations.

The message of the biblical narratives moves from creation, via the depths of alienation from God and fellow creatures, to reconciliation and eschatological completion. The perspective of evolutionary science moves along an ascending series of emergent levels of being. Thus from the Bible one cannot deduce emergence, and from science one cannot infer creation. But the biblical faith in creation can function as a hermeneutic context for scientific investigation. It can help us to view the idea of emergent evolution with greater openness than is usual in evolutionistic circles.

I regret that this openness is often lacking in discussions about evolution, hypnotized as many are by the dream of a one-dimensional evolutionary continuum in nature. Let us not forget that this dream, too, has a hermeneutic context and is inspired by faith. In fact a threefold faith is involved. It is the faith (1) that fundamental novelty is fully impossible, (2) that the method of the natural sciences is the deepest source of truth, and (3) that animate nature with all its levels of complexity can be completely reduced to inanimate nature. This faith covers up all the questions that I have posed in this chapter because its adherents know the answers from the outset.

Evolutionary naturalism is an unproven expectation that may accept the notion of emergence in terms of increasing complexification but that excludes the possibility of emergence in terms of idonomic and non-reductive innovation in advance. It contradicts explicitly the view that nature could transcend itself in favor of new configurations of being. It contradicts with even greater explicitness the view that in evolutionary history a perspective of meaning could delineate itself, a perspective that points to the crucial position of the human species. Upon closer examination, it contradicts the truth claim of science in this way, and thus also the validity claim of its own standpoint, as we saw earlier (see ch. 10, section 3).

After the failure of positivism with its belief in factual knowledge as the only source of rational and moral progression, and after the failure of Marxism with its belief in world revolution as the only entrance to the classless society of the future, evolutionary naturalism with its belief in the iron mechanisms of nature as the final solution of all riddles of life is the last great narrative from the past two centuries that is ready to be deflated.

CHAPTER 14

Enkapsis in nature. Is there an Omega point?

At the beginning of this book I posed the question: did the process of evolution produce living organisms including human beings strictly by chance? Or can evolution theory also be in harmony with the view that the world has a purpose and that human existence gives evidence of a plan or of divine intentions? Human history demonstrates such exceptional examples of wisdom, creativity, and moral dedication that the thought of an ultimate purpose of life forces itself upon us, even if these expectations are assailed by disappointment and bewilderment. For the world is presented to us in the Bible as a reality that has been created by God with a purpose: it is on the way toward its blessed final destiny, the kingdom of God.

In this final chapter we return to the quest for purpose and meaning. I want to focus our quest on these four questions: In nature, do perspectives of meaning not become apparent in the subordination of the physical to above-physical levels, and of nature as a whole to the actions of human beings as the bearers of culture (section 1)? Can these perspectives of meaning also transcend the interactions between nature and culture and be included in a religious perspective of meaning, in which we experience world events as subordinate to God's dealing with the world to open the path for His kingdom (section 2)? Can we on the basis of these experiences extend the idea of emergent evolution and conclude that the evolutionary process will reach its apotheosis in the expected kingdom of God (section 3)? Finally, are not all our experiences with respect to purpose and meaning ambiguous (section 4)?

Let us begin close to home and connect the quest for meaning, in the first instance, to the theme of self-subordination in nature. Everywhere in the living world, as we noted earlier, we encounter typical biotic laws: the laws of natural selection of Darwin, the laws of heredity of Mendel, the law of stable equilibrium between two gene alleles in large, undisturbed populations of Hardy and Weinberg, etc. But we also saw that in that same world physical laws continue to exert their influence. That is to say, physical laws maintain their validity, but not in complete autonomy. Physical nature is in one way or another enlaced in living organisms. It is present but has made itself serviceable to the principles and purposes of life. Think, for example, of the genetic mutations that can occur in the gametes, i.e. the germinal cell line in multicellular organisms. Such a gene mutation is, at first sight, nothing but a random event on the molecular level. Nevertheless, this mutation can only persist if it is of benefit to the group or, at least, if it is not harmful to it. In other words, the molecular processes are random and, nevertheless, subjected to the functional demands and the border conditions of the biological system of which they are part.

If it is clear anywhere that nature is a contingent occurrence and, simultaneously, more than that, then it is in this strange phenomenon of enkapsis[1] and self-subordination. With this phrase I mean that in living beings, despite their idionomic character, lower modal functions are interlaced and make themselves subservient to the purposes of higher modal functions. In the self-subordination of nature to successively higher levels, that is, to structures with supervenient properties and qualities, the lower structures acquire, in one way or another, foundational and preparatory significance.

We encounter the phenomenon of enkapsis and self-subordination in flora and fauna wherever we go. Tough plants are able to transform the most inhospitable places on earth into an Eden of ordered ecosystems. Thus, in the searing heat of Baja California in Mexico, gigantic barrel cacti fight the laws of thermodynamics to survive,

---

[1] "Enkapsis" is the Greek word for interlacement.

resisting a return to chaos. Animals, too, are able to make a hostile environment suit their own needs. Thus cheetahs in Tanzania's Serengeti desert are able to utilize the laws of gravity and motion in their hunt for speedy prey. In various ways, living creatures play with the inexorable laws of nature. It is as if they want to impress upon us that they can not only overcome mechanical laws of nature but can even exploit them for their own purposes and survival.

Self-subordination is even incorporated in the evolutionary principles of competition, variation, selection, and transmission. These principles are biotic in nature but often strike us as purely mechanical, blunt, and hard as a rock. Until we discover that there are, indeed, molecular mechanisms involved, but that these completely serve the maximization of the fitness of a population. Then the process of selection shows itself to be obedient to the rules for survival of the species. Then the striving of competition proves itself to be of service to the parenthood of animal pairs, the reciprocity of conspecifics, and the inclusive fitness of related individuals. Then the processes of variation and transmission, too, prove to be more than the random exchange of DNA molecules. For these molecules serve to support life, as I have tried to show with my example of gametes.

Do note, physical or mechanical laws do not lose their validity wherever life presents itself as an enkaptic whole; they are truly universal! But in the living world they are incorporated and over-ruled – no matter how unimaginable this may seem to one-dimensional evolutionists – by idionomic laws of a higher order, laws that reveal themselves in the kingdoms of unicellular and multicellular biosystems.

When we observe human culture and society we see similar examples of interlacement and subservience. It is noteworthy that this enkapsis in human society largely occurs unconsciously. As an example, take the traffic on our roads and the behavior of automobile drivers. Rules of traffic such as keeping to the right, giving right of way, stopping for red lights, and observing speed limits, we experience in our first driving lessons as rational instructions, rules that we carefully memorize. But when we obtain our driver's license and become experienced drivers these bothersome rules quickly become internalized reaction patterns. They become "second nature" to us, a set of standard behaviors and of well-used body reflexes. That is a good thing, for the automatic action pattern of accelerating, braking, stopping, and the like ensures that in hectic traffic situations we can concentrate on unexpected dangers. In short, driving an automobile is, for the most part, a well-balanced system of mechanical reactions, an unconscious disciplining of the lower levels of human nature to the benefit of society.

All of culture can be defined as a human attempt to accommodate nature to its own purposes and to subordinate it to higher goals. This becomes especially evident in science, technology, morals, and religion. Science, one could briefly say, is the attempt to subject nature to theoretical questions. Technology is the attempt to control nature and to make it subservient to practical purposes. Morality is the attempt to integrate the natural associations between people into a system of virtues and obligations. Even religion is based on subordination in that it bears witness to a God who turns the powers of nature and the natural passage of individual lives to human blessing, shalom.

Does that mean that miracles can occur? Perhaps. The Bible, in any case, tells us about many miracles. Let us examine some of them more closely.

2 "DESERT STORM" AND OTHER MIRACLES

The miracle that stands out in the Old Testament is the Exodus of Israel from Egypt and the passage through the Red Sea. When the Israelites reached the treacherous Sea of Reeds, as it is sometimes known, God's command to Moses was: "Raise your staff and stretch out your hand over the sea to divide the water so that the Israelites can go through the sea on dry ground." If one stops reading here, blind to the imagery of the Bible, one would picture the people of Israel in a fairy-tale-like setting, groping as they slowly move along an uneven sea-bottom between two walls of water, like the glass sides of an aquarium, that were divided by the intervention of Moses. In reality the passage through the Red Sea was a more prosaic event. For further in the passage we also read: "Then Moses stretched out his hand over the sea and all that night the Lord drove the sea back with a strong east wind and turned it into dry land.

The waters were divided and the Israelites went through the sea on dry ground, with a wall of water on their right and on their left" (Ex. 14:21). In the "dividing of the waters" God used a "desert storm."

Do not think that I'm using physical explanations to explain God's action away! Instead I'm trying to make clear that the domain of faith is supervenient to the domain of physics. To put it more simply, I'm attempting to show that, in the view of the Bible, God mobilizes the energies and laws of nature for purposes that can only be experienced in faith. The interlacement of matter in higher domains of being is a basic property of organic nature. It is also a basic feature of culture and civilization. And for those who have eyes to see, it is a characteristic too of how God interacts with nature. Many people protest when it comes to this last point. They consider God's exercise of power over nature to be untenable from a scientific point of view. But, oddly enough, they do not have this reservation when it comes to the possibilities of human intervention in nature.

I spoke of a miracle. There is no basis for the thought that God does make use of the laws of nature in His usual dealing with people, e.g. as an answer to their prayers, but that He, at a crucial moment, breaks them with a word of power in order to create a miracle. As if a miracle would go against nature! Theologians of scholastic persuasion do indeed suggest that the miracles in the Bible are *contra naturam* because they break the laws of nature. Do miracles violate the laws of nature? I call this an anachronistic representation of events. It reads the idea of a "closed system of nature," as it is presented by modern physics, into the biblical descriptions of nature. In this way, a miracle, by definition, acquires the character of an anomaly, a phenomenon that by means of an exception does not conform to the laws of nature as determined by science. But the modern concept of nature is lacking in the oriental worldview and was foreign to the authors of the Bible. Without embarrassment the Bible recounts that God, at the Sea of Reeds, did not switch off the powers of nature; rather he called on them, even overruled them by making them subservient to his seigniorial intents: the liberation of Pharaoh's slaves.

The great Reformers of the sixteenth century noted correctly that biblical miracles are not *contra naturam* but *contra peccatum* (against sin). A miracle does not oppose the rules of nature but the powers of sin and evil. God liberates us from them sometimes by means of a miracle, that is to say, in a manner that is not supernatural but wondrous or surprising. The miracle is, therefore, not recognizable in the cold-blooded analyses of science but in the warm-blooded experiences of faith, experiences that are receptive for surprises. We can only observe the miracle in a personal walk with God. As an objective fact it is ambiguous and arguable, and science cannot determine it unequivocally. Outside the realm of faith, even the great exodus from Egypt – so the prophet Amos impresses upon us in the Old Testament – is nothing more than an average event, as trivial as the exodus of the Philistines from Crete and of the Arameans from Iraq.[2]

This overpowering nature of God's actions also characterizes the miracles of Jesus, whether it concerns the so-called miracles of nature or the miracles of healing. Nowhere in the Bible do they have the character of extramundane phenomena or dazzling magic. Time and again, they are described as "signs" of the coming kingdom of God, that is, as healing acts that are laden with anticipatory meaning, as meaningful referrals to all those things that God may yet have in store for people on earth.

This anticipatory character is especially apparent in the pre-eminent miracle of the New Testament, the death and resurrection of Jesus. Jesus died a very cruel but also a very natural death. That's to say, God used natural mechanisms and human machinations – the plot of the Jewish leaders, the command of Pilate to execute Jesus – to complete his plan of salvation. When it comes to Jesus' resurrection, the Bible indeed depicts it as a turning-point in world history but not as an irregular and exceptional intervention in the creation order. The order of creation is dynamically described as pointing forward to the order of God's coming kingdom. For this reason the risen Lord is described in the imaginative language of the Bible as "first fruits" (1 Cor. 15:20), i.e. as an indication of the first fruits of a much more abundant harvest to come. In other words, Jesus' death and resurrection, no matter how unique, are not an

---

[2] This is how I interpret the Hebrew text in Amos 9:7.

exclusive but an inclusive event. In Jesus God is anticipating what He is intending to do with the world.[3]

In my account of miracles in the natural and human world, explained in terms of intertwinement, subordination, and anticipation, I simply pass on authentic experiences of meaning by people from many times and places. Philosophers can only reflect on the character of such experiences. Miraculous experiences surround our earthly existence on every level. I don't understand how a cactus in the desert turns the forces of nature to its advantage, but it happens. I don't fathom how an automobile driver utilizes the laws of nature to fight his or her way through traffic, but it happens. Most of all, I don't comprehend how the world with all its imposing orderings, but also with all its faults and failures, moves steadily toward the coming of God's kingdom. Yet, that is what the Bible shows us as a truth that we know by faith and that, from a scientific point of view, does not appear implausible or impossible.

3 THE KINGDOM OF GOD AS FINAL STAGE? TEILHARD AND LASZLO

In the evolutionary perspective, perhaps the most vexing question arises here. Can we, in scholarship and with the tools of science, present the kingdom of God as the highest stage of emergent evolution? Until now I have tried to maintain a distance between the theoretical insights of science and the practical certainties of faith. But can philosophical reflection not build a bridge between the theory of evolution and the religious expectation of God's kingdom? Suppose that evolution is emergent evolution, and that emergent evolution, despite factors of chance and randomness, is a process of gradual self-transcendence in the direction of increasingly higher levels of being. Would this assumption not form a valid ground for the theoretical conclusion that the expected kingdom of God can be considered to be the final result of the process of emergent evolution?

---

[3] See Rom. 6 and 1 Cor. 15. The miracle in Scripture is a sign that points forward, anticipating a greater reality that is still to come: "the powers of the coming age" (Hebr. 6:5).

In science the evolutionary process has proved to be a huge course of events that spans hundreds of millions of years and that reveals its secrets gradually, in bits and pieces. Matter transcends itself to become more than matter. Bacteria, plants, and animals transcend each other in successively higher systems of life. Human beings with their pre-functional status and functional competencies excel as the crown of creation. From a philosophical point of view there indeed seem to be indications – not to say valid reasons – here to speak of a purpose or a meaning. Can we draw this line of emergence further? Can we give the coming kingdom of God, a central intent in the Lord's prayer, a place in our theory of emergence now? Is the "New Jerusalem," the city of shalom where the struggle for life has been stilled and the pilgrimage of humankind is completed, not a novelty par excellence? In an earlier context I suggested that the kingdom of God is identical with creation but seen in the light of its blessed final destination. Doesn't such a description imply that we may conceptualize the kingdom of God as the concluding stage of the process of emergent development?

Here I touch a sensitive subject. I lay bare the deep concern of almost all the great historical writers from the Christian tradition, from Augustine, Joachim of Fiore, and Bossuet to Ernst Troeltsch, Herbert Butterfield, and Wolfhart Pannenberg. All these erudite scholars have thought about the crucial question of where world history is ultimately headed. From a purely theoretical point of view they are not able to solve this question, although they share the opinion of the Dutch philosopher of history Meijer C. Smit: *"world history does not bear its meaning within itself."*[4] They remind us of the dark side of earthly existence, of the human rebellion against God, of the massacres that have occurred in history, of the suffering of individuals and peoples, and of the future of humanity, threatened by the ever-increasing display of power of science and technology. They see all of this as a problem for which science does not have any wisdom, not to mention any solution. It is their conviction – a conviction derived from the Christian faith – that the world can

---

[4] M. C. Smit, *Toward a Christian Conception of History*, ed. and trans. H. D. Morton and H. Van Dyke (Lanham, MD: University Press of America, 2002), p. 339. Italics in the original.

only receive its ultimate meaning by a divine intervention, an intervention related to the unique position of Jesus as "firstborn" and forerunner in the kingdom of God. But the eschatological completion of world history escapes the conceptual framework of science. The Roman Catholic historian, Peter Meinhold, once said: "profane history does not escape the effect of the death on the cross of the Redeemer who transforms the world, although historical science in its scientific methods is powerless to 'grasp this adequately'."[5]

Lloyd Morgan, Alexander, and other emergence philosophers entertain expectations of science that are far too high. Expectations based on faith play a role with these thinkers, too, but these are readily transformed into arguments that seem to be scientific. From their view of emergent evolution they develop the thesis that all events in world history tend toward God. To give more force to this view they point to a *nisus*: the tendency or inclination of nature to articulate itself on higher and higher levels. At the highest level the consciousnesses of people would have grown toward a common understanding to such an extent that a divine consciousness manifests itself. I call this train of thought a complete reversal of what happened. Assuming that faith in God as the creator is as fundamental as the Bible presents it to us, there may be evolution based on divine creation but there cannot be divine consciousness based on creative evolution.

I propose to earmark this alternative and visionary type of evolutionary thinking as emergentism. It is important to make a distinction between emergence thinking as empirical philosophy and emergentism as speculative metaphysics. No thinker in the past century has given emergentism a sharper profile than the French Jesuit and paleontologist Pierre Teilhard de Chardin. For Teilhard human consciousness or the soul is a new concentration or synthesis in the process of evolution. In his view the soul has emerged from earlier syntheses or organic life forms and, ultimately, from inorganic matter, that is to say, from material particles in which a psychic moment or an element of consciousness would already lie hidden.

---

[5] The quotation is a shortened rendition of Meinhold's opinion by Smit in *Toward a Christian Conception of History*, pp. 337–38.

In the framework of this so-called "panpsychism," Teilhard also brings God into the discussion. He regards Him as the extension and completion of the preceding syntheses. There is, he boldly suggests, a new synthesis in the making, a soul of souls: the divine completion or the endpoint Omega. This Omega point is the emerging synthesis of all syntheses, the final apotheosis that is still coming forth, and that has already partially come forth, from the ascendance of the individual consciousnesses. God is the unity, the ultimate synthesis of all that is, the being that encompasses all that is. Teilhard concludes his major work, *The Phenomenon of Man*, therefore, with these words:

Modern thought is at last getting acclimatised once more to the idea of the creative value of synthesis in the evolutionary sense. It is beginning to see that there is definitely *more* in the molecule than in the atom, *more* in society than in the individual ... We are now inclined to admit that at each further degree of combination *something* which is irreducible to isolated elements *emerges* in a new order. And with this admission, consciousness, life and thought are on the threshold of acquiring a right to existence in terms of science ...

In conformity with this state of mind the idea that some Soul of souls should be developing at the summit of the world is not as strange as might be thought from the present-day views of human reason ... Yet we must be careful to note that under this evolutive facet Omega still reveals *only half of itself*. While being the last term of its series, it is also *outside all series*. Not only does it crown but it closes ... When, going beyond the elements, we come to speak of the conscious Pole of the world, it is not enough to say that it *emerges* from the rise of consciousnesses: we must add that from this genesis it has already undergone emergence.[6]

In the passage above we see how an originally Christian vision of faith conflates with scientific expectations regarding emergent evolution. And not only in Teilhard de Chardin's work! There are many emergence thinkers for whom the image of a unification of evolutionary development with divine agency has a magical fascination. I mention here the well-known Canadian philosopher Bernard Lonergan. In his major work, *Insight*, he not only places the natural and human order, but also the order of divine grace, in an

---

[6] P. Teilhard de Chardin, *Le Phénomène humain*, English: *The Phenomenon of Man* (New York: Harper and Brothers, 1959), pp. 267–68, 270. Italics in the original.

evolutionary perspective. That is to say, Lonergan considers also the coming of God's kingdom in Jesus Christ, the salvation of humankind, and the disclosure of faith, hope, and love, as a progressive articulation of "emergent probability."[7] Something similar occurs in the widely discussed book of Philip Clayton, *God and Contemporary Science.* Inspired by the process philosophy of A. N. Whitehead, Clayton imagines divine agency in the world as an example of emergentism and "strong supervenience." The relation between God's mind and the world he wants to understand by the analogy of the relation between the human mind and the human body; in both cases he speaks of a relationship of supervenience.[8]

I take distance from this emergentism. In my view it is a speculative picture of reality, a mix of faith and science that we encountered earlier in the views of C. Lloyd Morgan and Samuel Alexander. Nowadays such emergentism is also advocated by Ervin Laszlo, one of the contemporary founders of systems philosophy.

Laszlo is a prolific writer and in his books he develops an evolutionary vision with panpsychistic and almost pantheistic traits.[9] Thus he writes at the conclusion of *The Whispering Pond*:

We have now arrived at the deepest and most esoteric dimensions of human experience; at the outermost edges of the quasi-total vision emerging in the wake of the latest advances in the empirical sciences. That we could reach this far shore is significant in itself: it means that the separation between the natural sciences and the spiritual domains of experience is not permanent and irrecoverable. One day it may be bridged by the further advance of the scientific revolution that is unfolding before our eyes.

The paramount feature of the emerging quasi-total vision of cosmos, matter, life, and mind is subtle and constant interconnection. Evolution is not a blind groping toward nonexistent goals, a haphazard play with chance and accident. It is a systematic, indeed a systemic, development

---

[7] Lonergan, *Insight: A Study of Human Understanding*, pp. 718–25, 741.

[8] P. D. Clayton, *God and Contemporary Science.* Edinburgh Studies in Constructive Theology (Edinburgh: Edinburgh University Press, 1997), ch. 8.

[9] For this panpsychism see E. Laszlo *et al., The Reenchanted Cosmos: Welcome Home in the Universe* (Rochester, VT: Inner Traditions, 2005), ch. 4. One encounters pantheism by kindred spirits of Laszlo, such as Peter Russell, in ibid., Part 3. Laszlo represents a sort of panentheism. In his view the evolutionary process occurs *in* the mind of God. See E. Laszlo, *The Connectivity Hypothesis: Foundations of an Integral Science of Quantum, Cosmos, Life and Consciousness* (Albany, NY: SUNY Press, 2003).

toward goals generated in the process itself. It unfolds because, as humankind has intuitively known throughout the ages, we, as all elements of the universe, are linked with one another. We are partners in a cosmic dance that is constant and unceasing.[10]

I formulate four serious objections to evolutionary philosophies that have been caught in the trap of emergentism:

(1) Philosophy, at least academic philosophy, is a form of the-oretical knowledge. It is a scientific discipline in its own right. One may not identify scientific knowledge with expectations that regard God's kingdom or the "mysterious interconnection" of a coming age (Laszlo). It is the strong feature of emergence philosophy that it wants to do justice to experiences of newness. The expectation of God's kingdom is indeed an experience of newness; as such it can be a source of inspiration, also for philosophers. But it is an experience in hope, founded on promises that run counter to daily life experiences or even surpass them. Faith expectations are new but often contra-factual, not translatable into philosophical arguments or into a new scientific paradigm.

(2) World history is full of measureless suffering. This suffering may not be glossed over as an evolutionary pre-phase or as a necessary lesson in preparation for a future age of well-being for humankind. World conquerors have often propagated such ideas: they oppressed but in the meantime they promised mountains of gold. However, those who gloss over the blood and tears in history, depicting them as an unavoidable growing toward an ultimate unification or a final synthesis, mock the holiness of God and scorn the cries of the victims.

(3) The arguments of Teilhard, Whitehead, Clayton, and others include an everything-in-God theory, often indicated as panen-theism, a view that lies between theism and pantheism. Panenthe-ism rejects, on the one hand, the pantheistic idea that God's being coincides entirely with the being of the world or, to put it more poetically, that all things evolve but are kept together in a "sacred dance" (Laszlo). It rejects, on the other hand, the theistic idea that

[10] E. Laszlo, *The Whispering Pond: A Personal Guide to the Emerging Vision of Science* (Boston: Element Books, 1996), pp. 217–18; and *Science and the Akashic Field: An Integral Theory of Everything* (Rochester, VT: Inner Traditions, 2004).

God holds together the world and all it contains, but also transcends it. Teilhard assumes that the world evolves in such a manner that all things are united *in God*, or will be united in Him at some time. It seems difficult to unite this assumption with the biblical and theistic belief that God is the sovereign Lord of all created things.[11]

(4) The Bible does indeed proclaim a fundamental renewal at the end of times. But this renewal is described as an intervention from outside: a divine completion. The kingdom of God is not considered to be the ultimate realization of creaturely potentials. It is not a goal generated in the evolutionary process itself. It is not an evidence of emergence; it is, rather, a token of grace, an evidence of condescension. Isn't that the reason for the Bible ending with the strange vision of the apostle John, exiled on the island of Patmos? John did not see the New Jerusalem arising from the earth but descending from heaven.

4 HUMAN EXPERIENCES ARE AMBIGUOUS

Having arrived at the end of the book, I feel the need to look back at what we have discussed. I want to remind the reader of my philosophical point of departure. Philosophy is a scientific discipline and as such it has to base itself on the standpoint of experience. For scientific propositions without empirical basis are not testable; they degenerate into speculative metaphysics. In our search for a possible meaning of the living world and in our reflecting on creation and evolution, openness to experience in its abundant anatomical and structural diversity was for that reason the first prerequisite.

In this regard, philosophy has a different task from the special sciences. Philosophy does not analyze the content of experiences, say empirical phenomena. It analyzes the presuppositions of experience; to be more precise, it reflects upon the general conditions that determine how we experience the world.[12] A philosopher is – to

---

[11] J. W. Cooper, *Panentheism: The Other God of the Philosophers* (Grand Rapids, MI: Baker Academic, 2006).

[12] These conditions are the structural requirements that make the experience of the world and of things in the world possible. It does not pertain to purely *epistemic* principles, a priori's that would be inherent to the knowing subject and on the basis of which this subject, out

mention a point that was not unimportant for our study – interested in the question of how we, in the selection, ordering, comparing, interpreting, and evaluating of evolutionary phenomena, can make a distinction between physical, biological, and mental facts. She or he wants to know how we give account of this modal distinction and how this distinction can be of constitutive significance for the various organizational levels that we can observe in empirical reality.

Nowhere does the diversity of organizational levels come more clearly to the fore than in living nature. In this study that has been our main focus. We have tried to imagine how it was possible that, originally, physical things became involved in an evolutionary dynamic over hundreds of millions of years in such a way that they began to display above-physical properties without relinquishing their physical basis. It was this development that gave us opportunity to interpret evolution in terms of emergence, and to interpret emergent evolution as a process in which, at a critical moment, things began to display irreducibly new functions and properties in a hierarchy of ontological domains.

In this book I have brought forward a number of reasons for my main thesis, that emergent evolution is, at the same time, a random and a directional process. It is a process in which all kinds of contingent factors without doubt play an indispensable role. But they all function within an ordered framework, a scale of organizational levels of increasing complexity, determined by an ascending series of above-physical laws that propel the evolutionary process in the direction of human beings. This process of complexification and innovation allows us to speak of a "directed evolution" and of a "pathway of meaning." The more so since this purposefulness reflects itself in the microcosm of individual organisms. Every organism proves to be an enkaptic whole in which lower modal structures not only lay the ground for higher structures but also anticipate these higher modes and their controlling function. In this regard I can agree with Michael Denton's comment in

of a chaos of impressions, would constitute the world, as Kant suggests. It concerns *ontological* principles by which the human subject is able to experience the world as an ordered reality (see ch. 12, section 3).

his latest book, *Nature's Destiny*: "The entire process of biological evolution from the origin of life to the emergence of man was somehow directed from the beginning."[13]

Can science then conclude that the world's history has a purpose? What science can and cannot say about this point is a crucial question. Good reasons can be brought forward for the thesis that evolution is a directional process, a process in which a perspective of meaning becomes discernible, yes, in which random factors contribute to the realization of future purposes, including the emergence of phenomena that are typically human. But science is not in a position to determine the ultimate purpose of the world's history. Here its language and concepts fall short. A direction can be discerned, but what the final configuration or destination of the world will be completely exceeds human theoretical insight. To be sure, there are visionary scientists, busy in their field charting the purpose of world events. Do not be mistaken; these scientists have clad themselves in prophetic robes or they are restorers of natural theology.

I am of the opinion that only within the hermeneutic horizon of faith can we, tentatively, take the next step. Living in faith and in the hope for a messianic future, a Christian is able to see the evolutionary process as a disclosure of the creation in time, and time as the avenue that the Creator takes with the world toward the realization of His goal, the city of God. Here we can indeed speak of a goal. But remember: the imaginative language of the Bible exceeds the conceptual language of science. The Bible is not an extension of science for insiders.

When the imaginative language of Scripture and the conceptual language of science are not sharply distinguished, they become competitive. Then one sooner or later has to face the question: "Did God create by evolution?" The suggestion that is enclosed in this question has the charm of simplicity but it implies an uncritical accommodation of the Christian faith to the ideological expectations of evolutionary naturalism.[14] Faith in a divine creator, as we have seen, can be of inspiring and innovative significance for

---

[13] Denton's reasoning in favor of directed evolution is primarily determined by the argument of fine tuning.

[14] See W. Gitt, *Schuf Gott durch Evolution?* (Neuhausen/Stuttgart: Hänssler, 2005).

the evolution debate. But this faith cannot be reconciled to the evolutionistic doctrine that the origins of life and of all body forms are nothing else but random hits of nature.

The result of our findings may elicit contradiction. In the academic circuit, the thesis that evolution is accompanied by a sense of directionality, yes, by experiences of purpose and meaning, is controversial. One of the greatest stumbling blocks is the continuity argument of evolutionary naturalism. Indeed, no phylogenetic development is possible without continuity in the physical foundations of life. This makes naturalism as a methodological starting-point an exceedingly strong formula. But the ontological viewpoint hidden in this argument, the strictly physicalist explanatory model of the world, proves to be of a speculative nature. It is based on a naturalistic fallacy, a pseudo-religious trust in natural science as the deepest source of truth. Over against this we posit that life is more than its material basis. To put it more strongly, the idea of emergent evolution implies that continuity and discontinuity go hand in hand in the establishment of that hierarchy of arrangements of being that is characteristic of the multiformity and directionality of the living world.

Resistance to the idea of meaning and direction is also sustained by another consideration, a moral argument. I have not brought this moral argument into the discussion in this book until now, but I may not leave it totally unmentioned. That emergent levels of being and a perspective of meaning reveal themselves in the development of life on earth is implausible, so the critics say, for life on earth is drenched with meaningless violence and destruction. Especially the human realm, on which the perspective of meaning is focussed, gives evidence of excessive violence, injustice, and undeserved suffering. Investigators have called the last century the most violent in world history. According to a survey in *The Economist*, 37 million people became fatalities on battlefields alone. Many more succumbed to the terror of their own governments: 62 million in the Soviet Union, 35 million in communist China, and 21 million in Germany. These numbers do not include the countless victims of avoidable hunger, disease, and environmental destruction.[15] Reports

[15] *The Economist*, September 11, 1999.

from the World Health Organization tell much the same story. In the first issue of its *World Report on Violence and Health* the organization reports that in the twentieth century 191 million people died as a direct or indirect result of violence, the great majority of them civilians.[16] Apparently history does not bring out the best in human beings. How, then, can the process of evolution be connected with the experience of purpose and meaning?

With the 2004 tsunami in Southeast Asia and the recent catastrophes that spread death and destruction in Myanmar and China still in our memories, we have a great deal of difficulty with the pervasiveness of evil in history. We are confronted with explosions of violence and depths of suffering that witness to complete senselessness. At least they are events that fully surpass our comprehension. They give us the uncomfortable feeling that life, in the final analysis, could still be without any purpose. They suggest that humankind, too, isn't more than a violent extension of nature, is perhaps even able to destroy life on earth once and for all.

Against this moral argument there is little that can be objected to, apart from the difficulty it imposes upon us. We human beings indeed have difficulty with violence. We are stoop under the burden of suffering. We protest against injustice. We march together in tens or hundreds of thousands in the streets of Brussels, Seattle, or Rio de Janeiro and cry out: stop the oppression, the terror, the environmental destruction! Why do we see these world-wide protests? Why have some single individuals in world history even been willing to sacrifice their lives for a better world? I know only one convincing answer. The fight against violence and the longing for a world of shalom, unknown in the animal kingdom, are irrefutable indications of moral and religious emergence.

The ultimate result of the evolutionary process is hidden in the future. And as long as this final result is concealed, the experiences to which we appeal in scholarship remain ambiguous. They are open to more than one interpretation. To be sure, we are, as people, on a journey in a world that is on a journey, and the emerging facts of life give us much to think about. They offer an awareness of

---

[16] *World Report on Violence and Health* (Geneva: World Health Organization, October 2002).

meaning and directionality. They contain the suggestion that in the world secrets are hidden that await unveiling. Do they offer more than that?

I assume that the awareness of meaning is deepened in those who believe. Christians also have moral grounds for connecting their expectations and cares with the promised kingdom of God, even as they realize at the same time that this kingdom is not of this earth and exceeds our human expectations. The longing for this land strengthens their confidence that their existence is a pilgrimage, and that life on earth in all its brokenness is not without purpose. And yet, even a qualified faith in creation – the faith that creation will find its ultimate destination in the kingdom of God – does not take away from the fact that our experiences are ambivalent and that even our faith experiences remain puzzling, covered with a veil of ignorance.

It is time to take distance from all those eminent scholars who think they have solved the puzzle of life with the naturalistic conclusion that humankind and the world are random outcomes of blind natural forces. Let us also take distance from the opposite view, the visionary opinion of those scholars who think they have discovered in humankind a budding and steadily growing divine awareness. An unbridgeable difference remains between an appeal to facts that are part of our world of experience, no matter how puzzling these may be, and an appeal to facts that are not facts but fabrications of a naturalistic or emergentistic bent.

One does not need to see through experience in order to appeal to it. One must see through naturalism and emergentism so that one does not have to appeal to them.

Bibliography

Aertsen, J. A., "Thomas Aquinas (1224/5–1274)," in J. Klapwijk, S. Griffioen, and G. Groenewoud (eds.), *Bringing into Captivity Every Thought*, pp. 95–121.

Alexander, S., *Beauty and the Other Forms of Value* (London: Macmillan, 1933).

    Space, Time and Deity: The Gifford Lectures at Glasgow 1916–1918 (London: Macmillan, 1920; repr. Kila, MT: Kessinger Publishing, 2004).

Augustine, *Confessiones* [397–98]; English: *Confessions*, trans. R. S. Pine-Coffin (Harmondsworth: Penguin Books, 1961).

    De civitate Dei [413–26]; English: *The City of God*.

Barrow, J. D., and F. J. Tipler, *The Anthropic Cosmological Principle* (New York: Oxford University Press, 1986).

Behe, M. J., *Darwin's Black Box: The Biochemical Challenge to Chemical Evolution* (New York: The Free Press, 1996).

    The Edge of Evolution: The Search for the Limits of Darwinism (New York: The Free Press, 2007).

Bertalanffy, L. von, "General System Theory" (1956), in *General System Theory: Foundations, Development, Applications* (New York: Braziller, 1968).

Bos, A. P., "Augustine, 354–430," in J. Klapwijk, S. Griffioen, and G. Groenewoud (eds.), *Bringing into Captivity Every Thought*, pp. 49–66.

Boulding, K. E., "General Systems Theory – the Skeleton of Science," *Management Science* 2 (1956), 197–208.

Bowler, P. J., *Evolution: The History of an Idea* (Berkeley: University of California Press, 1983).

Brace, C. L., *The Stages Of Human Evolution: Human And Cultural Origins* (Englewood Cliffs, NJ: Prentice-Hall, 1967).

Brace, C. L., and M. F. Ashley Montagu, *An Introduction to Physical Anthropology* (New York: Macmillan, 1965).

Broad, C. D., *The Mind and Its Place in Nature* (New York: Routledge and Kegan Paul, 1925).

294   *Bibliography*

Brown, P., *et al.*, "A New Small-Bodied Hominin from the Late Pleis-
    tocene of Flores, Indonesia," *Nature* 431 (2004), 1055–61.
Brown, W. S., N. Murphy, and H. Newton Malony (eds.), *Whatever
    Happened to the Soul? Scientific and Theological Portraits of Human
    Nature* (Minneapolis, MN: Fortress Press, 1998).
Buber, M., *Ich und Du* (1923), in *Das dialogische Prinzip* (Heidelberg:
    Lambert Schneider, 1974).
Butterfield, H., *The Origins of Modern Science: 1300–1800* (New York: The
    Free Press, 1965).
Caird, E., *The Evolution of Theology in the Greek Philosophers*, Gifford
    lectures, vol. 11 (Glasgow: J. Maclehose, 1904).
Calvin, J., *Institutes of the Christian Religion*, trans. Henry Beveridge
    (Grand Rapids, MI: Eerdmans, 1964).
Capra, F., *The Tao of Physics* (Boulder, CO: Shambhala, 1975).
Cassirer, E., *Philosophie der symbolischen Formen*; English: *The Philosophy of
    Symbolic Forms*, 3 vols. (New Haven: Yale University Press, 1955–57).
Chalmers, D. J., *The Conscious Mind: In Search of a Fundamental Theory*
    (New York and Oxford: Oxford University Press, 1996).
    "The Puzzle of Conscious Experience," *Scientific American* 273
    (December 1995), 80–86.
Checkland, P., *Systems Thinking, Systems Practice* (Chichester: John Wiley,
    1981).
Churchland, P. M., *Matter and Consciousness* (Cambridge, MA: MIT
    Press, 1984).
    *A Neurocomputational Perspective: The Nature of Mind and the Structure
    of Science* (Cambridge, MA: MIT Press, 1989).
    Scientific Realism and the Plasticity of Mind (Cambridge, MA: MIT
    Press, 1979).
Churchland, P. S., *Neurophilosophy: Toward a Unified Science of the
    Mind-Brain* (Cambridge, MA: MIT Press, 1986).
Churchland, P. S., and T. J. Sejnowski, *The Computational Brain* (Cambridge,
    MA: MIT Press, 1992).
Cilliers, P., *Complexity and Postmodernism: Understanding Complex Systems*
    (London, New York: Routledge, 1998).
Clayton, P. D., *God and Contemporary Science.* Edinburgh Studies in Con-
    structive Theology (Edinburgh: Edinburgh University Press, 1997).
Clouser, R., "Is Theism Compatible with Evolution?," in Robert T. Pennock
    (ed.), *Intelligent Design Creationism and Its Critics: Philosophical, Theo-
    logical, and Scientific Perspectives* (Cambridge, MA: MIT Press, 2001),
    pp. 513–36.
    *The Myth of Religious Neutrality: An Essay on the Hidden Role of Religious
    Belief in Theories* (Notre Dame, IN: University of Notre Dame Press,
    2005).

Conway Morris, S., *Life's Solution: Inevitable Humans in a Lonely Universe* (Cambridge: Cambridge University Press, 2003).

Cook, H., "Wonderful Life: Burgess Shale and the History of Biology," *Perspectives on Science and Christian Faith* 47 (1995), 159–63.

Cook, H., and H. D. Bestman, "A Persistent View: Lamarckian Thought in Early Evolutionary Theories and in Modern Biology," *Perspectives on Science and Christian Faith* 52 (2000), 86–96.

Cooper, J. W., *Panentheism: The Other God of the Philosophers* (Grand Rapids, MI: Baker Academic, 2006).

Copeland, H. F., "The Kingdom of Organisms," *Quarterly Review of Biology* 13 (1938), 383–420.

Damasio, A. R., *The Feeling of What Happens: Body and Emotion in the Making of Consciousness* (New York: Harcourt Brace, 1999).

Danto, A. C., "Naturalism," in *The Encyclopedia of Philosophy*, vol. v (New York/London: Macmillan and The Free Press, 1972), p. 448.

Darwin, C. R., *The Autobiography of Charles Darwin: 1809–1882* [1887], N. Barlow (ed.) (New York: W. W. Norton, 1958; New York: Harcourt, Brace and Co., 1958).

 The Descent of Man, and Selection in Relation to Sex (London: John Murray, 1871).

 Journal of Researches into the Natural History and Geology of the Countries Visited During the Voyage of H.M.S. Beagle round the World [1845] (New York: Ward, Lock and Co., n.d.), known as *The Voyage of the Beagle*.

 On the Origin of Species by Means of Natural Selection, or the Preservation of Favoured Races in the Struggle for Life (London: John Murray, 1859).

Darwin, F. (ed.), *The Life and Letters of Charles Darwin*, 2 vols. [1887] (New York: D. Appleton, 1899; New York: Basic Books, 1959).

Davidson, D., *Essays on Actions and Events: The Philosophical Essays of Donald Davidson* (New York: Oxford University Press, 1980).

Davis, E. B., "Debating Darwin: The 'Intelligent Design' Movement," *The Christian Century*, July 15–22, 1998, 678–81.

Dawkins, R., *The Blind Watchmaker: Why the Evidence of Evolution Reveals a Universe without Design* (New York: W. W. Norton, 1986).

 The Selfish Gene: Why the Evidence of Evolution Reveals a Universe Without Design (Oxford: Oxford University Press, 1976, 2006).

 "Thoughts for the millennium: Richard Dawkins," *Microsoft Encarta Encyclopedia 2000* (1993).

Dembski, W. A., *The Design Inference: Eliminating Chance through Small Probabilities* (Cambridge: Cambridge University Press, 1998).

 The Design Revolution: Answering the Toughest Questions about Intelligent Design (Downers Grove, IL: InterVarsity Press, 2004).

  Intelligent Design: The Bridge between Science and Theology (Downer's Grove, IL: InterVarsity Press, 1999).

Dembski, W. A. (ed.), *Mere Creation: Science, Faith, and Intelligent Design* (Downers Grove, IL: InterVarsity Press, 1998).

Dennett, D. C., *Consciousness Explained* (Boston: Little, Brown & Co., 1991).

  Darwin's Dangerous Idea: Evolution and the Meanings of Life (New York: Simon & Schuster, 1995).

Denton, M., *Evolution: A Theory in Crisis* (Bethesda/Maryland: Adler and Adler, 1985).

  Nature's Destiny: How the Laws of Biology Reveal Purpose in the Universe (New York: The Free Press, 1998).

Diemer, J. H., *Natuur en wonder* (Amsterdam: Buijten & Schipperheijn, 1963).

Dodson, E. O., "The Kingdom of Organisms," *Systematic Zoology* 20 (1971), 265–81.

Doolittle, W. F., "Uprooting the Tree of Life," *Scientific American* 282 (February 2000), 90–95.

Dooyeweerd, H., *A New Critique of Theoretical Thought*, 4 vols. (Amsterdam: H. J. Paris, 1953–58; New York: Edwin Mellen Press, 1997).

  "Schepping en evolutie," *Philosophia Reformata* 24 (1959), 113–59.

  "Het substantiebegrip in de moderne natuurphilosophie," *Philosophia Reformata* 15 (1950), 66–139.

Drees, W. B., *Religion, Science and Naturalism* (Cambridge: Cambridge University Press, 1996).

Durkheim, E., *Les Formes élémentaires de la vie religieuse: Le système totémique en Australie* (Paris: Presses Universitaires de France, 1912).

Eigen, M., *Steps Toward Life: A Perspective on Evolution* (Oxford: Oxford University Press, 1992).

Eldredge, N., and S. J. Gould, "Biology Rules," *Civilization* 5 (1998), 86–88.

Feine, P., *et al.*, *Introduction to the New Testament* (Nashville, TN: Abingdon Press, 1965).

Fodor, J. A., *The Language of Thought* (New York: Thomas Y. Crowell, 1975).

Fox, S. W., and K. Dose, *Molecular Evolution and the Origin of Life* (New York: Marcel Dekker, 1977).

Gehring, W. J., *Master Control Genes in Development and Evolution: The Homeobox* (New Haven: Yale University Press, 1998).

Gehring, W. J., and K. Ikeo, "Pax 6: Mastering Eye Morphogenesis and Eye Evolution," *Trends in Genetics* 15 (1999), 371–77.

Gilbert, W., "The RNA World," *Nature* 319 (1986), 618.

Gitt, W., *In 6 Tagen vom Chaos zum Menschen: Logos oder Chaos* (Neuhausen/Stuttgart: Hänssler-Verlag, 1998).

  Schuf Gott durch Evolution? (Neuhausen/Stuttgart: Hänssler, 2005).

Goldie, P., *The Emotions: A Philosophical Exploration* (Oxford/New York: Clarendon Press, 2000).

Gorst, M., *Aeons: The Search for the Beginning of Time* (London: Fourth Estate, 2001).

Goudge, T. A., "Emergent Evolutionism," in *The Encyclopedia of Philosophy*, vol. III (New York: Macmillan and Free Press, 1972).

Gould, S. J., *Ever Since Darwin: Reflections in Natural History* (New York: W. W. Norton, 1977).

"Evolution's Erratic Pace," *Natural History* 86/5 (1977), 12–16.

The Flamingo's Smile: Reflections on Natural History (New York: W. W. Norton, 1985).

The Panda's Thumb: More Reflections in Natural History (New York: W. W. Norton & Co., 1980).

Wonderful Life: The Burgess Shale and the Nature of History (New York: W. W. Norton, 1989).

Grene, M., *The Understanding of Nature* (Dordrecht: D. Reidel, 1974).

Gunton, C. E., *The Triune Creator: A Historical and Systematic Study* (Grand Rapids, MI: Eerdmans, 1998).

Hare, R. M., *The Language of Morals* (Oxford: Clarendon Press, 1952).

Harold, F. M., "Biochemical Topology: From Vectorial Metabolism to Morphogenesis," *Bioscience Reports* 11, 347–85.

Harrison, P., *The Bible, Protestantism, and the Rise of Natural Science* (Cambridge: Cambridge University Press, 1998).

Harvey, W., *Exercitatio anatomica de motu cordis et sanguinis in animalibus* (Frankfurt: Fitzerl, 1628).

Haught, J., *Is Nature Enough? Meaning and Truth in the Age of Science* (Cambridge: Cambrige University Press, 2006).

Henshilwood, C., "Middle Stone Age Shell Beads from South Africa," *Science* 304 (2004), 404.

Herrick, C. J., *The Thinking Machine* (Chicago: University of Chicago Press, 1929).

Hooykaas, R., *Religion and the Rise of Modern Science* (Grand Rapids, MI: Eerdmans, 1972).

Jacob, F., *The Logic of Living Systems*, trans. from *La logique du vivant* (Paris: Gallimard, 1970; London: Allen Lane, 1974).

James, W., "What is an Emotion?," *Mind* 9 (1884), 188–205.

Jantsch, E., *The Self-Organizing Universe: Scientific and Human Implications of the Emerging Paradigm of Evolution* (New York: Pergamon Press, 1980).

John Paul II, "Message to the Pontifical Academy of Sciences," *The Quarterly Review of Biology* 72 (1997), 381–83.

Jongeling, T. B., *The Sceptical Biologist: An Inquiry into the Structure of Evolutionary Theory* (Amsterdam: Vrije Universiteit, 1991).

Kauffman, S. A., *At Home in the Universe: The Search for Laws of Self-Organization and Complexity* (New York: Viking, 1995).

The Origins of Order: Self Organization and Selection in Evolution (New York: Oxford University Press, 1993).

Kim, J., "Multiple Realization and the Metaphysics of Reduction," *Philosophy and Phenomenological Research* 52 (1992), 1–26.

Supervenience and Mind: Selected Philosophical Ideas (Cambridge and New York: Cambridge University Press, 2002).

Kirschenmann, P. P., "On Self-organization, Design, and the Almost-Inevitableness of Complex Order: Some Critical Assessments," *Studies in Science and Theology* 8 (2001–2), 17–42.

Klapwijk, J., "A la recherche d'une philosophie ouverte," *Hokma. Revue de réflexion théologique* 70–76 (Lausanne, 1999–2001).

"Honderd jaar filosofie aan de Vrije Universiteit," in M. van Os and W. J. Wieringa (eds.), *Wetenschap en Rekenschap 1880–1980: Een eeuw wetenschap ... aan de Vrije Universiteit* (Kampen: J. H. Kok, 1980), pp. 528–93.

"Pluralism of Norms and Values: On the Claim and Reception of the Universal," *Philosophia Reformata* 59 (1994), 158–92.

"Reformational Philosophy on the Boundary Between the Past and the Future," *Philosophia Reformata* 52 (1987), 101–34.

Klapwijk, J., S. Griffioen, and G. Groenewoud (eds.), *Bringing into Captivity Every Thought: Capita Selecta in the History of Christian Evaluations of Non-Christian Philosophy* (Lanham, MD: University Press of America, 1991).

Laszlo, E., *The Connectivity Hypothesis: Foundations of an Integral Science of Quantum, Cosmos, Life and Consciousness* (Albany, NY: SUNY Press, 2003).

Science and the Akashic Field: An Integral Theory of Everything (Rochester, VT: Inner Traditions, 2004).

The Whispering Pond: A Personal Guide to the Emerging Vision of Science (Boston: Element Books, 1996).

Laszlo, E., *et al.*, *The Reenchanted Cosmos: Welcome Home in the Universe* (Rochester, VT: Inner Traditions, 2005).

Legname, G., S. B. Prusiner *et al.*, "Synthetic Mammalian Prions," *Science* 305 (2004), 673–76.

Leipe, D., *et al.*, "Did DNA Replication Evolve Twice Independently?," *Nucleic Acids Research* 27 (1999), 3389.

Lever, J., *Creation and Evolution* (Grand Rapids, MI: International Publications, 1958).

Geïntegreerde Biologie (Utrecht: Oosthoek, 1973).

Lewin, R., "Biology is Not Postage Stamp Collecting," *Science* 216 (1982), 718–20.

Bibliography

299

Lewis, C. S., *Miracles: A Preliminary Study* (New York: Macmillan, 1947).

Lewontin, R. C., "Fallen Angels," *New York Review of Books*, June 14, 1990, 3–7.

Llinás, R., and P. S. Churchland (eds.), *The Mind-Brain Continuum* (Cambridge, MA: MIT Press, 1996).

Lonergan, B. J. F., *Insight: A Study of Human Understanding*, Collected Works (20 vols.), vol. III (1958) (Toronto: University of Toronto Press, 1992).

Looren de Jong, H., *Naturalism and Psychology: A Theoretical Study* (Kampen: J. H. Kok, 1992).

Lorenz, K., "Kant's Doctrine of the A Priori in the Light of Contemporary Biology" (German, 1941), in H. C. Plotkin (ed.), *Learning, Development, and Culture: Essays in Evolutionary Epistemology* (New York: Wiley, 1982).

Lyons, W., *Emotion* (New York: Cambridge University Press, 1980).

Malthus, T. R., *An Essay on the Principle of Population as it Affects the Future Improvement of Society* (London: J. Johnson, 1798).

Margulis, L., *Origin of Eukaryotic Cells* (New Haven: Yale University Press, 1970).

Mayr, E., *The Growth of Biological Thought: Diversity, Evolution, and Inheritance* (Cambridge, MA: The Belknap Press of Harvard University Press, 1982).

McDougall, I., *et al.*, "Stratigraphic Placement and Age of Modern Humans from Kibish, Ethiopia," *Nature* 433 (2005), 733–36.

McKay, D. S., *et al.*, "Search for Past Life on Mars: Possible Relic Biogenic Activity in Martian Meteorite ALH84001," *Science* 273 (1996), 924–30.

Meijers, A. W. M., "Mental Causation and Searle's Impossible Conception of Unconscious Intentionality," *International Journal of Philosophical Studies* 8 (2000), 155–70.

Miller, S. L., "A Production of Amino Acids under Possible Primitive Conditions," *Science* 117 (1953), 528–29.

Miller, S. L., and L. E. Orgel, *The Origins of Life on the Earth* (Englewood Cliffs, NJ: Prentice Hall, 1974).

Moleschott, J., *Der Kreislauf des Lebens* (Mainz: Von Zabern, 1852).

Monod, J., *Chance and Necessity*, trans. A. Wainhouse (New York: Vintage Books, 1972).

Morell, V., "Microbiology's Scarred Revolutionary," *Science* 276 (1997), 699–702.

Morgan, C. L., *Emergent Evolution* (London: Williams and Norgate, 1923; repr. New York: AMS Press, 1977).

Morris, H. M., *The Biblical Basis for Modern Science* (Grand Rapids, MI: Baker Book House, 1987).

Scientific Creationism (El Cajon, CA: Master Books, 1985).

Morwood, M. J., *et al.*, "Archaeology and Age of a New Hominin from Flores in Eastern Indonesia," *Nature* 431 (2004), 1087–91.

Nijkamp, H.J.J., *Genetica: Opwindend perspectief voor de samenleving* (Amsterdam: VU Boekhandel, 1992).

Nordenskiöld, E., *The History of Biology: A Survey* (New York: Alfred A. Knopf, 1932).

Numbers, R.L., *The Creationists: The Evolution of Scientific Creationism* (Berkeley, University of California Press, 1992).

Nussbaum, M., *Upheavals of Thought: The Intelligence of Emotions* (New York: Cambridge University Press, 2001).

O'Connor, T., and H.Y. Wong, "The Metaphysics of Emergence," *Noûs* 39 (2005), 658–78.

Oppenheim, P., and H. Putnam, "Unity of Science as a Working Hypothesis," in H. Feigl and M. Scriven (eds.), *Minnesota Studies in the Philosophy of Science* 2 (1958), 3–36.

Paley, W., *Natural Theology or Evidences of the Existence and Attributes of the Deity, Collected from the Appearances of Nature* (London: Wilks and Taylor, 1802).

Pennisi, E., "Molecular Approach to Mushroom Hunting," *Science* 293 (2001), 1027–28.

Pius XII, encyclical *Humani Generis, Acta Apostolicae Sedis* 42 (1950).

Plantinga, A., "Darwin, Mind and Meaning," *Books and Culture*, May/June 1996.

Warrant and Proper Function (New York: Oxford University Press, 1993).

Polanyi, M., "Life's Irreducible Structure," *Science* 160 (1968), 1308–12.

"Life Transcending Physics and Chemistry," *Chemical & Engineering News*, August 21, 1967, 54–66.

Polkinghorne, J., *The Way the World Is: The Christian Perspectives of a Scientist* (Grand Rapids, MI: Eerdmans, 1984).

Popper, K.R., *Objective Knowledge: An Evolutionary Approach* (Oxford: Clarendon Press, 1975).

Porter, A.P., "Naturalism, Naturalism by Other Means, and Alternatives to Naturalism," *Theology and Science* 1 (2003), 221–37.

Prum, R.O., "Palaeontology: Dinosaurs Take to the Air," *Nature* 421 (2003), 323–24.

Prusiner, S.B., "Detecting Mad Cow Disease," *Scientific American* 291 (July 2004), 86–93.

Putnam, H., "Minds and Machines," in S. Hook (ed.), *Dimensions of Mind* (New York: New York University Press, 1960), pp. 138–64.

Reason, Truth and History (Cambridge: Cambridge University Press, 1981).

Ratzsch, D.L., *Nature, Design, and Science: The Status of Design in Natural Science* (Albany: State University of New York Press, 2001).

Raven, P.H., *et al.*, *Biology* (New York: McGraw Hill, 2005, 7th edn.).

Roth, A.A., *Origins: Linking Science and Scripture* (Hagerstown, MD: Review and Herald Publishing Association, 1998).

Ruse, M., *The Evolution–Creation Struggle* (Cambridge, MA: Harvard University Press, 2005).

"Evolutionary Theory and Christian Ethics: Are They in Harmony?," *Zygon* 29 (1994), 5–24.

"Is Evolution a Secular Religion?," *Science* 299 (2003), 1523–24.

Taking Darwin Seriously: A Naturalistic Approach to Philosophy (Oxford: Blackwell, 1986).

Scherer, S., "Basic Types of Life," in W. A. Dembski (ed.), *Mere Creation*, pp. 195–211.

Searle, J. R., *Intentionality: An Essay in the Philosophy of Mind* (Cambridge: Cambridge University Press, 1983).

Minds, Brains, and Science (Cambridge, MA: Harvard University Press, 1984).

The Mystery of Consciousness (London: Granta Books, 1997).

The Rediscovery of the Mind (Cambridge, MA: MIT Press, 1992).

Seerveld, C., "Reformational Christian Philosophy and Christian College Education," *Pro Rege* (Dordt College, Sioux Center, Iowa) 30:3 (March 2002), 1–16.

Shanks, N., and K. H. Joplin, "Redundant Complexity: A Critical Analysis of Intelligent Design in Biochemistry," *Philosophy of Science* 66 (1999), 275.

Shapiro, R., *Origins: A Skeptic's Guide to the Creation of Life on Earth* (New York: Bantam, 1987; London: Penguin Books, 1988).

Planetary Dreams (New York: John Wiley and Sons, 1999).

Simpson, G. G., *The Meaning of Evolution* (New Haven: Yale University Press, 1949; revised edition, 1967).

Smit, M. C., *Toward a Christian Conception of History*, ed. and trans. H. D. Morton and H. Van Dyke (Lanham, MD: University Press of America, 2002).

Smuts, J. C., *Holism and Evolution* (London: Macmillan, 1926).

Snelders, H. A. M., *Darwins "strijd om het bestaaan" en de evolutie in de niet-levende natuur* (Amsterdam: Vrije Universiteit, 1984).

Solomon, R. C., *The Passions* (New York: Anchor Press/Doubleday, 1977).

Stafleu, M. D., *Een wereld vol relaties: Karakter en zin van natuurlijke dingen en processen* (Amsterdam: Buijten & Schipperheijn, 2002).

Stebbins, G. L., *Darwin to DNA, Molecules to Humanity* (San Francisco: Freeman, 1982).

Steen, W. J. van der, *Evolution as Natural History: A Philosophical Analysis* (Westport, CT: Praeger, 2000).

Swaab, D. F., "Wij zijn onze hersenen," *Trouw* (newspaper), September 30, 2000, 49.

Tattersall, I., *The Monkey in the Mirror: Essays on the Science of What Makes Us Human* (New York: Harcourt, 2002). ·

"Out of Africa Again . . . and Again?," *Scientific American* 276 (April 1997), 60–67.

Teilhard de Chardin, P., *Le Phénomène humain*; English: *The Phenomenon of Man* (New York: Harper and Brothers, 1959).

Templeton, J. M. (ed.), *Evidence of Purpose: Scientists Discover the Creator* (New York: Continuum Publishing, 1994).

Thewissen, J. G. M., *et al.*, "Skeletons of Terrestrial Cetaceans and the Relationship of Whales to Artiodactyls," *Nature* 413 (2001), 277–81.

Thomas Aquinas, *In librum Boethii De trinitate expositio* [1261]; English: *Commentary on Boethius's Book On the Trinity*.
Super Sententiis [1256].

Toulmin, S. E., "The Mentality of Man's Brain," in A. G. Karczmar and J. C. Eccles (eds.), *Brain and Human Behavior* (New York: Springer, 1972).

Ulam, S. M., *Adventures of a Mathematician* (New York: Charles Scribner's Sons, 1976).

Ussher, J., *The Annals of the World Deduced from the Origin of Time* (London: E. Tyler, 1658).

Voetius, G., *Selectarum disputationum theologicarum*, 5 vols. (Utrecht: Waesberge, 1648–69), vol. 1 (1648).

Vollenhoven, D. H. Th., "Problemen rondom de tijd," in A. Tol and K. A. Bril (eds.), *Vollenhoven als wijsgeer: Inleidingen en teksten* (Amsterdam: Buijten & Schipperheijn, 1992), pp. 160–98.

Vollmer, G., *Evolutionäre Erkenntnistheorie* (Stuttgart: Hirzel, 1975).

Watson, J. D., and F. H. C. Crick, "Molecular Structure of Nucleic Acids: A Structure for Deoxyribose Nucleic Acid," *Nature* 171 (1953), 737–38.

Weber, B. H., "Irreducible Complexity and the Problem of Biochemical Emergence," *Biology and Philosophy* 14 (1999), 593–605.

Weinberg, S., *Dreams of a Final Theory: The Scientist's Search for the Ultimate Laws of Nature* (New York: Pantheon Books, 1992).

Whitcomb, J. C., and H. M. Morris, *The Genesis Flood: The Biblical Record and Its Scientific Implications* (Philadelphia: Presbyterian and Reformed Publishing Co., 1962).

Whittaker, R. H., "New Concepts of Kingdoms of Organisms," *Science* 163 (1969), 150–60.

Woese, C. R., "A New Biology for a New Century," *Microbiology and Molecular Biology Reviews* (June 2004), 173–86.

Woese, C. R., and G. E. Fox, "Phylogenetic Structure of the Prokaryotic Domain: The Primary Kingdoms," *Proceedings of the National Academy of Sciences of the USA* 74 (1977), 5088–90.

Woltereck, R., *Ontologie des Lebendigen* (Stuttgart: F. Enke, 1940).

Woodger, J. H., *Biological Principles: A Critical Study* (New York: Harcourt, 1929).

World Report on Violence and Health (Geneva: World Health Organization, October 2002).

Xu, X., *et al.*, "Four-Winged Dinosaurs from China," *Nature* 421 (2003), 335–40.

Young, D., *Christianity and the Age of the Earth* (Grand Rapids, MI: Zondervan, 1982).

Zajonc, R. B., "Feeling and Thinking. Preferences Need No Inferences," in *The Selected Works of R. B. Zajonc* (New York: John Wiley & Sons, 2003).

Zhang, F., and Z. Zhou, "A Primitive Enantiornithine Bird and the Origin of Feathers," *Science* 290 (2000), 1955–59.

Zylstra, U., "Intelligent-Design Theory: An Argument for Biotic Laws," *Zygon* 39 (2004), 175–91.

  "Living Things as Hierarchically Organized Structures," *Synthese* 91 (1992), 111–33.

INTERNET RESOURCES

Behe, M. J., "Molecular Machines: Experimental Support for the Design Inference," http://www.arn.org/docs/behe/mb_mm92496.htm.

Center for Science and Culture, the Discovery Institute, Seattle, "Top questions," http://www.discovery.org/csc/topQuestions.php.

Haught, J., "Theology and Evolution: How Much Can Biology Explain?" http://www.metanexus.net/magazine/ArticleDetail/tabid/68/id/9598/Default.aspx.

Murphy, N., "A Hierarchy of Sciences," http://www.counterbalance.net/evp-mind/ahier-frame.html.

O'Connor, T., and H. Y. Wong, "Emergent Properties," http://plato.stanford.edu/entries/properties-emergent/.

Yahya, H., "Atlas of creation," http://www.harunyahya.net/V2/Lang/en.

Index